Lift Up Your Heads

Lift Up Your Heads

*Nonverbal Communication and Related
Body Imagery in the Bible*

John A. Davies

☙PICKWICK *Publications* • Eugene, Oregon

LIFT UP YOUR HEADS
Nonverbal Communication and Related Body Imagery in the Bible

Copyright © 2018 John A. Davies. All rights reserved. Except for brief quotations in critical publications or reviews, no part of this book may be reproduced in any manner without prior written permission from the publisher. Write: Permissions, Wipf and Stock Publishers, 199 W. 8th Ave., Suite 3, Eugene, OR 97401.

Pickwick Publications
An Imprint of Wipf and Stock Publishers
199 W. 8th Ave., Suite 3
Eugene, OR 97401

www.wipfandstock.com

PAPERBACK ISBN: 978-1-5326-1825-3
HARDCOVER ISBN: 978-1-4982-4366-7
EBOOK ISBN: 978-1-4982-4365-0

Cataloguing-in-Publication data:

Names: Davies, John A., author.

Title: Lift up your heads : nonverbal communication and related body imagery in the Bible / John A. Davies.

Description: Eugene, OR: Pickwick Publications, 2018 | Includes bibliographical references and index.

Identifiers: ISBN 978-1-5326-1825-3 (paperback) | ISBN 978-1-4982-4366-7 (hardcover) | ISBN 978-1-4982-4365-0 (ebook)

Subjects: LCSH: Human body in the Bible | Body image—Biblical teaching | Nonverbal communication | Body language | Bible—Hermeneutics | Bible. Old Testament—Criticism, interpretation, etc. | Bible. New Testament—Criticism, interpretation, etc.

Classification: BS680.B6 D385 2018 (print) | BS680.B6 (ebook)

Unless otherwise stated, all Bible quotations are from the New Revised Standard Version Bible, copyright 1989, Division of Christian Education of the National Council of the Churches of Christ in the United States of America. Used by permission. All rights reserved.

Illustrations from *The Symbolism of the Biblical World* by Othmar Keel are used with the permission of the author. Unless specified, references to Keel illustration numbers (Keel #) are to this work.

Manufactured in the U.S.A.   06/05/18

For my grandchildren

Charlotte, Ella, Harrison, Owen, Alice,
Cora, Theodore, and Bree

Lift up your heads, O gates!
and be lifted up, O ancient doors!
that the King of glory may come in.

—Psalm 24:7

Contents

List of Illustrations | ix
Preface | xi
Abbreviations | xiii

1 Introduction | 1
2 The Head | 15
3 The Eyes | 52
4 The Neck, Torso, and Whole Body | 67
5 The Arms and Hands | 96
6 The Legs and Feet | 129
7 Conclusion | 146

Bibliography | 153
Subject Index | 163
Scripture Index | 171

Illustrations

#1. A Syrian captive of Ramses III with arms above head in symbol of submission. Egyptian, twelfth century BC. Limestone relief from the mortuary temple of Sabu-Re at Abusir. Staatliche Museen, Berlin. Drawn by Charlotte Whitehouse. | 25

#2. A woman kisses the ground in homage. Egyptian Book of the Dead. Eleventh to tenth century BC. Keel #413. | 48

#3. A worshiper gazes in adoration at the deity. Note the enlarged eyes. Abu Tempel: Tell Asmar. Sumerian, third millennium BC. Drawn by Charlotte Whitehouse from Keel #411. | 59

#4. Pharaoh Ramses II triumphing over his enemy. Abu Simbel, Egypt, thirteenth century BC. Keel #404. | 69

#5. Worshipers in various stages of prostration. Egyptian, sixteenth to eleventh century BC. Keel #412. | 79

#6. Subjects of Ashurbanipal showing obeisance, including grasping his feet. Nineveh, seventh century BC. Keel #360a. | 81

#7. A tribute procession. Thebes, Egyptian, fifteenth century BC. Keel #408. | 83

#8. Pharaoh Haremhab seated at the right hand of the god Horus. Egyptian, fourteenth century BC. Keel #353. | 99

#9. The king is ushered into the presence of the deity. Cylinder seal of Ur-Nammu. Sumerian, twenty-first century BC. Drawn by Charlotte Whitehouse from Keel #272. | 109

ILLUSTRATIONS

#10. Desperate Libyan and Asiatics implore an official for food. Tomb of Horemheb. Sakkarah, Egyptian, fourteenth century BC. Keel #429. | 115

#11. Two kings clasp hands in alliance. Assyrian, ninth century BC. Keel #123. | 124

#12. Two men touch hands over what appear to be contract or treaty documents they are ratifying. Ras Shamra, fourteenth century BC. Keel #122. | 124

Preface

THIS WORK GREW OUT of some four decades of teaching the Bible and reflecting on a somewhat neglected aspect of the information it contains—that relating to the recorded posture and movement of the characters who inhabit its pages and the metaphorical use of gesture idioms such as raising the hand or covering the head. Often one looks in vain at the commentaries for some insight on what might be signified when a character stands or sits, falls to the ground, claps her hands, shakes her head, touches her throat, removes a sandal, or remains silent. Perhaps at times we are right to assume they act as we might act. Perhaps at times there are cultural elements we have not fully understood. Only through a careful compilation of the references to similar gestures and their contexts, and a comparison, where relevant, with other ancient texts from the milieu of the biblical writers, and with the iconography of Western Asia and the Mediterranean world, can we with more confidence lift up our own heads. I have become convinced of the need for such a book to address a blind spot in our reading of the Bible as more than one scholar, on hearing of my project, has remarked that he could only think of one or two places in the Bible where reference is made to a gesture!

I express my gratitude to Professor Othmar Keel for generously allowing the use of illustrations from his *The Symbolism of the Biblical World*. Sami and Samia Gerges assisted with understanding aspects of nonverbal communication in the living cultures of Egypt and Western Asia. Dr Carole Ferch-Johnson kindly provided me with a copy of her unpublished manuscript, "Human Hands and Feet and Their Functions as Media of Nonverbal Communication in the Narratives of Acts 3:1–11 and 9:1–19a." Steven Coxhead read the manuscript and made some helpful suggestions. My wife Julie assisted with the indexing.

Abbreviations

§	section number in this book
#	illustration number
AB	The Anchor Bible
ANEP	*The Ancient Near East in Pictures Relating to the Old Testament.* With Supplement. 2nd ed. By James B. Pritchard. Princeton: Princeton University Press, 1969.
ANET	*Ancient Near Eastern Texts Relating to the Old Testament.* 2nd ed. with Supplement. Edited by James B. Pritchard. Princeton: Princeton University Press, 1969.
AOAT	Alter Orient und Altes Testament
BDAG	Walter Bauer, Frederick W. Danker, W. F. Arndt, and F. W. Gingrich. *Greek–English Lexicon of the New Testament and Other Early Christian Literature.* 3rd ed. Chicago: University of Chicago Press, 2000.
BT	*The Bible Translator*
CBQ	*Catholic Biblical Quarterly*
CoS	*The Context of Scripture.* 3 vols. Edited by William W. Hallo. Leiden: Brill, 2003.
DCH	*The Dictionary of Classical Hebrew.* 8 vols. Edited by David J. A. Clines. Sheffield, UK: Sheffield Academic, 1993–2011.
NIDOTTE	*New International Dictionary of Old Testament Theology and Exegesis.* 5 vols., edited by Willem A. VanGemeren. Grand Rapids: Zondervan, 1997.

ABBREVIATIONS

ESV	*The Holy Bible Containing the Old and New Testaments: English Standard Version.* Wheaton, IL: Crossway, 2001.
HALOT	*The Hebrew and Aramaic Lexicon of the Old Testament.* 2 vols. Study edition. By Ludwig Koehler et al. Translated and edited under M. E. J. Richardson. Leiden: Brill, 2001.
HCSB	*Holman Christian Standard Bible.* Nashville, TN: B&H, 1989.
HTR	*Harvard Theological Review*
IBD	*The Illustrated Bible Dictionary.* 3 vols. Edited by J. D. Douglas et al. Leicester, UK: Inter-Varsity, 1980.
IEJ	*Israel Exploration Journal*
JANES	*Journal of the Ancient Near Eastern Society*
JAOS	*Journal of the American Oriental Society*
JBL	*Journal of Biblical Literature*
JETS	*Journal of the Evangelical Theological Society*
JNES	*Journal of Near Eastern Studies*
JNSL	*Journal of Northwest Semitic Languages*
JSOT	*Journal for the Study of the Old Testament*
JSOTS	Journal for the Study of the Old Testament Supplement Series
lit.	literally
LXX	Septuagint
Message	*The Message: The Bible in Contemporary Language.* By Eugene H. Peterson. Colorado Springs: Navpress, 2002.
NET	*The New English Translation of the Bible.* net.bible.org
NICNT	New International Commentary on the New Testament
NICOT	New International Commentary on the Old Testament
NTS	*New Testament Studies*
NIV11	*The Holy Bible: New International Version.* Grand Rapids: Zondervan, 2011.
NLT2	*The Holy Bible: New Living Translation.* 2nd ed. Wheaton, IL: Tyndale House, 2015.

ABBREVIATIONS

NRSV	*Holy Bible: New Revised Standard Version.* Grand Rapids: Zondervan, 1989.
OTL	The Old Testament Library
REB	*Revised English Bible with the Apocrypha.* Oxford: Oxford University Press, 1989.
s.v.	see under the word
TDNT	*Theological Dictionary of the New Testament.* 10 vols. Edited by Gerhard Kittel and Gerhard Friedrich. Translated by Geoffrey W. Bromiley. Grand Rapids: Eerdmans, 1964–1976.
TDOT	*Theological Dictionary of the Old Testament.* 14 vols. Edited by G. Johannes Botterweck and Helmer Ringgren. Translated by Geoffrey W. Bromiley et al. Grand Rapids: Eerdmans, 1974–2004.
VT	*Vetus Testamentum*
WBC	Word Biblical Commentary
WUNT	Wissenschaftliche Untersuchungen zum Neuen Testament

1

Introduction

"A GLAD HEART MAKES a cheerful countenance," as the proverb says (Prov 15:13). That is, an emotion (happiness) is likely to be evident through our body language (a smiling face).[1] Body language, or to use a term now commonly found in more formal discussion, nonverbal communication, covers the posture and movement of one's body or its members, such as head movements, facial expressions, hand gestures, and whole body positioning and movement, in such a manner as to communicate status, relationships, attitudes, emotions, intentions, and commands. These postures, gestures, actions, looks, etc., may stand alone (nonverbal) or may accompany speech (co-verbal) as meaningful acts. For the sake of brevity, further references to nonverbal communication are generally to be understood as including co-verbal.[2]

The term nonverbal communication is strictly too broad for our purposes if interpreted to include such communication events as smoke signals (Judg 20:38) or the display of Rahab's crimson cord in her window (Josh 2:18). The focus of this study will be on the references in the biblical text to the use of the body, apart from speech or in conjunction with speech, to aid the communication process. Of course, everything we do, or even fail to do, can potentially tell others something about us—our

---

1. The Greek writer now known as Pseudo-Aristotle (c. 300 BC) made the following general observation in his *Physiognomics*: "Gesture and the varieties of facial expression are interpreted by their affinity to different emotions" (Swain, *Seeing the Face*, 643). The contemporary psychiatrist Norman Doidge asserts, "Every emotion affects facial muscles and posture" (Doidge, *The Brain's Way of Healing*, 169–70).

2. The terms multi-modal communication and multimodality are also used, particularly by speech pathologists, but more commonly applied to the use of gesture and other modes by people with speech difficulties.

character, our emotions, our attitudes, our intentions, or expectations.[3] Even those who habitually lie in bed all day (Prov 6:9–10) are telling us (whether they intend to or not) a great deal about their character as lazybones. The offering by the magi of gifts of gold, frankincense, and myrrh (Matt 2:11) tells us something of their status, their estimation of the infant Jesus, and perhaps more if suggestions about the significance of the individual gifts are on the mark. We need to limit our focus to those actions which are more conventional or stylized; that is, those which generally have a meaning beyond a single context. To simple stances or movements of the body we might add actions involving items of clothing such as tearing one's garments (cf. §4.11) or removing one's sandals (cf. §6.3), and the use of other props which were ready to hand such as a ring or staff (chapter 5), items which are effectively extensions of the body.

We might also include as non-speech communication the utterance of sounds such as laughter, hissing, or whistling, which are not regarded as having a linguistic value, though the line between what is linguistic and non-linguistic vocalization is recognized to be very thin.[4] To limit the scope of this study, interjections ("aha," "woe," "alas," etc.) which are represented as lexemes in the text of the Bible (e.g., Gen 42:21; Ezek 16:23; Mark 15:29; Rev 18:19) will be excluded from further consideration.

This study then deals with nonverbal communication in the Bible. For the purposes of this study, the Bible will be taken to include the books of the Hebrew Bible (the OT) and the writings of the Greek NT, though all references will be given in English with English verse numberings.[5] The books of the Apocrypha contain much useful material on nonverbal communication but are not included here as being less accessible to many Protestants.

Unlike the classical Greek and Roman literary corpus, the Bible contains little that could be said to reflect at a theoretical level on nonverbal communication, and nothing to compare with the extensive how-to manuals on the use and interpretation of gesture in public speaking. There is a tendency in the classical authors to try to read too much into physical appearance (physiognomy) and body language.[6] It is possible to detect in

---

3. Cf. the "pansemiotic" view of the sociologist Erving Goffman as summarised by Lateiner: "The body, and therefore the person, can *never* not communicate" (Lateiner, *Sardonic Smile*, 7).

4. Wharton, *Pragmatics*, 70–106.

5. Unless otherwise indicated, English Bible citations are from the NRSV module of the *Accordance* Bible software.

6. See e.g., Cairns, *Body Language*, x–xii; Swain, *Seeing the Face*.

INTRODUCTION

Paul's language of 1 Cor 2:1-5, when he eschewed "human wisdom," a reference to the excessive reliance on oratorical technique, including gesture, by his contemporaries.[7] The biblical writers, and not least Paul, do, however, demonstrate an awareness of the role of the body in communicating meaning, either along with or independently of speech.[8]

A proverb reflects on the power of nonverbal communication: "One who winks the eyes plans perverse things; one who compresses the lips brings evil to pass" (Prov 16:30), where the point is probably that deception is possible without a word being spoken (cf. §2.11). The Bible abounds in references to the body and its members, and includes a rich vocabulary of function words associated with parts of the body (turn, raise, reach, touch, kiss, clap, kneel, bow, fall, sit, run, etc.), including words we might not immediately recognize as involving posture or gesture but where body language underlies them (worship, respect, show favor, be generous). Even the act of praying is likely to be perceived by modern Western readers as a mental or at most vocal activity. Earlier readers would have understood this to involve the body. Nehemiah prays: "Let your ear be attentive *and your eyes open* to hear the prayer of your servant that I now pray before you" (Neh 1:6, emphasis added). The prophets of Israel in particular are noted for their significant use of pantomime-like actions to accompany or to substitute for the spoken word, as Isaiah's "nakedness" (Isa 20:1-6), Jeremiah's yoke (Jer 27-28), and Ezekiel's mock siege of Jerusalem (Ezek 4:1-3), and while this is not a technical study of legal and prophetic gesture, reference will be made to some of these.[9]

When the writers of the Bible record an aspect of nonverbal communication by one party in a dialogue, and either explicitly or implicitly the other party takes note of this communication, we enter a shared realm of understanding between them and hopefully ourselves rightly understand this exchange, just as we hope through all of our lexical and grammatical studies to understand their recorded linguistic communication.

---

7. The works of Aristotle, Theophrastus, Cicero, and Quintilian, for example, include copious instruction on stance, facial expressions, hand gestures, and the like in oratory; see e.g., Corbeill, *Nature Embodied*; Kendon, *Gesture*, 17-19; Graf, "Gestures and Conventions," 36-58.

8. On Paul and rhetoric, see Porter, "Paul of Tarsus"; Welborn, *Paul, the Fool of Christ*, 90-99; Shi, *Paul's Message*, 112-42.

9. See Friebel, *Jeremiah's and Ezekiel's Sign-Acts*; Lundbom, *The Hebrew Prophets*, 209-17; Viberg, *Symbols of Law*.

Nonverbal communication can range from the finest of movements of facial muscles to the stance and movement of the body as a whole. Jacob could read in his father-in-law's face a change of attitude towards him (Gen 31:5). A silence, when speech is expected, can be quite eloquent (cf. §2.10). How close or far apart people position themselves can be instructive (cf. §6.7). When Joseph's estranged brothers draw nearer to him at his invitation (Gen 45:4), the emotional impact of the revelation of their brother's true identity is heightened.

Of course we only have a written account of all such communicative acts in the Bible, so we are at least one step removed at the outset from witnessing and being able to interpret such actions directly (insofar as the texts are historical rather than fictive). On the other hand, the written text offers us an advantage in the discernment of nonverbal communication. Whereas in face-to-face contact there could be any number of incidental movements which the observer must filter out to determine which ones convey information, whether intended or not, the biblical writers have done the filtering and included reference only to those gestures and expressions which they deem pertinent to the reader's understanding of the interaction.[10]

We need to exercise a degree of caution in endeavoring to reconstruct in any detail the physical gestures of the lived experience of the Israelites or their neighbors of the second or first millennium BC, or Jews, Christians, or pagans of the first century AD. Texts may use hyperbole, or stylize a character's actions for their own rhetorical purposes. There may be some literary conventions which take on a life of their own with little to anchor them in the social conventions of the era the texts represent. Did people really fall face-down on the ground as frequently as the texts suggest, or is this a literary device to highlight the drama of the events depicted?

We are further constrained by the fact that speech, and particularly its derivative, writing, lack the range of subtlety of which nonverbal communication is capable. Human lips alone have a dozen or so muscles to shape them into an astonishing array of distinguishable positions. If we read that a hand is stretched out, is it clenched or open, palm in or out or up, and is the movement fast or slow? Does stretching out the hand, then, suggest simply pointing out something, or an act of aggression, or an overture of friendship, or the commencement of a speech, or something else? There is a limited number of words to indicate raising the hand, touching, or looking, for example, whereas these actions can be performed in an infinitely subtly

---

10. Kendon, *Gesture*, 13.

variable range of ways and degrees, with corresponding gradation of intent. Written language is digital, whereas nonverbal communication is analogue, and spoken language a combination of the two (with the paralinguistic elements of gradation in volume, pitch, and pace).[11] The same Hebrew word can denote arrival (Gen 28:12), a reassuring touch (Dan 8:18), sexual molestation (Ruth 2:9), a beating (Prov 6:33), and affliction with plague or disease (Gen 12:17; 2 Chr 26:20). We are not going to be able neatly to correlate the communicative function of certain postures or gestures with particular vocabulary or to assign a one-gesture-one-meaning solution to the study of nonverbal communication in the Bible. However, through bringing together material in a more comprehensive manner than has been done to this point I hope to offer some insights and to stimulate further research. As David Calabro observes,

> Relationships and contrasts ... exist between the gestures described in ancient texts; paying attention to these allows one to tap a level of meaning beyond the analysis of isolated gestures. The meanings attached to these relationships and contrasts, like the grammatical rules of ancient languages, are rarely if ever stated explicitly in the texts, but they can be discovered through assembling examples of gestures and noting patterns of how they are used in context.[12]

As always, then, context plays a significant role in determining the meaning of the language employed to denote gesture, just as it must with the gestures themselves in real life.

Our expressions and gestures can be more or less instinctive and reflexive, such as smiling in response to a pleasing stimulus, turning or covering the face in shame, or putting a hand to the mouth to indicate silence. Such actions tend to be universal and hence more readily grasped by modern readers. Other gestures and body language are more voluntary, more culturally determined, and hence more open to misunderstanding. A modern Western reader might be inclined to interpret the phrase "shake his hand" (Isa 10:32 KJV) as a friendly initiative, whereas in context it indicates threatened judgment. Translators can ameliorate this by using the word "fist" for which there is no specific Hebrew equivalent. On the other hand, we may miss something of the significance of the "right hand of fellowship" (Gal 2:9) if we see it simply as a parting gesture of goodwill. And what is a

---

11. Cf. ibid., 70–71.
12. Calabro, "When You Spread Your Palms," 17.

modern reader to make of the intentions of one who places his hand "under the thigh" of another (Gen 24:2)? It is to these more ambiguous forms of nonverbal communication that we need to give greater attention.

No sharp distinction will be made here between gesture and body language as maintained by Cotterell and Turner.[13] Nor does this study make a sharp distinction between involuntary and voluntary movement in that both may be revealing. Charles Darwin (who effectively marks the beginning of the modern scientific study of nonverbal communication) demonstrated the relationship between reflex actions and acquired habits (including some observations based on biblical references), and tended to universalize gesture as a natural reaction to stimuli, minimizing cultural difference in expressions of gesture.[14] The philosopher of language E. P. Grice posited a polar distinction between natural (spontaneous) and non-natural (intentional) nonverbal communication, while others such as D. McNeill, Adam Kendon, and Tim Wharton have since refined this and demonstrated a continuum from gesticulation, through pantomime and culturally determined signaling, to signing.[15] Wharton draws on relevance theory to show how it is not a matter of simply coding and decoding specific items of nonverbal communication, but each gesture is context-dependent for its interpretation, and its meaning needs to be *inferred*, so is not necessarily reducible to words. Some would prefer to restrict the designation "nonverbal communication" to voluntary movements, using "nonverbal information" to refer to involuntary ones.[16] But natural gestures can be intentionally displayed or concealed with varying degrees of success. Sarah tried unsuccessfully to conceal her laughter at the news she would have a son (Gen 18:12–15), whereas Habakkuk pictures the advancing Babylonians who very openly "laugh at every fortress, and heap up earth to take it" (Hab 1:10). On recognizing his brothers (Gen 42:7), Joseph managed for quite some time to contain his emotion in front of them but, after a couple of bouts of secret weeping (Gen 42:24; 43:30), eventually he could "no longer control himself" (Gen 45:1) and wept loudly (Gen 45:2; cf. §3.2.2). Smiling is both innate and universal on the one hand, and

13. By gesture they mean the expressions and movement of parts of the body, while body language refers more generally to posture and proxemics (the closeness of people when interacting) (Cotterell and Turner, *Linguistics*, 49–51).

14. Darwin, *Expression*, 321.

15. Grice, "Meaning"; McNeill, *Hand and Mind*; Kendon, *Gesture*; Wharton, *Pragmatics*.

16. Kruger, "'Nonverbal Communication' in the Hebrew Bible," 144.

learned and cultural on the other, and as many as nineteen different smiles have been identified by researchers.[17]

There is also in the languages of the Bible (as in most languages) a vast range of metaphorical expressions employing words for body parts or movements.[18] Walking is a standard metaphor for conduct or lifestyle (Ps 1:1; Mic 6:8; John 12:35), and standing for endurance (Exod 14:13; Eph 6:13; Phil 4:1). Some of these may owe their origin to physiological correlations of emotions and parts of the body.[19] Many may have had their origin in cultural communicative gesture, but it is not always clear whether an element of this survives in the actual texts under consideration. Are we to picture a physical gesture in all references to raising the hand in an oath-taking context, e.g., Gen 14:22 where NRSV simply has "I have sworn to the LORD"? Given that the key Hebrew and Greek words usually translated "worship" refer in their etymology to the physical action of bowing or falling to the ground, are we to envisage this as taking place every time the word "worship" occurs or do some instances refer to an inner attitude alone (cf. §4.6)? We need to be open to the possibility that what we consider a purely internal process (as evidenced by some of our modern translations) may, in a different culture, have survived as a genuine act of nonverbal communication.

We recognize the reference to heaping burning coals on heads (Rom 12:20) as a metaphor. But what about Paul's injunctions regarding head coverings for men and women in 1 Cor 11:4–7? And what could Jesus have meant when he taught that "the eye is the lamp of the body. So, if your eye is healthy, your whole body will be full of light" (Matt 6:22; cf. §3.2.1)?

This book does not endeavor to deal with the wealth of references to internal organs (heart, liver, kidneys, womb, intestines, blood, bones, etc.) which are frequently associated with various cognitive and emotional functions, but by their hidden nature are not normally involved with any nonverbal communicative actions.[20] Where idiomatic expressions are based on gestures, some of these will be touched on in the discussion that follows.[21] A typical body idiom refers to a body part and an action

---

17. Wiemann and Harrison, *Nonverbal Interaction*, 280–81.

18. Cf. Griffin, "Investigation."

19. See e.g., Dhorme, *L'emploi*; Plutchik, *Psychology*; Hupka et al., "Anger"; Smith, "Heart"; Kotzé, "A Cognitive Linguistic Approach."

20. For this material see, e.g., Schroer and Staubli, *Body Symbolism*; Smith, "Heart."

21. Van Den Heever defines an idiom as "a conventionalised multi-word symbolic

or state predicated of the body part and where we understand that the reference is not "literal"; that is, the meaning of the whole is not immediately transparent from its components. Translations differ in the way they treat such idioms. Particularly where translators apparently feel the idiom may be reasonably transparent to a modern English reader, they may render the components of the Hebrew or Greek expression in a formally equivalent way. So we get: "Within three days Pharaoh will lift up your head" (Gen 40:13 NRSV; cf. §2.3), or "You stiff-necked people, uncircumcised in heart and ears" (Acts 7:51 NRSV). Elsewhere, particularly where translators believe the idiom is opaque, or in translations where more dynamic equivalence is preferred in general, body idioms may be rendered without reference to the body. Thus Acts 7:51 (cited above from NRSV) becomes: "You stubborn people! You are heathen at heart and deaf to the truth" (NLT2). The Message renders heaping coals on the head as: "Your generosity will surprise him with goodness" (Rom 12:20), but is this understanding correct (cf. §2.6)? There is a gradation from literal to metonymic or metaphorical uses of body terminology as well as a gradation from involuntary through to voluntary body movements. Thus it will not always be possible to tell if a writer intends us to picture a literal action, or to infer the idiomatic meaning of the expression. When God stretches out his hands, that is, to plead or entreat (Isa 65:2), we know it is an idiom, but what about when Moses is said to do the same (Exod 9:33)?

The biblical texts frequently describe particular gestures such as raising the head or hand, and, whether or not we envisage a literal action, we need mentally to supply an emotion or disposition as an interpretation of the gesture. Occasionally we even have nothing but a reference to a change of facial expression, for example, where the reader is left to infer the nature of the change, and hence the character of the emotion, from the context. When Hannah received some reassurance from the priest Eli that her prayer had been heard, we are told (lit.) that "she no longer had her face," that is, "her countenance was sad no longer" (1 Sam 1:18 NRSV).

On the other hand, there is also of course in the Bible a vast array of descriptors of emotional response or mental disposition, from terror to amazement, from perplexity to recognition, from wariness to adoration. In general, emotions and attitudes betray themselves in nonverbal

---

unit with a verbal nucleus and a content message, whose global meaning is a semantic extension of the combined meanings of its constituent elements" (Van Den Heever, "Idioms," 177).

communication, whether or not such bodily movement is expressly referred to in the text. We picture the exuberance in the faces of the magi at the realization that the star had stopped and their mission was over and "they were overwhelmed with joy" (Matt 2:10). When the ark is brought to Jerusalem "with great rejoicing" (2 Sam 6:12), we see the joy in the faces of the people without expressly being given any outward description. Elisha stared at Hazael "until he [Hazael] was ashamed" (2 Kgs 8:11), and the prophet must have seen the awkward embarrassment in his face at the news he has been given.[22] We know that the shepherds in the Bethlehem fields were terrified at the sight of the angels (and we picture this in their faces) only because the narrator tells us of their emotion, not of their facial expression (Luke 2:9). No facial expressions are indicated in the text, but when Jesus was accused before Pilate, "he gave him no answer, not even to a single charge, so that the governor was greatly amazed" (Matt 27:14). When a rich man heard Jesus' response to his question about eternal life, "he was shocked and went away grieving, for he had many possessions" (Mark 10:22). When the risen Jesus encounters his disciples and tells them not to be afraid, we infer that Jesus recognizes in their reaction at seeing him an element of fear (Matt 28:9–10). Sometimes, with masterly understatement in the text, the situation alone is sufficient to make us very aware of the emotions the characters may be expressing or seeking to suppress. When Isaac questioned Abraham about the sacrifice they were traveling to offer on Mount Moriah and we read that "the two of them walked on together" (Gen 22:6), we picture the awkward silence and Abraham struggling to keep his emotions in check.

Of particular interest in what follows will be those places where a bodily expression, such as a "fallen face" (Gen 4:5), trembling (Mark 5:33), or the lifting up of hands (Ps 141:2) can, from the context, be associated with an emotion or inner process (anger, fear, prayer) as these associations then help us to interpret those instances where body language alone is referred to.

The field of nonverbal communication has a vast and expanding literature. Already in 1980 there was a book-length bibliography of over four thousand items of nonverbal communication research.[23] The majority of this deals with study of contemporary observable nonverbal

---

22. See commentaries; the Hebrew uses the pronoun "he" throughout this verse so it is an interpretation to supply the names.

23. Frye, *FIND*. For a discussion on the history and status of nonverbal research, see also Wiemann and Harrison, *Nonverbal Interaction*, 271–85.

communication and much less attention has been given to the role that references to nonverbal activity play in literature, in ancient societies, and in the Bible in particular.

A number of studies on gesture in the ancient world, covering literary texts as well as iconography, should be mentioned as providing a valuable wider context within which to situate a study of the biblical material. In his Introduction to a volume of essays on the role of gesture in history generally, Keith Thomas notes that "gesture formed an indispensable element in the social interaction of the past."[24] Richard Wilkinson includes a study of gesture in his comprehensive treatment of Egyptian iconography, noting that "there is a remarkable consistency and continuation in the use and meaning of Egyptian gestures."[25] Mayer Gruber has produced a study of a limited range of gestures in ancient Western Asia, mainly those associated with certain emotions such as mourning, joy, and anger, striving to sharply differentiate genuine body language from idiomatic uses of the descriptors of that body language.[26] But there is much more to nonverbal communication than the emotions Gruber deals with. He does not, for example, cover gestures of shame or contempt, and performative gestures like swearing an oath are outside his purview. Gruber may at times be too quick to assume a universality in the forms of emotional expression across cultures, but there is a wealth of comparative material for the Hebrew Bible from Mesopotamia and Ugarit (a kingdom on the coast of Syria with cultural affinities with Israel's immediate neighbors, the Canaanites).

Another important contributor to the discussion is Othmar Keel, whose work illustrating the symbolism of the book of Psalms from the iconography of the ancient world includes some material on gesture, though this is not the focus of his book. Like Gruber, Keel works from a premise of substantial cultural continuity across the Mediterranean and Western Asia.[27] Another work which deals with body symbolism in the Bible more generally, with less of a focus on nonverbal communication, is that of Schroer

---

24. Thomas, "Introduction," 5.

25. Wilkinson, *Symbol and Magic*, 195.

26. Gruber, *Aspects*. Gruber's organizing principle is to group gestures according to their intended function. Thus gestures of worship and supplication are treated separately from those of obeisance, which obscures the range of functions of a common gesture and Gruber too neatly categorizes some complex emotions. For a critique of Gruber's confident differentiation of idiomatic and literal references, see Calabro, "Ritual Gestures," 132–36.

27. Keel, *Symbolism*.

and Staubli, which includes some good illustrations from the iconography of the cultures surrounding the lands of the Bible's setting.[28]

There is a growing number of studies of gesture in the classical Mediterranean cultures of Greece and Rome which (as well as the Semitic cultural milieu) form a significant background for the world of the NT.[29] These include studies of gesture in classical art as well as in literary texts, and texts describing gesture in drama and oratory. In this world, gestures formed a strong means of differentiating social ranking, and we will note some comparisons with corresponding gestures in the biblical world.

Studies of biblical narrative may include brief reference to gesture as an aspect of characterization. For Robert Alter, gesture is at the less explicit end of a spectrum of information disclosure (from inferences which may be drawn from the account of the characters' actions through to statements by the reliable narrator on what the characters feel, intend, etc.).[30] However, there is little in Alter's subsequent discussion which could be regarded as related to gesture. Shimon Bar-Efrat devotes half a page to the function of gesture in characterization.[31] There is also now a considerable number of specialized studies on specific gestures or particular portions of Scripture to which reference will be made later. One is worth mentioning at this point. David Calabro's recent thesis on hand gestures in the Northwest Semitic cultural sphere is a particularly useful collation of material relating to the OT and its more immediate cultural environment.[32] The work covers in depth a limited range of gestures, with close attention to context, and should serve as a model for future research into other forms of nonverbal communication relevant to the interpretation of the Bible.

To this we may add studies of idiomatic expressions. A number of these draw on theoretical study of idioms and consider biblical idioms including those based on gesture in the light of the theory. While much has been done, a more systematic treatment of idioms in the lexicons and a more consistent approach to the translation of idioms are much to be

---

28. Schroer and Staubli, *Body Symbolism*.

29. See, e.g., Brilliant, *Gesture and Rank*; Davies, "Significance"; Graf, "Gestures and Conventions"; Lateiner, *Sardonic Smile*; Aldrete, *Gestures and Acclamations*; Cairns, *Body Language*; Corbeill, *Nature Embodied*; Clark, Foster, and Hallett, *Kinesis*.

30. Alter, *Art*, 116–17.

31. Bar-Efrat, *Narrative Art*, 84.

32. Calabro, "Ritual Gestures."

desired.³³ It is to be hoped that this work, limited though its treatment of idioms is to those related to gesture, will stimulate further reflection on this important area of linguistic study.

Since, then, the biblical writers have included numerous references to nonverbal communicative activity, a more comprehensive and systematic treatment of the subject is called for. The main source for this study, as will be evident from the foregoing, is the consideration of biblical passages containing expressions of nonverbal forms of communication, comparing texts within the Bible with uses of the same or similar actions in an endeavor to understand their significance. More of the examples are drawn from the OT because the OT abounds in narrative involving the behavior of people, though in the NT the Gospels and Acts furnish us with further material, and other parts of Scripture include idioms and imagery drawn from body language. It has been calculated, for example, that 5.7 percent of the words occurring in the Psalms are from the semantic domain of the body and its members.³⁴ While we may detect instances of development within the pages of Scripture, particularly as the Semitic world meets the Hellenistic culture of the NT period, there is a reasonable level of continuity in the recorded body language of pre-exilic Israelites, Second Temple Jews, and early Christians.

To this we may add any light that may be shed by other literature from the ancient world. There are dangers in this, in that gesture, insofar as it has a cultural element, might not be identical across national boundaries or over time. Comparative material is included here where it serves to illustrate or elucidate the gestures of the biblical text without assuming a close identity of culture.³⁵ There are many cultural differences in nonverbal communication between, say, Iron Age Israel and Egypt, or the early church and classical Greece, which are not mentioned in this study. However, it is a reasonable hypothesis (and borne out by observation) that some gestures are likely to have similar force throughout much of ancient Western Asia and the Mediterranean, the more so in areas of close geographical proximity, hegemony, and linguistic milieu. Regular contact for trade and other purposes would have rendered invaluable the use of "sign language" as an

---

33. Griffin, "Investigation"; Lübbe, "Idioms"; Babut, *Idiomatic Expressions*; Warren-Rothlin, "Body Idioms"; Van Den Heever, "Idioms"; Tilford, *Sensing World, Sensing Wisdom*.

34. Gillmayr-Bucher, "Body Images," 302.

35. For the issue of cultural difference in the study of gesture, see Kendon, *Gesture*, 326–54.

aid to communication in situations where the command of the other's spoken language was not strong.[36]

There is also the evidence afforded by ancient art. While we do not have much in the way of depictions of people from ancient Israel or the primitive church, we have a wealth of images of bodies portrayed in situations of everyday life in Egyptian, Mesopotamian, Levantine, Greek, and Roman art. Of course in these we only have a frozen moment in time, rather than an indication of movement, but there is sometimes enough to suggest comparison with biblical expressions, such as postures for prayer.

A further possibility is to consider body language in the living cultures of Western Asia today or the accounts of observers of relatively recent times.[37] This would presuppose some continuity between ancient and modern gestures and idioms relating to the body and its movements in this part of the world, analogous to the survival of linguistic forms, and is to be used with caution.[38] It is a method exploited by Kenneth Bailey, for example, in his works on the cultural background to the parables of Jesus.[39]

This study is not a general discussion of manners and customs in biblical times. Occasionally a cultural mode (e.g., the normal treatment of hair) may be mentioned as the backdrop for those abnormal treatments (such as shaving the head or pulling out the hair) which then constitute a statement. An area that will be largely excluded from this survey is that of cultic activity, particularly the rituals of sacrifice and offering, blood manipulation, etc., practiced at the sanctuary, and covenant signs or sacraments such as circumcision and baptism. Cultic gesture is a specialized discipline and one which is the subject of a number of admirable studies.[40] However, since some cultic gestures may be derivatives of everyday gestures, just as the gestures in Roman oratory or acting were often stylizations and exaggerations of gestures from daily life, aspects of these may be mentioned for illustrative purposes.

---

36. Cf. Wilkinson, *Symbol and Magic*, 200.

37. For this we have the useful taxonomy of Arabic gestures compiled by Barakat, "Arabic Gestures."

38. E.g., Tristram, *The Land of Israel*. On the issue of cultural continuity of gesture, see Thomas, "Introduction," 10.

39. Bailey, *Poet and Peasant* and *Through Peasant Eyes*.

40. Haran, *Temples and Temple Service*; Gorman, *The Ideology of Ritual*; Jenson, *Graded Holiness*; Milgrom, *Studies*; Milgrom, *Leviticus 1–16*; Milgrom, *Leviticus 17–22*; Milgrom, *Leviticus 23–27*.

The plan of this book is broadly to group the elements of nonverbal communication according to body part mentioned (or implied) in the biblical text and discuss these in relation to the function words (raising, turning, falling, clapping, etc.) used to indicate their position or movement, and their significance as indicated by their contexts, with some mention of the idioms and metaphors associated with these. Parallel expressions, direct or indirect speech, and associated purpose and result clauses may form part of the elucidating context. We deal in turn with the head, the eyes (treated separately because of their prominent use in gesture phrases),[41] the neck, torso, and body as a whole, the arms and hands, and the legs and feet. This is to some extent simplistic as many emotions and dispositions are communicated with a complex of gestures. To limit weeping to a function of the eyes overlooks other aspects of facial expression, vocalization, head movement, and hand movements that may accompany the tears. Anger involves more than a reddening of the face though this is often the facial characteristic to which the narrator draws attention. Sometimes two or more aspects of nonverbal communication are mentioned in a passage, as when Job tore his robe, shaved his head, and threw himself face-down on the ground (Job 1:20) or when the tax collector "standing far off, would not even look up to heaven, but was beating his breast and saying, 'God, be merciful to me, a sinner!'" (Luke 18:13). But often one aspect suffices for mention by the narrator and we picture the others. When Reuben returned to find his brother Joseph missing, all we are told is that "he tore his clothes" (Gen 37:29), but we surely picture the distress in his face as well. We surmise from ancient images that the gesture of surrender involved a tilt of the head as well as the stretching out of the arms, but only the arms are mentioned in the biblical texts (cf. §5.9).

I have endeavored to make the material accessible to the general reader. Reference to Hebrew and Greek and other technical matters has been kept to an absolute minimum in the body of the text, though the reader who wishes to pursue particular issues in greater depth will find the footnotes useful.

While body language can thus only be represented in biblical text in the most reductionist and stylized of ways, the fact that it is mentioned at all, particularly in a corpus of literature that is not noted for its descriptive language or unnecessary coloration, makes it a topic worthy of our careful attention.

---

41. The second-century-AD writer Polemon of Laodicea devoted one of his two books on physiognomy to the eyes; see Swain, *Seeing the Face*, 177.

2

The Head

OUR ATTENTION IS NATURALLY drawn to the head as the feature we find the most distinguishing and most expressive in other people. Through the tensioning or relaxing of muscles resulting in a great variety of head movements and facial expressions we convey a vast range of moods and attitudes. The head, with the face and its features and functions, is then the source of a considerable store of idioms. Because the eyes receive more attention than other features of the head and face, they will be dealt with separately in a subsequent chapter.

The head may represent the whole person.[1] Achish engaged David as his bodyguard or (lit.) "keeper of his head" (1 Sam 28:2). The spoils of the Israelite conquest were to be distributed to (lit.) each "head of a man" (Judg 5:30). Responsibility for one's actions rests on one's own head (1 Kgs 2:32, 37, 44; 8:32; Esth 9:25; Ps 7:16; Ezek 11:21; Joel 3:7; Obad 15; Acts 18:6). Being essential for viability, the head can stand for a person's life. The official responsible for Daniel's provisions at the Babylonian court was reluctant to "endanger his head" by contravening a royal directive (Dan 1:10). When the image of the Philistine god Dagon fell face down in front of the ark of the LORD, the severing of its head would have suggested to the Israelite reader the lifelessness of the deity it represented (1 Sam 5:4). Similarly, human beheadings, rare in the Bible, constitute a gruesome statement of power over life and death; the severed head is a trophy. David's beheading of Goliath (when piercing the chest would have been quicker) and subsequent display of the severed head induced fear in the Philistines and emboldened the Israelite troops (1 Sam 17:51–54).[2] Second Samuel

---

1. Gruber, "Many Faces," 252.

2. Cf. the depiction of Pompey's beheading in Lucan, *Pharsalia* viii 667–73; beheading was not a quick and easy procedure with ancient weaponry.

4:7–12 relates the beheading of Ishbaal by those who wrongly thought they would impress David and consolidate his kingship over all Israel (cf. 2 Sam 20:22). Herod's beheading of John the Baptist was a dramatic gesture (and contrary to Jewish law) prompted by his wife, demonstrably silencing the unwelcome prophetic voice (Matt 14:8–12; Mark 6:17–29).

The head is then the locus for such symbolic actions, referring to the well-being or role of the whole person, as anointing and laying on of hands in healing, in blessing, in consecrating, and the like. Because it is on the head that hands might physically be placed in an act of blessing, by metonymy the blessings themselves can be said to be on the head (Gen 49:26; Prov 10:6; 11:26).

The head then can serve as a natural image of leadership, primacy, or source. Jephthah was made "head and commander" over the people of Gilead (Judg 11:11), and "Christ is the head of the church" (Eph 5:23; cf. Num 30:1; 36:1; Deut 20:9; Josh 11:10; 2 Sam 22:44; Neh 12:46; Job 29:25; Isa 7:8–9; 9:15; Jer 13:21; 31:7; Ezek 38:2–3; Matt 21:42; 1 Cor 11:3; Eph 1:22; 4:15; Col 1:18; 2:10). In the Bible, the head is not thought of as the locus for reasoning; thinking is rather with the "heart" (Ps 10:6, 11), though it is in the head that one sees visions (Dan 2:28).

2.1 The Hair and Beard

The hair can be regarded as a physically attractive feature of both men and women (Lam 4:7; Song 4:1; 1 Cor 11:15), though too much attention to one's hairdo and outward appearance in general is discouraged in early Christian teaching (1 Pet 3:3; 1 Tim 2:9). The arrangement (or disarrangement) of the hair can communicate one's status or state of mind. Isaiah pictures well-groomed hair as part of the normality of daily life in Jerusalem in contrast to the (self-inflicted) baldness and other signs of distress that are coming (Isa 3:24). Israelites were to have an identifiable hairstyle in relation to the other nations (Lev 19:27; Jer 9:26; 25:23; 49:32), perhaps to avoid associations with idolatry. It is possible that Israelite prophets had a distinctive hairstyle or tonsure, for a prophet (who was unlikely to have been known to Ahab personally, given that the prophets had been in hiding) was recognized by the king to be a prophet when he removed a head bandage which had served as a disguise (1 Kgs 20:41; cf. 2 Kgs 2:23).[3] Paul regards it as "natural" for men and women to have different hairstyles

---

3. Davies, *1 Kings*, 384–85.

(1 Cor 11:14–15). Gray hair, a natural indicator of aging, in the cultures of the Bible connotes respect: "Gray hair is a crown of glory; it is gained in a righteous life" (Prov 16:31; cf. 20:29).

Ancient societies (as many contemporary cultures) could be quite demonstrative in mourning rites involving the hair, with some differentiation between men and women.[4] Any departure from normal grooming of the hair indicates an abnormal state of affairs, a public demonstration of a temporary change in an individual's status in relation to the community.[5] In Israel, self-inflicted baldness or a shaved head speaks of humiliation, mourning, or ritual uncleanness (Lev 10:6; 13:45; 21:5, 10; Deut 14:1; Isa 3:24; 7:20; Jer 7:29; 16:6; 48:37; Ezek 5:1; 44:20; Amos 8:10; Mic 1:16). Job's response at the news of the calamities that had befallen him was to tear his robe, shave his head, and throw himself face down on the ground (Job 1:20). Ezra pulled his hair out in reaction to the news of the mixed marriages among the people of Judah (Ezra 9:3), while Nehemiah even enforced this expression of mourning in pulling out the hair of those responsible for such compromising behavior (Neh 13:25). If the reading of Jer 2:16 adopted by ESV is correct, the shaving of the crown of the head which would be inflicted by the Egyptians on the Israelites is a metaphor for the embarrassment Israel would suffer if they should rely on Egypt for aid.[6] Nebuchadnezzar is pictured as having unkempt hair as a sign of his madness or affinity with the animals (Dan 4:33).

Paul's teaching on men's and women's roles in worship includes the following observation: "But any woman who prays or prophesies with her head unveiled disgraces her head—it is one and the same thing as having her head shaved" (1 Cor 11:5). We know from an ancient source that a shaved head was regarded as shameful for a woman at Corinth.[7]

---

4. This included displaying unbound or dishevelled hair, shaving the head, and (particularly by women) pulling out the hair (Homer, *Iliad* 23.46; Euripides, *Andromeda* 1209–10; Euripides, *Alcestis* 216, 427, 512; Ovid, *Metamorphoses* 11.682); see Keener, "Head Coverings"; Corbeill, *Nature Embodied*, 72–83.

5. See Olyan, "What Do Shaving Rites Accomplish?"

6. This either involves reading a Hebrew word which normally means "graze" in the extended sense of "shave" or else transposing two letters to yield a word from the root ʿrr meaning "lay bare, expose."

7. A comedy of the Greek dramatist Menander, the *Perikeiromene* ("The Girl with Her Hair Cut Short"), set in Corinth, concerns a jealous lover who committed the outrage of cutting short his girlfriend's hair.

Both priests and those undertaking a nazirite vow symbolized their holiness through their distinctive hairstyles (Num 6:1–21; Judg 13:5; Ezek 44:20). Paul shaved his hair at Cenchreae in fulfillment of a vow, presumably after letting it grow long for a time in a manner analogous to a nazirite, and probably as an outward demonstration of thanksgiving for his safety at Corinth (Acts 18:18; cf. 21:24). Priests and nazirites were forbidden to perform some of the otherwise normal mourning rituals involving the hair (Lev 21:10). The prophet Ezekiel, who is forbidden to mourn his wife, is told to keep his turban fastened (Ezek 24:17).

Respectable Jewish women did not let their hair down in public, so the scandalous actions of a woman, probably a former prostitute, in wiping Jesus' feet with her hair was a very unselfconscious act of humility and gratitude (Luke 7:38, 44; cf. John 11:2; 12:3).[8]

Facial hair was common for mature males throughout much of the ancient world. Bearded figures are the norm in Mesopotamian and early Greek iconography. Egyptians on the other hand were clean-shaven (Gen 41:14) though a false beard served as a status symbol for men of high rank. Alexander had his soldiers shave to make it harder for an enemy to grab the head (cf. Joab's tactic with Amasa: 2 Sam 20:9–10), and other Greeks in Hellenistic times followed suit. Romans, by NT times, were clean-shaven. Israelite men generally had beards and moustaches, which were a mark of their manliness (Ps 133:2), and normally kept them trimmed, so Mephibosheth's failure to trim his moustache displayed his distress (2 Sam 19:24). Beards might be shaved off or plucked in times of grief or great distress, perhaps coupled with tearing one's clothes or wearing sackcloth (cf. §4.11), common indicators of mourning (Ezra 9:3; Isa 15:2; Jer 48:37) or in certain cleansing rituals (Lev 13:33; 14:8, 9). Priests, who (among other things) represented the ideal of manliness,[9] were prevented from carrying out the otherwise customary beard shaving associated with mourning other than for very close relatives (Lev 21:5). To pluck hairs from another's beard or partially shave a beard is to commit a great indignity as the Ammonites did to David's envoys (2 Sam 10:4; 1 Chr 19:4).[10] Ezekiel's prophetic action in shaving his hair and beard and dealing in different ways with the hair

---

8. Bailey, *Through Peasant Eyes*, 8.

9. Cheung, "Priest."

10. For an analogous custom in Arabic societies of cutting off the beard of conquered enemies, see Barakat, "Arabic Gestures," 782.

symbolizes a coming judgment on Jerusalem and may combine elements of grief and disgrace (Ezek 5:1–4).

2.2 The Ears

An OT idiom for disclosing or revealing something to another is to uncover or open their ears: "He opens their ears to instruction, and commands that they return from iniquity" (Job 36:10; cf. Ruth 4:4; 1 Sam 9:15; 20:2; 20:12; 20:13; 22:8; 22:17; 2 Sam 7:27; 1 Chr 17:25; Job 33:16; 36:15; Isa 22:14).[11] In a more dramatic image, the ear is said to be "dug out" or "excavated" though NRSV tones down the image and renders it by "an open ear" (Ps 40:6). The notion of having a hole drilled in one's ear, emblematic of facilitating listening with a view to obedience, has been thought by some to lie behind the custom mentioned in Exod 21:2–6 (cf. Deut 15:12–18) where a slave who willingly submits to a master for life has his earlobe pierced, though the practice is otherwise unknown.[12]

One's choice to listen can be expressed by inclining or bending one's ear, an idiom based on the natural gesture of turning an ear closer to the source of the sound: "I will incline my ear to a proverb" (Ps 49:4), and an appeal to another to listen is to call upon them to incline their ear (Prov 4:20; 5:1, 13; 22:17; Isa 55:3). This becomes a standard form of plea to God to heed a petitioner's prayer (2 Kgs 19:16; Pss 10:17; 17:6; 31:2; 45:10; 71:2; 86:1; 88:2; 102:2; 116:2; Isa 37:17; Dan 9:18). The converse, a refusal to listen or obey, can be expressed as closing or stopping one's ear (Isa 6:10; 33:15; Prov 21:13; Lam 3:56). Other idioms for failing to listen are to have dull or heavy ears: "See, the Lord's hand is not too short to save, nor his ear too dull to hear" (Isa 59:1; cf. Matt 13:15; Acts 28:27; Heb 5:11), or uncircumcised ears (Acts 7:51).

To refuse to listen can be expressed as "blocking the ears." The righteous "stop their ears from hearing of bloodshed" (Isa 33:15). The Jewish crowd who had heard enough of Stephen's testimony "covered their ears, and with a loud shout all rushed together against him" (Acts 7:57). This is almost certainly referring to hands or fingers placed over the ears in a deliberate show of refusal to listen to what they regarded as blasphemy.

---

11. The Akkadian parallel is "to open the ears," meaning "to inform, reveal" (Oppenheim, "Idiomatic Accadian," 263).

12. For the practice, see Viberg, *Symbols of Law*, 77–88.

2.3 Head Movements

Head movements from the neck are among the most expressive of gestures as the head is raised, lowered, nodded, or shaken. The Roman writer Quintillian identified shame, doubt, admiration, and indignation as emotions that can be signaled by particular head movements.[13]

Raising one's head may express an attitude of joyful confidence. The Ugaritic Ba'lu epic depicts the gods lowering their heads to their knees in distress, then lifting them up upon receiving encouragement.[14] The ruler seated at God's right hand lifts up his head at the prospect of victory (Ps 110:7; cf. 3:3; 27:6; Zech 1:21). The temple doors are addressed as the LORD (represented by his ark) approaches in triumphal procession, "Lift up your heads, O gates! and be lifted up, O ancient doors! that the King of glory may come in" (Ps 24:7). The coming of the Son of Man likewise should give Jesus' followers confidence to "stand up and raise your heads, because your redemption is drawing near" (Luke 21:28). There can be a negative connotation to such head raising in proud self-exaltation. Israel's enemies exhibit hubris when they raise their heads in conspiracy against God's people (Ps 83:2), and such an image lies behind the description of the aspiration of the architects of Babel, who aspired to build "a city and a tower with its top [head] in the heavens" (Gen 11:4).

The head can figuratively be lifted by others in an act of exaltation. Pharaoh's cupbearer is promised that his head would be lifted, that is, he would be released from prison and restored to his office (Gen 40:13; cf. 2 Kgs 25:27; Pss 3:3; 27:6; Jer 52:31). In a dark play on words, his fellow-prisoner, the royal baker, had his head "lifted" from him on the gallows (Gen 40:19–20).

Shame or grief (regarded as closely related emotions in the ancient world)[15] results in a lowering of the head (as in the Ba'lu myth above). In *The Babylonian Theodicy* the sufferer complains that when his prayers for relief remained unanswered, "I did not hold my head high, I would look at the ground."[16] The Midianites were no longer able to hold their heads high after the slaughter of their kings (Judg 8:28). Lowering the head may accompany

---

13. Quintilian, *Institutio Oratoria* 71.
14. *The Ba'lu Myth* i 20–25 (*CoS*, 1:246); Gruber, *Aspects*, 598–614.
15. See e.g., Homer, *Odyssey* 8.84–85, 92; Euripides, *Hippolytus* 243–46; Epictetus, *Discourses* 1.11.27; Aulus Gellius, *Noctes Atticae* 19.6.1.
16. *The Babylonian Theodicy* xxvii (*CoS*, 1:495).

shedding tears (cf. §3.2.2), fasting (cf. §2.10), and wearing sackcloth (cf. §4.11). In parallel with the Jerusalem elders who in a time of distress "sit on the ground in silence" with "dust on their heads and . . . [wearing] sackcloth," "the young girls of Jerusalem have bowed their heads to the ground" (Lam 2:10; cf. Job 10:15; Isa 58:5).[17] Daniel's reaction to an angelic revelation is to turn his face to the ground and be at a loss for words (Dan 10:15). A similar response is shown by the frightened women at Jesus' empty tomb who "bowed their faces to the ground" when they encountered the angels (Luke 24:5). Plutarch similarly identifies a lowering of the face with dejection.[18] Jesus' bowing of his head on the cross (rather than raising it to gasp for air) is generally understood as an indication of the voluntary character of his death (John 19:30; cf. 10:17).[19] Bowing the head (and closing the eyes) as a general posture for prayer is a later Christian practice and unknown in the Bible. The one verse which could be taken this way is Ps 35:13: "But as for me, when they were sick, I wore sackcloth; I afflicted myself with fasting. I prayed with head bowed on my bosom" (NRSV). However, there is no mention of the head in Hebrew. The words are more literally, "My prayer kept returning to my breast," that is, where it started, in the "heart" (cf. Matt 10:13), so a reference to unanswered prayer.

Assent or a signal to proceed could be indicated by nodding the head.[20] Paul declined an invitation to stay longer in Ephesus, or (lit.) "did not nod" (Acts 18:20). When it was time for Paul to commence his defense before Felix, "the governor . . . nodded to him to speak" (Acts 24:10), and a more complex communication takes place at the last supper, when "Simon Peter . . . motioned to him [John] to ask Jesus of whom he was speaking" (John 13:24). While the word in both of these passages originally referred to head nodding, it is possible that (as NRSV's translation suggests) other gestures might have been involved.

A movement of the head (shaking or wagging from side to side) may indicate pity or sympathetic grief. Job's friends shake their heads in sympathy with his sufferings (Job 2:11). Jeremiah laments the condition of the land under God's judgment: "All who pass by it are horrified and shake their heads" (Jer 18:16). The word head is implied in other texts: "Who will have pity on you, O Jerusalem, or who will bemoan you [lit.: who will

---

17. For Ugaritic parallels, see Gruber, *Aspects*, 350–54.
18. Plutarch, *De vitioso pudore* 1.15.
19. BDAG, s.v. κλίνω.
20. Cf. the similar Homeric gesture (*Odyssey* 12:194; 15:463–64; 16:283).

shake (the head) at you]?" (Jer 15:5), and English translations often employ words for the attitude expressed (sympathy, comfort) rather than the physical movement (cf. Job 2:11; 42:11; Pss 64:8; 69:20; Isa 51:19; Jer 16:5; 22:10; 31:18; 48:17, 27; Nah 3:7).

Indications of derision or scorn (mock pity?) can also be expressed by a wagging or shaking of the head. A psalmist laments, "I am an object of scorn to my accusers; when they see me, they shake their heads" (Ps 109:25; cf. 2 Kgs 19:21; Job 16:4; 44:14; Isa 37:22; Jer 18:16; Lam 1:8; 2:15). Those who witnessed Jesus' crucifixion wagged their heads at him in derision (Matt 27:39; Mark 15:29; cf. Ps 22:7).

2.4 Covering the Head

As in many cultures, head covering or adornment in the Bible can serve as a symbol of status.[21] In particular several words generally translated "crown" refer to the distinctive headdress of royalty and of the priesthood. Kings and queens wore a "crown" on ceremonial occasions (2 Sam 1:10; 2 Kgs 11:12; 2 Chr 23:11; Esth 1:11; 2:17; 6:8; 8:15). In the OT the word rendered crown generally refers more accurately to a rosette affixed to a turban (Exod 29:6). In a judgment oracle against king Zedekiah, God says, "Remove the turban, take off the crown; things shall not remain as they are" (Ezek 21:26). The crown taken by David from the king of Rabbah is described as consisting of a talent of gold containing a precious stone (2 Sam 12:30; 1 Chr 20:2). Priests in Israel were dressed in the fashion of royalty and represented what it meant for Israel to be a royal priesthood (Exod 19:6).[22] The high priest Joshua was to have made for him a crown of silver and gold to symbolize the renewed acceptance and dignity in the sight of God of the returnees from exile (Zech 6:11). Bridegrooms also wore a head adornment akin to that of priests as the Hebrew of Isa 61:10 indicates. In the Hellenistic world, as well as serving as symbols of royal office, crowns (or wreaths placed on the head) were bestowed on victors in athletic contests or battles, and as civic honors.[23]

A wide range of metaphorical uses of crown imagery is to be found in the Bible. "A good wife is the crown of her husband" (Prov 12:4). "The

21. See Keener, "Head Coverings."
22. See Davies, *A Royal Priesthood*, 157–61.
23. For the background and significance of crown imagery in the NT, see Stevenson, "Conceptual Background."

crown of the wise is their wealth" (Prov 14:24). "Grandchildren are the crown of the elderly" (Prov 17:6). Both the people of God and God himself are depicted with crown imagery (Isa 28:5; 62:3). Those who continue faithful win or are given "the crown of righteousness" (2 Tim 4:8), "the crown of life" (Jas 1:12; Rev 2:10), or "a crown of glory" (1 Pet 5:4; cf. Job 19:9; Ps 21:3; Prov 4:9; Lam 5:16; Ezek 16:12). Jesus' crown at his crucifixion, like so much of his messianic role, represented a subverting of expectations, the thorns with which it was twisted a reminder that the road to glory lay in suffering (Matt 27:29).

This is not the place to engage in a full discussion of headwear in general in the Bible, nor a particular discussion of 1 Cor 11:2–16 dealing with men's and women's head covering and/or hair in Christian worship. The maintenance of gender differentiation (symbolized by means of the conventions of hairstyle) with regard to roles in the church remains a reasonable understanding of Paul's concern.[24] The way men and women appear in the semi-public environment of a church meeting (though held in a home) carries communicative value and is to be appropriate to the created order and/or social mores.

To pour dust or dirt (sometimes rendered ashes) on the head is an expression of distress, grief, and sympathy. In the Ugaritic myth, the high god 'Ilu, on learning of Ba'lu's death, "descends from the throne, sits on the footstool, (descends) from the footstool, sits on the earth. He pours dirt of mourning on his head, dust of humiliation on his cranium."[25] Jeremiah envisages farmers covering their heads, presumably with the dry earth that is the cause of their distress (Jer 14:4).[26] When Job's companions saw his condition, "they raised their voices and wept aloud; they tore their robes and threw dust in the air upon their heads" (Job 2:12; cf. Josh 7:6; 1 Sam 4:12; 2 Sam 1:2; 13:19; 15:32; Neh 9:1; Job 16:15; Lam 2:10; Ezek 27:30; Rev 18:19).[27] Dust in Scripture is the humble raw material from which humanity is constituted and to which we return (Gen 2:7; 3:19; 18:27; Job 10:9; 17:16; 20:11; 34:15; Pss 103:14; 104:29; Eccl 3:20; 12:7; 1 Cor 15:47–49), and covering oneself (from the head down) with dust is a form of self-abasement. One

---

24. For this, see Keener, "Head Coverings"; Fee, *The First Epistle to the Corinthians*, 491–530; Garland, *1 Corinthians*, 505–32; Bailey, *Paul through Mediterranean Eyes*, 303–8.

25. *The Ba'lu Myth* vi 11–16 (*CoS*, 1:267).

26. Lynch, "Neglected Physical Dimensions," 502.

27. For alternative explanations of the gesture in Job 2:12, see Clines, *Job 1–20*, 62–63.

instance where ash (or "soot") is thrown is when Moses threw it in the air to cause boils throughout Egypt (Exod 9:8–11). The plague-initiating sign may be an echo of the grief gesture, and we note that the ash is thrown "in the sight of Pharaoh," or more literally, "in Pharaoh's eyes," so perhaps a deliberate wordplay hinting at an insult.

Another mourning custom is to cover the head with the hand as Tamar did, along with dust on the head, tearing clothing, and wailing (2 Sam 13:19; cf. 15:30; Esth 6:12). An Egyptian tomb painting and the sarcophagus of King Ahiram of Byblos both show female mourners covering their heads with their hands, and in the Egyptian tale of *The Two Brothers* the elder brother mourns the tragic fate of the younger with "his hand on his head and smeared with dirt."[28] In Greek depictions of mourning, women commonly raise both hands to their head, though only in one known example does a man do so.[29] Plutarch records a Roman mourning practice in which men covered their heads.[30] In Jer 2:37 the placing of hands on the head is a sign of Israel's shame at foolishly relying on Egypt, and Egyptian reliefs show prisoners covering their heads with their arms.[31] A difficult verse is Mark 14:72 where Mark records Peter's remorse following the second cockcrow, reminding him of Jesus' prophecy of Peter's threefold denial. NRSV reads, "And he broke down and wept." Other suggestions for the meaning of the first verb include "covered (his head)," perhaps with similar force to "buried his face in his hands."[32]

---

28. *CoS*, 1:87; see "Head" in *IBD*, 615–16.
29. Corbeill, *Nature Embodied*, 72.
30. Plutarch, *Quaestiones Romanae* 14.
31. *ANEP*, #1, #7.
32. See Evans, *Mark 8:27—16:20*, 466–67.

THE HEAD

#1. *A Syrian captive of Ramses III with arms above head in symbol of submission. Egyptian, twelfth century BC. Limestone relief from the mortuary temple of Sabu-Re at Abusir. Staatliche Museen, Berlin. Drawn by Charlotte Whitehouse.*

2.5 Anointing

Anointing is treated here as it is typically applied to the head (Exod 29:7; Lev 8:12; 1 Sam 10:1; 2 Kgs 9:3; Ps 23:5). More generally, anointing is the application of oil to an object or person, particularly with the significance of rendering the object or person ritually holy, that is, fit for access to the presence of God or for employment in his service.[33] The oil is generally olive oil with added spices or fragrances (Exod 25:6; 30:25). Occasionally the word anoint is used for the application of non-oil-based substances as when Jesus smeared a mud mixture on a blind man's eyes (John 9:6). Objects such as pillars, altars, the tabernacle, and its furnishings could also be

---

33. See de Vaux, *Ancient Israel*, 103–6; Mettinger, *King and Messiah*, 185–232; Viberg, *Symbols of Law*, 89–119; Davies, *A Royal Priesthood*, 99–100; Fleming, "Anointing."

consecrated or declared ritually holy through anointing (Gen 31:13; Exod 29:36; 30:26; 40:10, 11; Lev 8:10, 11).

Fragrant oil was also applied to the skin as a cosmetic. Naomi encourages her daughter-in-law Ruth to apply perfume prior to her night-time encounter with Boaz (Ruth 3:3; cf. Ps 104:15; Ezek 16:9; Dan 10:3; Amos 6:6; Micah 6:15; Matt 6:17). An extended beauty treatment of twelve months' duration is prescribed for the women selected as potential replacements for Queen Vashti at the court of Xerxes (Esth 2:3–12). The image of oil on the head speaks of joy and the celebration of special occasions. A woman poured the contents of a bottle of perfume on Jesus' head in an extravagant display of devotion (Matt 26:7; cf. Pss 23:5; 141:5; Eccl 9:8; Isa 61:3). Presumably the woman who anointed Jesus' feet (the lowest and dirtiest part of the body) did so because she considered that to anoint his head would be presumptuous on her part (Luke 7:38).[34]

Oil is also applied in connection with cleansing and healing. James urges those who are sick to "call for the elders of the church and have them pray over them, anointing them with oil in the name of the Lord" (Jas 5:14; cf. Lev 14:18; Mark 6:13; Luke 10:34). Burial customs also involved anointing the body, as the women who came to Jesus' tomb had prepared to do (Mark 16:1; cf. Amos 6:10; Mark 14:8).

Ritual anointing of persons is attested in Hittite, Egyptian, and Canaanite contexts.[35] In Israel it was performed on persons designated for office, notably monarchs (Judg 9:8, 15; 1 Sam 9:16; 10:1; 16:13; 1 Kgs 1:39; 19:15, 16; 2 Kgs 9:3, 6; 11:12) and priests (Exod 28:41; 29:7, 21; 30:30; Lev 8:30; 21:10; Ps 133:2). The symbolism points to the bestowal of God's Spirit empowering the individual (1 Sam 10:10; 16:13; Luke 4:18; Acts 10:38). The phrase "anointed of the LORD" (or "his anointed") could then be used particularly to refer to the incumbent king in Israel (1 Sam 24:6, 10; 26:9, 11, 16, 23; 2 Sam 1:14,16; 2 Chr 6:42; Pss 45:7; 89:20), even a foreign king designated by God to accomplish his purpose (Isa 45:1) or, in time, to an ideal future ruler, a messiah or Christ (the Aramaic and Greek words for anointed: Matt 16:16; 26:63; Luke 4:41; John 1:41; 4:25; 11:27; 20:31). Several times anointing is associated with the prophetic office, though the references may be more metaphorical as we do not have an unambiguous account of a prophet being anointed (1 Kgs 19: 16; 1 Chr 16:22; Ps 105:15; Isa 61:1).

---

34. Bailey, *Through Peasant Eyes*, 8.
35. See χρίω in *TDNT* 9:493–580 (497); Fleming, "Biblical Tradition."

While there is some discussion as to whether the designation of Jesus as the Christ, prevalent throughout the NT, particularly the epistles, has weakened to become almost a "surname," we should not lose sight of its force as designating a role Jesus fulfilled, albeit one he and his followers radically redefined.[36]

The people of God collectively seem to be in view in Hab 3:13 when they are described as his "anointed" (cf. Exod 19:6). Christians have received an anointing of the Holy Spirit, providing understanding and assurance of their relationship with God (2 Cor 1:21–22; 1 John 2:20, 27).

2.6 Heaping Coals on the Head

There is a curious expression, said to be the consequence of performing acts of kindness towards one's enemies: "you will heap coals of fire on their heads" (Prov 25:22; Rom 12:20). A popular understanding of this is that it is a figurative way of speaking of arousing their conscience and causing shame, perhaps leading to repentance. An Egyptian ritual of carrying a pan of burning charcoal on one's head in a show of repentance has been adduced as a possible background. This is unlikely, however, and the context and general biblical background on the function of fire suggests an eschatological judgment is in view.[37]

2.7 The Face

Faces can be very expressive as a result of a combination of subtle voluntary and involuntary muscle actions, draining of or suffusing with blood, and secretion of tears. The Bible describes some faces as hard (Prov 7:13; Eccl 8:1), pale (Nah 2:10), red (Job 16:16), beaming (Job 29:24; Eccl 8:1), haughty (Ps 10:4), tearful (Luke 7:38), downcast (Gen 40:7; 1 Sam 1:18), and even "angelic" (Acts 6:15), and facial expressions are said to demonstrate a full range of emotions from joy and tenderness to indifference, resentment, pride, hostility, and shame. A change of emotion or disposition may be indicated simply by the writer's telling us that a face changed (though English translations may feel the need to be more specific as to the

---

36. See, e.g., Wright, *Paul and the Faithfulness of God*, 2:815–908.
37. See Klassen, "Coals of Fire"; Kio, "What Does 'You Will Heap Burning Coals upon His Head' Mean?"; Day, "Coals of Fire"; Martens, "Burning Questions."

nature of the change). When Jacob tells his wives, "I see that your father does not regard me as favorably as he did before" (Gen 31:5), a more literal rendering is: "I see the face of your father that it is not towards me as before" (cf. 1 Sam 1:18; Job 9:27; 14:20).

A couple of descriptions of faces indicate the effect they have on others without describing the facial characteristics. We have one description of a face, that of Stephen before the council, as being "like the face of an angel" (Acts 6:15). The only description of an angel's face we have elsewhere in Scripture is in Rev 10:1, where it is described as being "like the sun," and elsewhere angels are said to be in white or to be associated with shining glory (Luke 2:9; John 20:12), so perhaps those who saw Stephen detected a confident radiance under interrogation.

The opposite is also evident, as it is possible to have a guilty look. Isaiah writes of the people of Jerusalem and Judah, "The look on their faces bears witness against them; they proclaim their sin like Sodom, they do not hide it. Woe to them! For they have brought evil on themselves" (Isa 3:9). The Roman orator Cicero likewise took it for granted that a man's offences could be seen in his expression.[38] According to Hosea, there are telltale signs of a prostitute in her face. In an extended metaphorical treatment of Israel's unfaithfulness, he urges the prostitute's children to plead with their mother to "put away her whoring from her face" (Hos 2:2). While this might be a reference to her "wanton looks" (NEB), it might equally refer to her painted and otherwise ornamented face (Jer 4:30; Ezek 23:40).

To face something or turn towards something is implicitly to give it one's attention, whether favorably, or with critical appraisal or with hostility. Qoheleth "turned [faced] to consider wisdom and madness and folly" (Eccl 2:12). Through Hosea God reminds Israel that "their deeds surround them, they are before my face" (Hos 7:2; cf. Num 16:15; Job 6:28; 21:5). With God as subject, the turning or facing is predominantly favorable. A psalmist is confident that God "will regard [lit.: face] the prayer of the destitute" (Ps 102:17; cf. Deut 9:27; 2 Sam 9:8; 2 Kgs 13:23; 2 Chr 6:19; Pss 25:16; 69:16; 86:16; 119:132; Ezek 36:9; Acts 13:46).[39] Seeing the face of a loved one brings joy: "Israel said to Joseph, 'I can die now, having seen for myself [lit.: after seeing your face] that you are still alive'" (Gen 46:30), and Paul writes of a congregation he has established, "We longed with great

---

38. Cicero, *In Verrem* 2:3.22.

39. For a similar idiom in Akkadian, "set the face" in the sense of "look favorably upon", see Oppenheim, "Idiomatic Accadian," 256.

eagerness to see you face to face" (cf. Gen 48:11; Song 2:14; 1 Thess 2:17; 3:10; 2 Tim 1:4). The prospect of not seeing a beloved face brings sorrow as when the Ephesian elders realized they were seeing Paul for the last time (Acts 20:38). When people interact, faces of course are generally turned towards one another. This facial engagement can be suggestive of friendly and intimate dealings, and such face-to-face encounters are, when possible, much to be preferred over other forms of contact, such as letter writing, to foster the bonds of friendship and fellowship (1 Thess 2:17; 3:10; 2 John 12; 3 John 13–14).

To see the face of royalty is to have the privilege of access to the court. The Persian king consulted his advisers "who had access to the king [lit.: who saw the face of the king]" (Esth 1:14; cf. Gen 43:3, 5), and the same language is applied to worshipers appearing at God's sanctuary at festival times: "No one shall appear before me [lit.: see my face] empty-handed" (Exod 23:15; 34:20). God is said to have had dealings with Moses "face to face, as a man speaks to his friend" (Exod 33:11; Deut 34:10). God's close relationship with Israel at the exodus was "face to face" (Deut 5:4; Num 14:14), and the righteous are promised that they will "behold his [God's] face" (Ps 11:7).

Such a close encounter with God, however, is fraught with danger. Jacob is grateful to be alive after meeting God "face to face" (Gen 32:30). Moses' dealings with God are qualified: "You cannot see my face; for no one shall see me and live" (Exod 33:20), and Gideon is dismayed at a face-to-face meeting with the "angel of the LORD" (Judg 6:22). Ezekiel envisages a face-to-face encounter between God and Israel in the wilderness in a new exodus as a prelude to a purging judgment (Ezek 20:35). Paul contrasts the clarity of face-to-face knowledge at the coming of perfection with our present partial knowledge which is like looking at a dull metallic mirror surface (1 Cor 13:12; cf. Rev 22:4).

To seek the face of those in authority is to look to them for justice or favor: "Many seek the favor [lit.: face] of a ruler, but it is from the LORD that one gets justice" (Prov 29:26). "The whole earth sought the presence [lit.: face] of Solomon to hear his wisdom, which God had put into his mind" (1 Kgs 10:24). To turn to or seek the face of God is then an idiom for wanting a relationship with God and particularly connotes prayer and repentance: "If my people who are called by my name humble themselves, pray, seek my face, and turn from their wicked ways, then I will hear from heaven, and will forgive their sin and heal their land" (2 Chr 7:14; cf. 2 Sam

21:1; Pss 24:6; 27:8; Isa 45:22; Hos 5:15; Dan 9:3). In the NT to "turn to God" is an idiom for Christian conversion from Judaism as well as paganism (Acts 3:19; 9:35; 15:19; 26:20; 1 Thess 1:9).

Conversely the turning away of one's face signals distress, disinterest, disengagement, a breaking off of an encounter and, perhaps more than that, of cordial relations. When Ahab was resentful of Naboth's refusal to sell his orchard, he "lay down on his bed, turned away his face, and would not eat" (1 Kgs 21:4). In response to the prophet Isaiah's devastating message that he would not recover from his illness, "Hezekiah turned his face to the wall and prayed to the Lord" (Isa 38:2; cf. 2:22). The idiom of turning away is frequently used in Scripture for renouncing evil or idolatry on the one hand (Prov 3:7; 4:15; 13:19; 14:16; Ezek 14:6; 18:21; Acts 14:15; 26:18; 2 Tim 2:19; 1 Pet 3:11), or God and righteousness on the other hand (Josh 22:18, 23; 2 Chr 29:6; 34:33; Jer 17:13; Ezek 18:24, 26). The possibility that God might himself turn his face away is always to be reckoned with (Deut 23:14; 2 Chr 30:9; Ezek 7:22). To turn another's face away is to refuse to pay attention to them. Bathsheba entreated Solomon, "I have one small request to make of you; do not refuse me [lit.: do not turn my face]" (1 Kgs 2:20).

Facial expression can be used to show resolute determination, or steadfast defiance and hostility. Isaiah describes a confident person, who has no cause to be ashamed, as having a face "like flint," that is, firm and unflinching (Isa 50:7). With a negative nuance, Jeremiah says of the stubborn inhabitants of Jerusalem, "They have made their faces harder than rock" (Jer 5:3), and Daniel has a vision of "a king of bold countenance," that is, determined with hostile intent (Dan 8:23). The graphic portrayal of a brazen prostitute in Proverbs includes a description of her "impudent face" (Prov 7:13; cf. 21:29), where the word translated "impudent" is from a root meaning "hard, strong." To set one's face is to be determined on a course of action, perhaps a journey, and often with conflict in view. "Hazael set his face to go up against Jerusalem" (2 Kgs 12:17), and Jesus, with rather different intent, "set his face to go to Jerusalem" (Luke 9:51; cf. Gen 31:21; Lev 17:10; 20:3, 5, 6; 26:17; Num 24:1; 2 Chr 20:3; Ps 34:16; Prov 17:24; Jer 21:10; 44:11; Ezek 3:8; 4:3, 7; 6:2; 13:17; 14:8; 15:7; 20:46; 21:2; 25:2; 28:21; 29:2; 35:2; 38:2; Dan 11:17; Luke 9:53; 1 Pet 3:12). Similarly, to "look someone in the face" is military language for engaging in hostilities (2 Kgs 14:8, 11; 2 Chr 25:17). A rigid face can suggest scrutiny with a penetrating gaze. "He fixed his gaze [lit.: made his face stand] and stared at him, until he was ashamed" (2 Kgs 8:11).

"Hardness of face" can be the polar opposite of the shining (smiling) face which one acquires through wisdom (Eccl 8:1).

Faces can be "lifted up" or "lowered" in pleasure or displeasure respectively. To lift up one's face can mean to show one's face in a potentially awkward, embarrassing, or dangerous situation, as when Abner urges Asahel, "Turn away from following me; why should I strike you to the ground? How then could I show [lit.: lift up] my face to your brother Joab?" (2 Sam 2:22). In his prayer of public confession, Ezra prays, "O my God, I am too ashamed and embarrassed to lift my face to you, my God, for our iniquities have risen higher than our heads, and our guilt has mounted up to the heavens" (Ezra 9:6). This idiom is similar to lifting the head (cf. §2.3).

More commonly lifting one's face (using facial muscles to raise the edges of lips and other facial features) signifies "smiling" with various connotations including displaying confidence (Job 11:15), and showing favor or respect towards the one smiled upon. Moses warns Israel of the coming of "a grim-faced nation showing no respect [lit.: not lifting the face] to the old or favor to the young" (Deut 28:50), that is, the invaders will spare no-one.[40]

To lift another person's face, then, is to cause them to smile or show them acceptance, respect, or favor.[41] Jacob is hopeful of being favorably received by Esau or (lit.) that "he might lift my face" (Gen 32:20). Elisha acknowledges his regard for (lit.: lifting the face of) King Jehoshaphat (2 Kgs 3:14; cf. Gen 19:21; 33:10; Job 42:8–10; Prov 6:35; Lam 4:16). As a passive expression, a person "raised of face" is one on whom favor has been bestowed, a dignitary or high official (2 Kgs 5:1; Job 22:8; Isa 3:3; 9:15). With a negative nuance, to lift the face of another can mean to show partiality, a particularly serious offence on the part of judges (Lev 19:15; Deut 10:17; 2 Chr 19:7; Job 13:8, 10; 32:21; 34:19; Ps 82:2; Prov 18:5; Mal 2:9).

In a slight variation of the idiom, partiality can also be expressed in the OT as "recognizing, or regarding a face" (Deut 1:17; 16:19; Prov 24:23), while the NT idiom for deference or partiality is "receive a face" (Luke 20:21; Acts 10:34; Rom 2:11; Eph 6:9; Col 3:25; Jas 2:1, 9) or "admire a face" (Jude 16).

A smiling or favorable disposition is also one in which a face "lights up" so we have the expression "the light of your countenance" (Ps 44:3), or

---

40. Gruber, "Many Faces," 253.
41. Ibid.

references to beaming faces.⁴² Job reflects on his former role as one of society's leading lights, "I smiled on them when they had no confidence; and the light of my countenance they did not extinguish" (Job 29:24; cf. Pss 4:6; 31:16; 39:13; 44:3; 67:1; 80:3, 7, 19; 89:15; 119:135; Prov 16:15; Eccl 8:1; Isa 60:1; Dan 9:17). The Aaronic blessing includes the words "the LORD make his face to shine upon you, and be gracious to you" (Num 6:25; cf. Pss 31:16; 67:1; 80:3, 19; Dan 9:17). It is against this background that Moses' shining face makes sense (Exod 34:29-30). Moses' encounter with God secured forgiveness and favor for the people after the golden calf incident (Exodus 32), and Moses reflected (albeit in an impermanent way; cf. 2 Cor 3:7-13) the favorable disposition of God.

To drop or lower one's face suggests the inverse of lifting it, so rather than smiling, a fallen face is a gesture of displeasure, such as scowling. On having his offering rejected by God, Cain was angry and his face dropped (Gen 4:5-6), and God assures his people through Jeremiah, "I will not look on you in anger [lit.: I will not cause my face to fall]" (Jer 3:12). A rebuke may be indicated by or accompanied by a gesture such as this; a psalmist prays with reference to those who have brought devastation to God's people, "May they perish at the rebuke of your countenance" (Ps 80:16). A sad face may be referred to simply as (lit.) a "bad face." Joseph noted the hangdog look of his fellow prisoners after their troubling dreams (Gen 40:7), and Artaxerxes was concerned about the doleful look on Nehemiah's face, reminding him of the look of someone suffering an illness (Neh 2:2, 3), while Qoheleth, in his typically contrarian manner, sees a sad face as ultimately salutary (Eccl 7:3). The disciples on the road to Emmaus displayed their response to Jesus' death by their sad facial expressions (Luke 24:17). Jesus speaks of hypocrites who affect a dismal appearance by their facial disfiguration to advertise the fact that they are fasting (Matt 6:16). As well as possibly putting on an artificially pained expression, this appears to include failure to wash so as to present a squalid unkempt appearance, and Jesus teaches his disciples to wash their faces when fasting (Matt 6:17).

Anger or indignation is displayed in facial expression: "The north wind produces rain, and a backbiting tongue, angry looks [lit.: face]" (Prov 25:23). A face can become contorted with anger. When Nebuchadnezzar heard of the refusal of Shadrach, Meshach, and Abednego to bow

---

42. Cf. the Egyptian *Dream Oracle* 3/3 (*CoS*, 1:53): "His hair having become long. Good. It means something at which his face will light up (i.e., 'be joyful')."

down to his statue, he "was so filled with rage ... that his face was distorted [changed]" (Dan 3:19).

A proud attitude is shown in the face: "In the pride of their countenance the wicked say, 'God will not seek it out'; all their thoughts are, 'There is no God'" (Ps 10:4; see also neck, §4.1).

A pale or white face (drained of its normal blood supply) can be an involuntary response to situations of distress, associated particularly with fear or shame. The Egyptian pharaoh is praised thus: "A face that sees you shall not pale, Eyes that see you shall not fear!"[43] Jeremiah describes a scene of terror in store for Israel: "Ask now, and see, can a man bear a child? Why then do I see every man with his hands on his loins like a woman in labor? Why has every face turned pale?" (Jer 30:6), and Isaiah identifies shame with a pale face: "No longer shall Jacob be ashamed, no longer shall his face grow pale" (Isa 29:22). Belshazzar's fearful reaction to seeing the writing on the wall was in part that "the king's face turned pale, and his thoughts terrified him: Dan 5:6; cf. vv. 9, 10; 7:28; Job 14:20). While the Aramaic of the Daniel passages and the Hebrew of the Job passage more literally refer to a change of face, we infer the nature of the change from the context.[44]

Isaiah pictures flaming faces, anguished at the coming cosmic upheaval: "They will be dismayed. Pangs and agony will seize them; they will be in anguish like a woman in labor. They will look aghast at one another; their faces will be aflame" (Isa 13:8).

A veil usually covered the face, or at least the head, of a married woman when in public in patriarchal times.[45] Rebekah veiled herself on learning that she was approaching her intended husband Isaac (Gen 24:65). All the more curious, then, is Tamar's behavior as rendered by NRSV at Gen 38:15, "When Judah saw her, he thought her to be a prostitute, for she had covered her face." However, it makes better sense if the correct translation is "... although she had covered her face." While Tamar presented as a prostitute in some ways, she needed to cover her face so as not to be recognized. We know that (at least certain classes of) prostitutes uncovered their faces in Mesopotamia.[46] It is also possible that Tamar's veil was suggestive of a bridal veil (a statement of her design); it is Judah, not the narrator, who identifies

---

43. *Sinuhe* 278 (*CoS*, 1:82).
44. See Gruber, *Aspects*, 360–62.
45. For a survey of head covering customs, see Keener, "Head Coverings."
46. Cf. Andersen and Freedman, *Hosea*, 224–25.

her as a prostitute (Gen 38:15, 21–22).[47] There is also perhaps a clever play on words in the description of Tamar's location in that "at the entrance to Enaim [Springs]" is capable of another meaning: "invitingly" (lit.: "with opening of eyes," something Judah had failed to do!; v. 14), that is, with a pose suggestive of that of a prostitute.[48]

Covering or hiding one's face can be a natural response to fear. In a work of social criticism, an Egyptian sage offers this observation of his people: "Yet they cover their faces in fear of tomorrow."[49] In the Bible, to hide one's face is particularly a response to being in the awesome presence of God, so as not to risk seeing God. At the burning bush encounter, "Moses hid his face, for he was afraid to look at God" (Exod 3:6), and Elijah's wrapping his face in his mantle may be similarly motivated (1 Kgs 19:13). The seraphs of Isaiah's vision who attend God's throne likewise cover their faces with their wings (Isa 6:2). Roman iconography depicts people shielding their eyes with their hands, in awe of the radiance of the gods.[50]

Covering the face may also be a gesture of shame. When Haman is condemned for approaching the queen in violation of court etiquette, the courtiers "covered Haman's face" (Esth 7:8). Some have suggested this is the sign of a man under a death sentence, though it is not clear precisely what the significance of this action is other than that it is associated with Haman's shame and reversal of fortunes. Jeremiah's prophecy regarding the calamity facing Jerusalem involves a doubly shaming action on God's part: "I myself will lift up your skirts over your face, and your shame will be seen" (Jer 13:26; cf. Nah 3:5). Jesus' face was covered at one stage in his trial. Besides being a prelude to the demand for a "prophecy" as to who struck him, the action was itself insulting (Mark 14:65; Luke 22:64). To cover the face of another person is an idiom for appeasement or pacification, so perhaps akin to shaming them (by entreaty or gifts) into relenting from anger. Jacob hoped to appease (lit.: cover the face of) Esau with his generous gift (Gen 32:20; cf. Prov 16:14).

Shame may itself be said to cover the face, that is, one may detect in a person's facial expression their sense of embarrassment or dishonor. Jeremiah laments, "We are put to shame, for we have heard insults; dishonor

---

47. See the discussion of the Judah–Tamar pericope in Matthews, *More Than Meets the Ear*, 27–66.

48. Robinson, "Genesis 38:14"; Matthews, *More Than Meets the Ear*, 47.

49. *The Admonitions of Ipuwer*, Sixth Poem (CoS, 1:98).

50. Brilliant, *Gesture and Rank*, 11.

has covered our face, for aliens have come into the holy places of the LORD's house" (Jer 51:51; cf. 7:19; 2 Sam 19:5; Ps 69:7; Ezek 7:18).

Closely related to shame is grief, and similar gestures are used in its expression. In his grief at his son Absalom's death in battle, David "covered his face" (2 Sam 19:4). For this and his other gestures of mourning, David is criticized by Joab, for what should have been a time of celebration of victory has been turned into an exhibition of what the people regard as humiliating shame.[51] Ezekiel, who is prevented from publicly mourning his wife's death is told, "Do not cover your upper lip" (Ezek 24:17).

To hide one's face may mean simply to ignore someone and in Scripture is used particularly of God's unresponsiveness towards his people, often said to be as a result of his anger at their unfaithfulness. Micah warns, "Then they will cry to the LORD, but he will not answer them; he will hide his face from them at that time, because they have acted wickedly" (Mic 3:4; cf. Deut 31:17, 18; 32:20; Job 13:24; 34:29; Pss 10:11; 13:1; 22:24; 27:9; 30:7; 44:24; 69:17; 88:14; 102:2; 104:29; 143:7; Isa 8:17; 54:8; 57:17; 59:2; 64:7; Jer 33:5; Ezek 39:23, 24, 29).

An emotional expression of joy at a family reunion is to fall on another's face. Joseph "threw himself on his father's face and wept over him and kissed him" (Gen 50:1; cf. §2.11; §4.11). As it involves the whole body, falling on one's own face is treated under prostration (cf. §4.6).

To strike someone on the face (or cheek or mouth) is a humiliating action.[52] Under a Mesopotamian law, such a social insult incurred a penalty of 10 shekels of silver.[53] "To give one's cheek to the smiter" is parallel with to "be filled with insults" (Lam 3:30). Job complains, "They have gaped at me with their mouths; they have struck me insolently on the cheek; they mass themselves together against me" (Job 16:10). We observe this form of insult carried out in an altercation between two rival prophetic claimants: "Then Zedekiah son of Chenaanah came up to Micaiah, slapped him on the cheek, and said, 'Which way did the spirit of the LORD pass from me to speak to you?'" (1 Kgs 22:24; cf. Ps 3:7; Mic 5:1). In an echo of this incident, Jesus suffered such treatment at his trial before the high priest (Matt 26:67-68; Luke 22:64; John 18:22) as later did Paul (Acts 23:2) and Paul reminds his readers in Corinth that they "put up with it when someone

---

51. See Olyan, "Honor, Shame, and Covenant Relations, 208–11.

52. A similar idiom for humiliation is found in Akkadian; see Greenstein, "To Grasp the Hem," 217.

53. *Laws of Eshnunna* 42 (*CoS*, 2:334).

makes slaves of you, or preys upon you, or takes advantage of you, or puts on airs, or gives you a slap in the face" (2 Cor 11:20). Jesus teaches a general attitude of patience under provocation when he encourages his disciples, "Do not resist an evildoer. But if anyone strikes you on the right cheek, turn the other also" (Matt 5:39; cf. Luke 6:29).

The cheeks can also have warm and tender associations. Hosea evokes the tender care of a parent for a child in his description of God's parental nurture of his people: "I led them with cords of human kindness, with bands of love. I was to them like those who lift infants to their cheeks. I bent down to them and fed them" (Hos 11:4; cf. Song 1:10; 4:3; 5:13; 6:7).

2.8 The Forehead

The forehead or brow can be expressive of emotions through control of the muscles that tighten or relax it. A rigid expression, compared with brass or described as "harder than flint," can convey resolute determination or obstinacy, depending on one's perspective: "I know that you are obstinate, and your neck is an iron sinew and your forehead brass" (Isa 48:4; cf. Ezek 3:7–9). A shameless person can be accused of having the "forehead of a whore" (Jer 3:3).

As a prominent feature at the top of the face, the brow is used in a number of biblical images for marks of identification. The Aaronic high priest wore a rosette on his forehead, affixed to his turban engraved with the words "Holy to the Lord" (Exod 28:36–38). As a symbol of personal identity and behavior, God's commandments are to be fixed to one's forehead (Exod 13:9; Deut 6:8; 11:18). While doubtless originally intended as a metaphorical reference, later orthodox Judaism interpreted this literally, so tefillin or phylacteries, small leather containers, were worn on the forehead containing Scripture verses (Matt 23:5). In visionary accounts, a mark on the forehead identified those who belonged either to God or a substitute for God like the "beast" of Revelation (Rev 14:9; cf. Ezek 9:4; Rev 7:3; 9:4; 14:1; 20:4; 22:4).

2.9 The Nose and Breath

Women of higher social rank in OT times, such as Rebekah, might adorn their noses with gold nose rings (Gen 24:22, 30, 47; cf. Isa 3:21). God reminds his people that he metaphorically adorned them with nose rings, among other luxury items (Ezek 16:12).

The nose is the source of breath (Gen 7:22), and a recurrent theme of Scripture is that the breath of life comes from God. At the creation of humankind, God "breathed into his nostrils the breath of life; and the man became a living being" (Gen 2:7; cf. 7:15, 22; Job 33:4; Isa 42:5; 57:16; Ezek 37:5; Acts 17:25; Rev 11:11). Abnormal breathing patterns can send signals. Lying behind an expression for impatience or irascibility is an idiom which is literally "shortness of nose/breath" (Num 21:4; Judg 10:16; 16:16; Zech 11:8), the opposite of patience or "length of nose/breath" (Exod 34:6; Num 14:18; Neh 9:17; Pss 86:15; 103:8; 145:8; Prov 14:29; 15:18; 16:32; 25:15; 19:11; Isa 48:9; Jer 15:15; Joel 2:13; Jonah 4:2; Nah 1:3). A proverb uses two different expressions for patience or self-control where breath is at least a secondary meaning of the words: "One who is slow to anger [long of breath] is better than the mighty, and one whose temper [breath/wind] is controlled than one who captures a city" (Prov 16:32). Words for breath or nose can indicate anger, so perhaps snorting or heavy breathing is in view: "When he said this, their anger [lit.: breath/wind] against him subsided" (Judg 8:3); "Then the channels of the sea were seen, the foundations of the world were laid bare at the rebuke of the LORD, at the blast of the breath of his nostrils" (2 Sam 22:16; cf. Gen 27:45; 49:6; 49:7; 2 Kgs 24:20; Job 4:9; Ps 18:15).[54] See also below for a "burning nose."

In both Hebrew and Greek the words for breath and spirit are the same. Jesus imparts the Spirit to his disciples by the act of breathing on them (John 20:22). While God's breath, or that of the glorified LORD Jesus, is powerful and potentially dangerous (2 Sam 22:9, 16; Ps 18:8, 15; Isa 11:4, 15; 27:8; 30:28, 33; 40:7; 2 Thess 2:8), human breath represents that which is fleeting and insubstantial (Job 7:16; Pss 39:5, 11; 62:9; 78:33; 94:11; 104:29; 144:4; Isa 2:22). The LORD's anointed, the king who represented the dashed hopes of Judah, is likened to "the breath of our nostrils" (Lam 4:20).

A nose gesture underlies an expression of contempt. When the Jewish leaders scoffed at Jesus, the word for "scoffed" has as its root the word for "nose," so something like "turning up one's nose" would have been a non-verbal indication of scornful rejection of that which one finds distasteful (Luke 23:35).

Some common idioms (several expressions) for the display of anger in the OT have at their root the idea of a red-hot or "burning" nose or face

---

54. Cf. אף II, in *HALOT*; Dhorme, *L'emploi*, 80–81; Van Den Heever, "Idioms," 146.

(that is, flushed): "Who can stand before his indignation? Who can endure the heat of his anger? His wrath is poured out like fire, and by him the rocks are broken in pieces" (Nah 1:6; cf. Exod 32:12; Num 25:4; Deut 13:17; 32:22; Josh 7:26; 1 Sam 28:18; 2 Kgs 23:26; 2 Chr 28:11; Ezra 10:14; Job 20:23; Pss 2:5; 69:24; 78:49; 85:3; Isa 13:9; 30:27; Jer 4:8; 15:14; 17:4; Hos 11:9; Jonah 3:9; Zeph 2:2). Poetically, smoke can be depicted as issuing from nostrils in a display of anger (2 Sam 22:9; Job 41:20; Ps 18:8; Isa 65:5). There is a variant idiom in Hebrew which uses the verb "to burn" without the noun "nose," also generally understood as referring to anger, e.g., "Cain was very angry [burned], and his countenance fell" (Gen 4:5; cf. 18:30, 32; 31:36; 34:7; Num 16:15; 1 Sam 15:11; 18:8; 20:7; 2 Sam 3:8; 6:8; 13:21; 19:42; 22:8; 1 Chr 13:11; Neh 4:1, 7; 5:6; Ps 18:7; Jonah 4:1, 4, 9).[55] Gruber argues on the basis of Akkadian analogies that these are all more accurately references to depression.[56] It is indeed quite possible that in most cases the reference is to a more internalized emotion rather than a fiery outburst, but it is difficult not to feel the outrage, for example, when Jacob's sons learn of the rape of their sister (Gen 34:7).

The reference to those condemned for "putting the branch to their nose" (Ezek 8:17) is obscure, but may refer to a pagan religious practice. We have texts from Mesopotamia referring to an analogous practice and images depicting people holding what appear to be branches or stalks with flowers before their faces in worship chiefly of the sun god.[57] Alternatively, it may be an idiomatic allusion to an obscene gesture (reading "my [i.e. God's] nose"), summarizing a generally insulting attitude towards God.[58]

2.10 The Mouth

The mouth has several natural associations in Scripture, including eating and drinking, breathing, speaking, and kissing which give rise to a number of images.

Eating and drinking are associated with fellowship, celebration, overindulgence, and destruction. We have one glimpse of an adulterous diner who has had her fill and wipes her mouth in smug self-satisfaction (Prov 30:20),

---

55. For the physiological correlation of anger with sensation in the face, see Hupka, "Anger," 250.
56. Gruber, *Aspects*, 370–79.
57. See *ANEP*, #281; Saggs, "The Branch to the Nose."
58. See Daniel I. Block, *Ezekiel 1–24*, 298–99.

and feasting might at times get out of hand and be associated with excess (Eccl 10:16, 17; John 2:10; 1 Cor 11:21; 1 Pet 4:3). But eating and drinking are predominantly presented in Scripture in a positive light: "Go, eat your bread with enjoyment, and drink your wine with a merry heart; for God has long ago approved what you do" (Eccl 9:7; cf. Ps 104:14–15; Amos 9:14). Sharing a meal with family and guests is a universal expression of bonding and hospitality and the Bible reflects this in numerous ways. Abraham, for example, is eager to show himself a generous host to his three unexpected visitors (Gen 18:6–8; cf. 19:3; 24:54; Judg 19:4–8; 21; Ruth 2:14; 1 Sam 9:24; 2 Sam 9:11; 2 Kgs 4:8; Luke 14:1; 22:8; 1 Cor 10:27). Feasting or banqueting with ample food and wine (for those who can afford it or are invited by those who can) are expressions of joy and give people the opportunity to celebrate an occasion such as a wedding (Song 2:4; Matt 22:4; 25:10; Luke 12:36; John 2:1–10; Rev 19:9) or a victory (Gen 14:18–19; Ps 23:5; Isa 25:6; 55:1–5; Rev 19:17–18), or to honor someone (Gen 21:8; 29:22; 40:20; Judg 14:10–12; 1 Sam 25:36; 2 Sam 3:20; 13:27; 1 Kgs 1:41; 3:15; 1 Chr 29:22; Esth 9:17–19; Job 1:4; Mark 6:21; Luke 5:29). Banquets, notably royal banquets, were occasions for display of power and rank (Esth 1:3–9; Dan 5:1; Matt 22:1–14). Jesus' invitation to eat of his flesh (John 6:51–58) in context suggests close identification with his sacrificial death.

Eating together may suggest initiating or confirming a more formal alliance, as elsewhere in the Semitic world, though the boundaries between hospitality and covenant meal are rather fluid as the symbolism is that of bringing non-family into the intimacy of a family setting (Gen 14:18; 26:28–31; 31:48–54; Exod 18:12; 24:11; Josh 9:14; 2 Sam 3:20; Isa 25:6–8).[59] This helps explain Ps 41:9: "Even my bosom friend in whom I trusted, who ate of my bread, has lifted the heel against me," and the words of Jesus at the Last Supper with his disciples: "The one who has dipped his hand into the bowl with me will betray me" (Matt 26:23; cf. Luke 22:21).[60] An aspect of the OT ritual of the tabernacle and temple was the institution of the sacrifice of well-being at which the worshipers shared in a fellowship meal (Lev 3; 7:11–35) and there are other meals in the Bible with covenantal associations, presenting an image of the kingdom of God or the messianic age

---

59. McCree, "The Covenant Meal"; Kruger, "Nonverbal Communication and Symbolic Gestures," 220–21; Hagelia, "Meal."

60. For a parallel sentiment in Egyptian literature, cf. the lament put into the mouth of Pharaoh Amenemhet: "But he who ate my food raised opposition, He whom I gave my trust used it to plot" (*CoS* 1:67).

(Exod 24:11; Isa 25:6; Matt 22:2; 25:1–10; 26:26–29; Mark 14:22–25; Luke 14:15; 22:14–20; 1 Cor 10:16–17).

Jesus' eating with tax collectors and "sinners," those considered beyond the bounds of social acceptability (Matt 9:10–11, 11:19; Mark 2:15–16; Luke 5:30), makes a statement as to the inclusive character of his kingdom. As the early church struggled to come to terms with the inclusion of gentiles without requiring them to take on Jewish identity, this came to expression in different attitudes to table fellowship. Paul took Peter to task for his reversion to an exclusively Jewish table (Gal 2:11–14).

Eating or devouring is also a common idiom of destruction. The image of ferocious animals consuming their prey (Gen 49:27; Num 23:25; 1 Kgs 14:11; Jer 15:3, Ezek 19:6; 22:25; Dan 7:5; Zeph 3:3; Acts 20:29; 1 Pet 5:8) can be extended to such instrumentalities as heat and fire, sword and plague (Gen 31:40; Exod 22:6; 24:17; Lev 9:24; Num 11:1; Deut 32:24, 42; 2 Sam 2:26; 2 Kgs 1:14; Isa 26:11; Luke 9:54; Heb 10:27; Rev 11:5; 20:9), emotions such as anger and zeal (Exod 15:7; Esth 1:12; Pss 69:9; 90:7; Ezek 43:8; Zeph 3:8; John 2:17), the earth or underworld as a hungry predator (Num 26:10; Isa 5:14), and even people may be said to "devour" one another (Deut 7:16; Isa 9:12; Gal 5:15). God in his zeal for purity is described as a "devouring fire" (Deut 4:24; cf. Exod 24:17; Deut 9:3; Isa 29:6; 30:30).

When failure to eat is mentioned, this may be an expression of grief or anxiety. In her distress at the provocation of her rival Peninah, Hannah would not eat at the annual festival (1 Sam 1:7, 8; cf. 28:20; 2 Sam 3:35; 12:17). Ahab's refusal to eat when Naboth declined to sell him his ancestral property reveals something of Ahab's character as a sulky and manipulative man (1 Kgs 21:4, 5; cf. Ps 102:4).[61] Fasting, or abstaining from food for a period, was a corporate, and at times individual, religious practice in Israel and the early church, and could mark times of grief, national humiliation, repentance, and seeking the favor of God (Lev 16:29, 31; 2 Sam 12:16–17; Esth 4:16; Zech 8:19; Matt 9:14–15; Luke 2:37; 18:12; Acts 13:2, 3; 14:23; 27:9).[62] As noted above, Jesus discouraged making an outward show of fasting (Matt 6:16–18).

Eating can serve as a metaphor of taking in a message (cf. English "digest"). Ezekiel is instructed in a vision to eat a scroll containing the words of God (Ezek 3:1–3; cf. Rev 10:8–10). Jesus similarly draws on the dual functions of the mouth of eating and speaking in his saying that "it

---

61. Kruger, "Depression," 192.
62. Lambert, "Fasting."

is not what goes into the mouth that defiles a person, but what comes out of the mouth" (Matt 15:11).

In contrast with the generally active and at times aggressive associations of eating, drinking functions passively. In an idiom common throughout the ancient world, one is handed a "cup" in life to drink, that is, a particular set of life experiences, positive or negative. A psalmist finds his cup in God (Ps 16:5) or rejoices in an overflowing cup (Ps 23:5). Or the cup can be one of wrath and judgment (Isa 51:17, 22; Jer 14:12; 25:15, 16; Ezek 23:33, 34; 1 Cor 11:29; Rev 14:10; 16:19). As a judgment, the Israelites were made to drink water scattered with the burned and ground-up remains of the idol they had made (Exod 32:20). Jesus speaks of the future events of his humiliation and death as his "cup," one to be shared with his followers (Matt 26:39, 42; Mark 10:38, 39; 14:36; Luke 22:4; John 18:11). Jesus invites his followers to drink his blood (John 6:53–56), that is, to partake of that wherein life is to be found (Lev 17:11) through identification with his death.

To offer a cup of water to a stranger in the arid climate of Israel is the most basic of courtesies and normally unremarkable (e.g., Gen 24:14; 1 Kgs 17:10). All the more remarkable, then, is Jesus' promise of a reward for those who offer even this smallest gesture of support to his disciples as they pursue his mission (Matt 10:42; Mark 9:41).

The impulse to have food and drink in our mouths can suggest other needs or cravings which, as Qoheleth observes, are never satisfied (Eccl 6:7). The psalmists express their desire for God as a "thirst" (Pss 42:2; 63:1; 143:6), and Isaiah urges his readers to avail themselves of the "food," "wine," and "milk" that truly satisfy (Isa 55:1–2). Jesus declares blessed "those who hunger and thirst for righteousness, for they shall be satisfied" (Matt 5:6). He offers himself as "the bread of life" and promises "those who drink of the water that I will give them will never be thirsty" (John 4:14), and "whoever comes to me shall not hunger, and whoever believes in me shall never be thirsty" (John 6:35; cf. Rev 7:16; cf. throat, §4.1).

A strong image of subservience is that of putting one's mouth in the dust (Lam 3:29), that is, total prostration (cf. §4.6). The serpent in the Garden is condemned to "eat dust" (Gen 3:14; Isa 65:25).[63]

The mouth may by metonymy refer to the content of its speech. The mouth can condemn or curse (Job 9:20; 15:6; 23:4); it can be full of true instruction or deceit (Ps 50:19; Mal 2:6), and praise or laughter (Pss 34:1;

---

63. *ANEP*, #45, #46, #47.

126:2). The power of words is likened to a sharp sword issuing from the mouth (Job 5:15; Isa 49:2; Rev 1:16; 2:16; 19:15, 21).

A frequently occurring idiom for initiating speech is the expression "[he] opened his mouth and said" or similar words (Job 3:1; 33:2; Dan 10:16; Matt 5:2; Acts 8:35; 10:34; 18:14; Rev 13:6). This has the effect of slowing down the action and drawing attention to the speech. By itself, the expression "open the mouth" may refer to taking a vow (Judg 11:35, 36).[64]

The mouth is sometimes paired with the heart to indicate that speech either correlates with thought or else is deceptively at odds with it. A psalmist prays, "Let the words of my mouth and the meditation of my heart be acceptable to you, O LORD, my rock and my redeemer" (Ps 19:14; cf. Deut 30:14; 1 Sam 2:1; Ps 49:3; Eccl 5:2; Jer 9:8; Ezek 33:31; Matt 12:34; 15:18; Luke 6:45; Rom 10:8–10), and Isaiah records God's complaint, "These people draw near with their mouths and honor me with their lips, while their hearts are far from me" (Isa 29:13). The mouth can also be paired with the hand in the idiom "speak with the mouth, and fulfill with the hand," that is, accomplish what has been promised (1 Kgs 8:15, 24; 2 Chr 6:4, 15; Jer 44:25).

The mouth also figures in idioms of agency in speech. To speak "from the mouth of the LORD" indicates the prophetic role of mediating the divine message (2 Chr 36:12, 21; 36:22; Ezra 1:1; Luke 1:70; Acts 1:16; 3:18, 21; 4:25; 15:7). Similarly, we read of Jeremiah's perception that God had touched his mouth and put words into it (Jer 1:9).

In the caricature portrait of a "scoundrel and a villain" (Prov 6:12; cf. 4:24), his perverse or deceptive speech is displayed (lit.) in his "crooked mouth."

There are a number of references to non-linguistic noises emanating from the mouth such as sighing, hissing, or whistling. The action of hissing, or making a sound through the rapid forcing of air (in or out) through a narrow aperture of tongue, teeth, dental ridge and/or lips, is an unsympathetic or derisive response to another's misfortune, particularly a horrifying large-scale devastation. Accompanying gestures can include hand clapping (cf. §5.12) or fist-brandishing (cf. §5.3), head-wagging (cf. §2.3), and teeth-gnashing (cf. §2.13). The book of Lamentations pictures such a reaction by Judah's enemies to the downfall of Jerusalem (Lam 2:15–16; cf. 1 Kgs 9:8;

---

64. The Akkadian equivalent "open the mouth" can mean "make a promise" (Oppenheim, "Idiomatic Accadian," 262).

2 Chr 29:8; Job 27:23; Jer 18:16; 19:8; 25:9; 25:18; 29:18; 49:17; 50:13; 51:37; Ezek 27:36; Mic 6:16; Zeph 2:15).

Whistling (the same word as translated hissing in the examples above) can be used for signaling over long distances. Isaiah uses military language in depicting God summoning foreign armies: "He will raise a signal for a nation far away, and whistle for a people at the ends of the earth" (Isa 5:26; cf. 7:18).

A universal human response to a variety of emotional dispositions (from anguish to exuberance) is to utter sound (without necessarily forming words). Scripture makes reference to sighing, moaning, groaning, crying out, and the like in association with grief, sorrow, labor pains, the deprivations of imprisonment, and life's frustrations in general. Job laments, "For my sighing comes like my bread, and my groanings are poured out like water" (Job 3:24). Jesus' response to the demand for a sign was a deep sigh (Mark 8:12; cf. Exod 15:25; Pss 31:10; 32:3; 38:9; 90:9; 102:5; Prov 5:11; 29:2; Isa 15:4; 35:10; 51:11; Ezek 9:4; 24:17; Lam 1:4; Mic 4:9; 10; Heb 13:17). The unclean spirit, which Jesus commanded to come out of a man in the synagogue, used his last moment of possession to utter a cry of defeat (Mark 1:26). Even where there is verbal content, where the volume of an utterance is indicated this may constitute a paralinguistic aspect of the communication. While sometimes volume is simply a function of the distance sound may need to travel (as when addressing a crowd, or calling to someone up on a town wall), at other times it marks emotional intensity as when David uttered his lament at the death of his son Absalom "with a loud voice" (2 Sam 19:4). Cries of distress can in Scripture be directed to God, and so be tantamount to prayer, as the Israelites' groaning under oppression in Egypt (Exod 2:23, 24; 6:5). Paul speaks of the sort of prayer that consists of "sighs too deep for words" (Rom 8:26). Prior to Jesus' healing of the deaf mute, "looking up to heaven, he sighed and said to him, 'Ephphatha,' that is, 'Be opened'" (Mark 7:34; cf. 2 Kgs 20:11; 1 Chr 5:20; Pss 5:1; 12:5; 79:11; 102:20; 2 Cor 5:2, 4; for wailing associated with weeping, see §3.2.2).

Shouting can also serve as an indication of joyful exuberance as at harvest and festival times (Isa 16:10; Jer 25:30; 48:33), in military or mob contexts to instill fear, and to celebrate a triumphal or joyous occasion (Josh 6:5, 10, 16, 20; Judg 15:14; 2 Chr 13:15; 15:14; Ezra 3:11; Ps 35:27; Jer 50:15; 51:14, 48; Acts 7:57; Rev 10:3). Isaiah 8:9 reads in NRSV: "Band together, you peoples, and be dismayed; listen, all you far countries; gird yourselves and be dismayed"; however, the first verb is better understood as "Raise the war cry" (NIV11). Shouting greets the triumphal processional entry of the ark into Jerusalem (2 Sam 6:15; 1 Chr 15:28). Jesus' final cry from the cross, which in Matthew and Mark is wordless (Matt 27:50; Mark 15:37), suggests a triumphant shout of victory (cf. Luke 23:46; John 19:30). God's people are then encouraged to shout in joyful celebration of God's salvation: "Rejoice greatly, O daughter Zion! Shout aloud, O daughter Jerusalem!" (Zech 9:9; cf. 1 Sam 4:5; Ezra 3:11–13; Pss 20:5; 32:11; 33:3; 47:1, 5; 60:8; 71:23; 81:1; 89:15; 95:1; 98:4, 6; 100:1; 108:9; 132:9; 132:16; Isa 12:6; 24:14; 42:11–13; 44:23; 48:20; 54:1; Zeph 3:14; Gal 4:27; 1 Pet 4:13).

Laughter likewise is a form of nonverbal communication on the broader definition adopted here of an action of the body, voluntary or involuntary, which expresses something of our disposition.[65] Through laughter we display a spectrum of emotions and attitudes, depending on context. It is not so much associated with comic humor in the Bible (though the Bible is not lacking in humor). Laughter is a natural, though controllable, outlet for joy or pleasure and can be associated with times of feasting. Because the same Hebrew word may be translated laugh or smile, we cannot always be sure whether vocalization is involved in the expression of pleasure or a favorable disposition (e.g., Job 29:24; cf. smiling, §2.7). With his simplistic view of the moral order of the world, Bildad assures Job that God's attitude to the righteous ensures that "he will yet fill your mouth with laughter, and your lips with shouts of joy" (Job 8:21; cf. Ps 126:2; Prov 14:13; Eccl 2:2; 7:3; 10:19; Luke 6:21, 25; Jas 4:9). There is a more hollow form of laughter associated with fools, likened to "the crackling of thorns under a pot" (Eccl 7:6). Abraham's and Sarah's response to being informed that they would have a child is the laughter of disbelief (Gen 17:17; 18:12–15). Sarah's cynical laughter turns to joyous laughter at the birth of her son Isaac ("He laughs," Gen 21:6). The response of the onlookers to Jesus' observation that Jairus's daughter was not dead but sleeping was that of scornful laughter or ridicule (Luke 8:53; cf. Gen 38:23; 2 Chr 30:10; Neh 2:19; Job 5:22; 9:23; 12:4; 22:19; 41:29; Pss 2:4; 22:7; 37:13; 52:6; 59:8; 80:6; Prov 1:26; 29:9; Isa 37:22; Ezek 23:32; Hab 1:10; Matt 9:24; Mark 5:40).

A reference to shutting one's mouth can suggest that one has been overwhelmed or shamed or outclassed in an argument (Ezek 16:63). When God acts, Eliphaz observes, "the poor have hope, and injustice shuts its mouth" (Job 5:16). When kings are said to shut their mouths at the sight of

---

65. Kendon, *Gesture*, 8.

God's servant (Isa 52:15), they may simply be amazed or perplexed, though an alternative suggestion is that it is a stronger metaphor of subjugation (cf. Job 5:16; Ps 107:42; Ezek 16:63).[66] One of the purposes of the law, according to Paul, is that "every mouth may be stopped, and the whole world may be held accountable to God" (Rom 3:19). Ezekiel's period of silence was to serve as a prophetic sign to the exiles in Babylon (Ezek 3:22–27; 24:25–27; 33:21–22)[67] and Zechariah, the father of John the Baptist, experienced a period of being unable to speak as a consequence of his reluctance to believe the angelic message, so this may be seen as a period of enforced submission to the word of God (Luke 1:20–22; 62–64). Saul's traveling companions were rendered speechless through amazement or fear on hearing a voice but seeing no-one on the road to Damascus (Acts 9:7).

Some figurative ways of speaking of the exercise of restraint in speech are to set a guard at the doorway of the mouth or to muzzle the mouth (Pss 39:1; 141:3; Prov 13:3; Mic 7:5). Further animal imagery is employed in the image of a bit placed in the mouth, as in a horse, by which to steer one in the right direction (2 Kgs 19:28; Isa 37:29; Jas 3:3).

To draw attention to the fact that one declines to speak, a hand might be placed over or near the mouth. This then serves as a gesture of respect and submission, perhaps even of shame, in the presence of a more worthy and eloquent social superior (Job 29:9; Mic 7:16). An Egyptian father instructs his son: "When you enter a man's house, / And he's busy with someone before you, / Sit with your hand over your mouth."[68]

An appalling or overwhelming situation might lead to emotional overload and render one speechless, perhaps with the bringing of a hand to the mouth (Job 21:5). Job's words to God before God's speech from the whirlwind are "See, I am of small account; what shall I answer you? I lay my hand on my mouth. I have spoken once, and I will not answer; twice, but will proceed no further" (Job 40:4–5). The significance of Job's action is disputed (contemptuous revulsion? capitulation? precaution?) but we note that God's barrage of questions in Job 41–42 elicits no response from Job and Job's next words to God are: "I know that you can do all things, and

---

66. Watts, "Meaning."

67. For approaches to some of the difficulties raised by the motif of Ezekiel's dumbness, see Greenberg, "On Ezekiel's Dumbness"; Wilson, "Interpretation."

68. *Dua-khety* or *The Satire on the Trades* (*CoS*, 1:125); A relief from Persepolis shows a Median dignitary approaching the enthroned king Darius with his hand to his mouth, *ANEP*, #463.

that no purpose of yours can be thwarted" (Job 42:2).[69] The proverb urges us to "put your hand on your mouth" in the face of temptation to boast or say something harmful (Prov 30:32). When Micah's priest challenged the Danites who were stealing Micah's idol, "they said to him, 'Keep quiet! Put your hand over your mouth, and come with us, and be to us a father and a priest'" (Judg 18:19). This may be as much a call for stealth as it is a call to desist from his challenge and to submit to their offer to become the priest of the whole Danite tribe. Aaron was stunned into silence at the dramatic death of his two sons (Lev 10:3).[70]

Silence can be eloquent when speech is anticipated and there is a significant body of literature on the role of silence in communication. When Elijah challenged the people of Israel on Mount Carmel and we are informed that "the people did not answer him a word" (1 Kgs 18:21), we detect a bewildered and perhaps guilty silence. The last-minute wedding guest of Jesus' parable in Matt 22:12 is understandably speechless at being challenged for not being appropriately clothed for a wedding. Those who sought to trap Jesus by their questions were amazed and reduced to silence by his answers (Luke 20:26; cf. Matt 22:34; Mark 3:4; Luke 14:4; Acts 11:18). One of the ways silence is indicated in the Bible is when the normal turn-taking in conversation is subverted and, after a pause, the first speaker resumes. Thus we read, "He [God] brought him [Abram] outside and said, 'Look toward heaven and count the stars, if you are able to count them.' Then he [God] said to him, 'So shall your descendants be'" (Gen 15:5). The resumptive formula "Then he said to him" suggests Abram was rendered speechless by the enormity of the undertaking he has been given. Jesus' silence in the face of the charges against him before the high priest and Pilate (Mark 14:61; 15:5) suggests his acceptance of the messianic suffering to which he understood he was called, probably in imitation of the silence of the servant of Isa 53:7.

---

69. For this crucial verse for understanding the book of Job, and the "hand to mouth" texts in general, see Newell, "Job"; Glazov, "Significance."

70. See Levine, "Silence." Levine and *DCH* posit a root דמם II meaning "mourn" in this and other passages, homonymous with דמם I "be silent," though as shocked silence is often the initial stage of grief, it is reasonable to see a single root in play here.

2.11 The Lips

Along with the tongue, the lips represent the power of speech (Gen 11:1; Ps 81:5; Isa 33:19; Ezek 3:5, 6) which of course can be wholesome and beneficial (Pss 17:1; 40:9; 51:15; Prov 8:6; 10:13; Zeph 3:9; Mal 2:6, 7) or deceitful, flattering, and dangerous (Job 27:4; Pss 12:2, 3; 31:18; 34:13; 59:12; 140:3; Prov 5:3; Isa 59:3; Matt 15:8; Mark 7:6; Rom 3:13; 1 Pet 3:10). Those who speak unguardedly, or "open wide their lips," come to ruin (Prov 13:3). To "make mouths [lit.: make an opening with the lip]" (Ps 22:7) is a form of mockery. Job complains that his treatment by God has resulted in people gaping at him with their mouths and abusing him (Job 16:10).

Moses acknowledges his "uncircumcised" lips, that is, his inadequacy as a speaker (Exod 6:12), and Isaiah, recognizing his and his people's "unclean" lips, receives a touch of the purifying altar coal on his lips (Isa 6:5–7). A trembling lip can indicate fear (Hab 3:16) or sympathy (Job 16:5). The reassuring touch on Daniel's lips brought a restoration of his ability to speak after he had been rendered speechless for a time (Dan 10:16).

Kissing may of course have sexual connotations (Prov 7:13; Song 1:2; 7:9) or be a gesture of family intimacy used particularly in greetings, farewells, and blessings, sometimes in conjunction with an embrace and/or tears. We hear of the emotional reunion of Jacob and Esau in the following terms: "But Esau ran to meet him, and embraced him, and fell on his neck and kissed him, and they wept" (Gen 33:4; cf. 27:26, 27; 29:11, 13; 31:28; 45:15; 48:10; 50:1; Exod 4:27; 18:7; Ruth 1:9, 14; 2 Sam 14:33; 20:9; 1 Kgs 19:20; Song 8:1).[71] When the father in Jesus' parable kissed his prodigal son on his return, the verb is an intensive and perhaps suggests repeated kisses (Luke 15:20).[72] More rarely a kiss may mark a close friendship or signify an honor from a king to his subject (1 Sam 20:41; 2 Sam 19:39). Absalom's practice of kissing all who approached would seem to be mentioned to illustrate his inappropriate behavior as he sought to promote his pretensions to the throne (2 Sam 15:5).

In ancient Western Asia, kissing, particularly on the feet or the ground in front of the feet, was an expression of obeisance towards one of high rank or deity and such a display of reverence for the icons is still practiced in some Eastern churches. As the Egyptian god Osiris receives

---

71. An image on a limestone fragment from Amarna (Egypt) from the fourteenth century BC depicts queen Nefertiti kissing her daughter on the lips; see Keel, *Song*, 42, #3.

72. Bailey, *Poet and Peasant*, 183.

homage, "The Nine Gods adore him, / Those in the *Duat* kiss the ground, / Those on high bow down."⁷³ Samuel kissed Saul on anointing him as king (1 Sam 10:1). The rebellious kings of Ps 2 are urged to pay homage either to the divinely anointed ruler or to the LORD: "Kiss the Son" (Ps 2:12 KJV), or, with emended text, "kiss his [the LORD's] feet" (NRSV). When images of deity are involved kissing is considered an idolatrous practice (1 Kgs 19:18; Hos 13:2), though whether the image is kissed with the lips, or a kiss to the hand which is then "thrown" towards the image is in view, is not clear. As the NRSV has it, Job says, "If . . . my mouth has kissed my hand, this also would be an iniquity to be punished by the judges" (Job 31:26–28). Kissing one's hand has been understood as an act of vanity or as a ritual associated with idolatry. The practice of throwing kisses to the object of one's adoration is known from places as far apart as Arabia and Rome.⁷⁴ Stephen Langdon explains images of the curved palm to the mouth and those with the hand pointing to the deity as successive stages in throwing kisses to the deity and interprets Job 31:27 accordingly.⁷⁵ However, there are difficulties with this reading. For a start the word "hand" is more naturally read as the subject of the verb. An alternative explanation is that Job denies ever having put his hand to his mouth to seal it up, that is, to display awe in the presence of false gods.⁷⁶

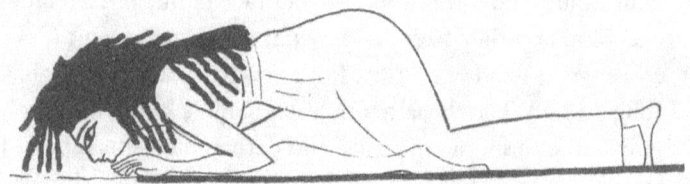

#2. *A woman kisses the ground in homage. Egyptian Book of the Dead. Eleventh to tenth century BC. Keel #413.*

In the NT, as well as signaling affection within the family circle, a kiss was to be expected as a greeting between host and guest, and disciple and teacher (Luke 7:45; 22:47). The woman who anointed Jesus' feet at a banquet carried on kissing them in a show of humility and gratitude (Luke

73. *The Great Hymn to Osiris* (*CoS*, 1:41).
74. Tur-Sinai, *Job*, 444; Corbeill, *Nature Embodied*, 26.
75. Langdon, "Gesture," 546–48; Keel, #418; *ANEP*, #463, #493, #533, #609.
76. Cf. Cohen, "An Unrecognized Connotation," 423–24.

7:38). The holy kiss or kiss of love was a form of greeting encouraged in the early church (Rom 16:16; 1 Cor 16:20; 2 Cor 13:12; 1 Thess 5:26; 1 Pet 5:14), and we are probably to picture kissing in other references to greeting in family and Christian community contexts (Matt 5:47; Acts 21:7; 21:19; Rom 16:3-15; 2 Tim 4:19). This gesture then treats members of the church as extended family, in keeping with a motif of the NT of Christian brotherhood and sisterhood (Matt 12:50; Rom 7:1; 1 Pet 2:17; 5:8; Rev 1:9).[77] To give an honest answer is (according to NRSV) likened to "a kiss on the lips" (Prov 24:26), that is, the person who answers truthfully is a true friend.[78] If this reading is correct, this is the only place in the OT where the lips are explicitly mentioned in connection with kissing, though another reading, based on an understanding of the core meaning of the verb as "close up, seal," is "He that gives forthright judgment will silence all hostile lips."[79] It is ironic that a gesture of friendship and respect should be turned into a traitorous sign when Judas used his kiss to identify Jesus in the Garden of Gethsemane (Matt 26:48; Mark 14:44; Luke 7:45; 22:47-48).

As noted in the Introduction, the proverb, "One who winks the eyes plans perverse things; one who compresses the lips brings evil to pass" (Prov 16:30), is probably not a reference to some specific symbolism involving the lips, but a general reference to being tight-lipped, that is, silent, and so a comment on the power of body language alone to convey a deceptive message.

2.12 The Tongue

The tongue, like the lips, stands for the power of speech: "See, I open my mouth; the tongue in my mouth speaks" (Job 33:2). A tongue can be like a sharp razor in its treachery (Ps 52:2), or mischievous, boastful, flattering, arrogant, slanderous, and deceitful (Pss 5:9; 10:7; 12:4; 15:3; 73:9; 109:2; 140:3; Rom 3:13). Or the tongue can be used for praise, dispensing justice, and imparting wisdom (Pss 35:28; 37:30; 51:14; Rom 10:9; 14:11; Phil 2:11). James likens the power of the tongue to that of a bushfire (Jas 3:5-9). When Jeremiah's enemies wished to silence him, they conspired: "Come, let us bring charges against him, and let us not heed any of his words" (Jer 18:18). At least that is the NRSV's paraphrase. The words are literally, however,

---

77. See Stählin, φιλέω, 125-27, 138-40.
78. Cf. Gruber, *Aspects*, 328-29.
79. Cohen, "An Unrecognized Connotation," 422.

"Come, let us strike his tongue . . ." and a case can be made that the expressed intention is really to cut out the prophet's tongue as a drastic means of silencing his unwelcome words.[80]

As well as its speech function, the tongue can be used in gesture. Isaiah asks those who have been mocking the faithful, "Whom are you mocking? Against whom do you open your mouth wide and stick out your tongue?" (Isa 57:4).

To "lick the dust" in front of the feet of the victor is the fate of the vanquished (Ps 72:9; Isa 49:23; Mic 7:17). The latter verse alludes to the serpent of Gen 3:14 being condemned to "eat dust," a common expression in ancient Western Asia for subservience (cf. Lam 3:29–30).[81]

2.13 The Teeth

Teeth represent the power of biting and devouring, so the baring, snapping, or grinding of teeth in front of another is a threatening gesture. A psalmist laments, "The wicked plot against the righteous, and gnash their teeth at them" (Ps 37:12; cf. Pss 35:16; 112:10; Lam 2:16; Acts 7:54). Even God can be said to gnash his teeth in an antagonistic gesture (Job 16:9). The grinding of teeth is also an indicator of extreme pain and characterizes the suffering of those who, according to Jesus, are cast out into darkness (Matt 8:12; cf. 13:42; 13:50; 22:13; 24:51; 25:30; Luke 13:28).

2.14 Spitting

Spitting is an almost universal sign of disgust and spitting at another person, particularly spitting in the face, is an extremely insulting action. In the Ugaritic myth, Baʻlu complains of his treatment by the other gods: "they stood up and cast scorn upon me, they arose and spat upon me."[82] In Israel, spitting is associated with social exclusion when performed as a ritual act of diminishment.[83] It was part of the prescribed humiliation of those who refused to carry out their family responsibilities under the levirate law (Deut 25:9). Isaiah speaks of one who declares, "I gave my back to those who

---

80. Foreman, "Strike the Tongue."
81. Gruber, *Aspects*, 288–91.
82. *The Baʻlu Myth* iii 10–22 (CoS, 1:258).
83. Cf. Darwin, *Expression*, 258; Lynch, "Neglected Physical Dimensions," 514–16; Barakat, "Arabic Gestures," 783.

struck me, and my cheeks to those who pulled out the beard; I did not hide my face from insult and spitting" (Isa 50:6; cf. Num 12:14; Job 17:6; 30:10), and Jesus suffered just such degrading treatment at the hands of the hostile participants in his trial and crucifixion in accordance with his prediction (Matt 26:67; 27:30; Mark 10:34; 14:65; 15:19; Luke 18:32). Jesus subverts the normal associations of spittle, or saliva, in his use of it to bring healing to a blind man (Mark 8:23; John 9:6).

3

The Eyes

"THE EYES ARE THE windows of the soul" as the saying goes.¹ We believe we can glean a lot about the disposition, emotions, and intentions of others from the way they look at us, or avoid looking at us, the fixity or shiftiness of their gaze, the moisture content of their eyeballs, and other subtle eye features and movements. The Bible also frequently links the eyes with the soul (or heart, mind, or spirit; e.g., Deut 28:65; 29:4; 1 Kgs 9:3; 2 Chr 7:16; Job 15:12; 31:7; Pss 19:8; 36:1; 38:10; 131:1; Prov 15:30; 21:4; 23:26; Eccl 2:10; 11:9; Isa 6:10; 44:18; Jer 5:21; 22:17; Lam 5:17; Matt 13:15; John 12:40; Rom 11:8; Acts 28:27; 1 Cor 2:9; Eph 1:18; 2 Pet 2:14; Rev 5:6), confirming our belief that eyes can reveal a great deal about our inner world.

The pupil, or more poetically the "apple" of the eye, is something precious which we seek to protect, so serves as a fitting metaphor for God's estimation of his people, or of that which they should value, such as wisdom (Deut 32:10; Ps 17:8; Prov 7:2; Zech 2:12).² Our pupils react not simply to changing light conditions (appearing larger in dim light), but also in response to various emotional stimuli. We betray our emotions through their dilation (when we are excited, for example) and contraction (when

---

1. Pliny observes: "No other part of the body supplies greater indications of the mind" (*Natural History* xi 145); cf. Cicero, *De oratore* 3.221: "But all depends on the countenance; and even in that the eyes bear sovereign sway . . . for all the powers of action proceed from the mind, and the countenance is the image of the mind, and the eyes are its interpreters. This, indeed, is the only part of the body that can effectually display as infinite a number of significations and changes, as there is of emotions in the soul"; Polemon's treatise *Physiognomy* begins (in one of its transmission traditions): "Know that the eyes are the gateway to the heart, from which arise the cares of the soul" (Swain, *Seeing the Face*, 341).

2. Finley, "The Apple of His Eye," 337–38; Finley sees a pun on the word Zechariah uses for pupil (*bābat* "gate") and the city of Babylon, Judah's oppressor.

resentful, for example). We also narrow or widen the aperture of the eyelids, exposing more or less of the eyeballs as indications of responses such as astonishment or suspicion. We may assume that pupil size and degree of opening of the eyes is a contributing factor to many of the observed facial expressions in the Bible; for example, when the king of Israel was "resentful and sullen" (1 Kgs 20:43; cf. 21:4), or when Rhoda was excited at seeing Peter at the gate (Acts 12:14), or when, on seeing the risen Jesus, the disciples "were startled and terrified, and thought that they were seeing a ghost" (Luke 24:37). We possibly have explicit reference to the body language involved in 1 Samuel 2:32 when Samuel declares to Eli who has turned a blind eye to his sons' greed, "Then in distress you will look with greedy eye on all the prosperity that shall be bestowed upon Israel." The word NRSV has translated "in distress" is perhaps better taken as an adverbial use of the adjective *ṣar* meaning "narrowly," qualifying "look," so perhaps indicating that the looking will be through narrowed eyelids. Psalm 68 speaks poetically of the mountains of Bashan looking enviously at God's mountain abode (Ps 68:16). A verbal form of the word for eye, meaning to view with suspicion (presumably through narrowed eyelids) occurs only once in the Bible: "So Saul eyed David from that day on" (1 Sam 18:9).

It is to the eyes of others above all that our own are most naturally drawn. Eyes (or eyelashes) are singled out as a feature of both men and women to which we may be attracted (1 Sam 16:12; Prov 6:25; Song 1:15, 4:1; 5:12). The lover of the Song declares of his beloved, "You have ravished my heart with a glance of your eyes" (Song 4:9). There was something about Leah's eyes considered worthy of the narrator's notice, though we are not actually sure if it is their attractiveness or some other quality that is in view (Gen 29:17 NRSV: "Leah's eyes were lovely"; NIV11: "Leah had weak eyes"). In what is more a physiognomical than a gestural comment, a psalmist portrays the arrogant as having eyes that "swell out with fatness" or perhaps "glisten more than milk" (Ps 73:7).[3]

As is the case in many contemporary cultures, eye cosmetics were widely used, particularly by women, in ancient Western Asia and the Mediterranean world. In an Egyptian tomb painting, Asiatics (the ethnic grouping to which the Hebrews belonged) are depicted as offering eyeshadow to

---

3. See discussion of alternatives in Tate, *Psalms 51–100*, 228. A possible parallel is to be found in Polemon, *Physiognomy*, 57 (Swain, *Seeing the Face*, 449): "The sign of the man with little modesty is that he has puffed up eyes."

the pharaoh Khnum-hotep III.[4] Eyeshadow (applied to the eyelids or under the eyebrows) drew attention to the eyes with a view to enhancing their appeal. Such painting of the eyes, while not condemned, is particularly associated in the Bible with unwholesome forms of sexual allure, a practice of loose or desperate women (2 Kgs 9:30; Jer 4:30; Ezek 23:40).

Eyes can stand for the presence of a person as in Ephron's offer to Abraham, "I give you the field, and I give you the cave that is in it; in the presence [lit.: eyes] of my people I give it to you; bury your dead" (Gen 23:11; cf. 2 Sam 22:25; Acts 1:9; Rom 3:18; Gal 3:1). God's glorious presence and authority can be expressed via the idiom "the eyes of his glory" (Isa 3:8).

In the ancient world, the eye was commonly imagined to be the source of light rather than its receptor.[5] Eyes brighten or light up, that is, exhibit joy, at good news or a pleasurable experience, or general well-being. Jonathan's eyes brightened on eating some honey in unwitting contravention of his father's orders (1 Sam 14:27, 29), and Ezra's prayer of confession on behalf of his people includes a reference to the evidence of the favor of God "who has left us a remnant, and given us a stake in his holy place, in order that he may brighten our eyes and grant us a little sustenance in our slavery" (Ezra 9:8; cf. Pss 13:3; 19:8; 38:10; Prov 29:13). The converse is to have dull or dark eyes, that is, a gloomy expression (Job 17:7; Lam 5:17). Other passages sometimes interpreted as referring to dim or failing eyes are treated below under weeping (§3.2.2; Deut 28:65; Job 11:20; 17:5; 31:16; Ps 119:82, 123; Jer 14:6; Lam 4:17).

3.1 Eyes Open and Shut

The most obvious eye movement is that of opening them (or in several instances having them opened or kept open by divine agency). A troubled psalmist moans to God, "You keep my eyelids from closing" (Ps 77:4). Though Jesus urged his disciples to stay awake in the Garden of Gethsemane, "he came and found them sleeping, for their eyes were heavy" (Matt 26:43; cf. Mark 14:40). Beyond normal wakefulness "opening the eyes" is used in the Bible in connection with the restoration of sight to the blind (e.g., Ps 146:8; Isa 35:5; 42:7; Matt 9:30; John 9:17, 26; 10:21; 11:37)

---

4. *ANEP*, #3.

5. Among those who expounded this "extramission" theory were Plato, Ptolemy, and Galen.

and in the rare recorded instances of awakening from the sleep of death (2 Kgs 4:35; Acts 9:40). Opening the eyes is used to refer to observing or paying attention to something otherwise unnoticed. Of Adam and Eve we read, "Then the eyes of both were opened, and they knew that they were naked" (Gen 3:7). Hagar and her son were in danger of dying of thirst until "God opened her eyes and she saw a well of water" (Gen 21:19). Hezekiah even called on the LORD to be observant, "Incline your ear, O LORD, and hear; open your eyes, O LORD, and see; and hear the words of Sennacherib, which he has sent to mock the living God" (2 Kgs 19:16). The two disciples on the road to Emmaus initially failed to recognize the risen Jesus until "their eyes were opened, and they recognized him" (Luke 24:31).

Having one's eyes opened can suggest gaining visionary insight, enabling one to see things not perceptible to normal vision. It was only when "the LORD opened the eyes of Balaam" that he saw the angel in front of him (Num 22:31). Elijah prayed that his servant's eyes would be opened to see the surrounding army of horses and fiery chariots (2 Kgs 6:17). Opening the eyes can be used as an idiom for being attentive even when the reference is primarily to a verbal plea: "Let your eyes be open to the plea of your servant, and to the plea of your people Israel, listening to them whenever they call to you" (1 Kgs 8:52), so perhaps drawing attention to the nonverbal elements involved in prayer (cf. Neh 1:6; 2 Chr 6:40; 7:15; 1 Pet 3:12). Conversely, closing the eyes, apart from regular sleep, may refer to death. Jacob is promised, "Joseph's own hand shall close your eyes" (Gen 46:4). To "close one's eyes" can be willfully to ignore something (e.g., Lev 20:4), and God is said as an act of judgment to close the eyes of the prophets so they fail to perceive what is coming and warn the people (Isa 29:10; cf. 6:10; 44:18; Matt 13:15; Acts 28:27). Bribery causes metaphorical "blindness" on the part of judges (Exod 23:8; Deut 16:19; 1 Sam 12:3), and those lacking spiritual insight are equally "blind" (Isa 42:18–19; 43:8; 56:10; Matt 23:16–26; John 9:39–41; 2 Pet 1:9; 1 John 2:11; Rev 3:17).

One of the more poetic Hebrew words for eyes may suggest fluttering or flashing eyes. A proverb warns of the enticing behavior of an adulteress, "Do not desire her beauty in your heart, and do not let her capture you with her eyelashes" (Prov 6:25).[6]

The rapid eyelid movement of closing and opening one or both eyes by winking or blinking can constitute a number of meaningful acts of communication. In Ps 35:19 the psalmist prays for deliverance from

---

6. See עפעפים, in *DOTTE*, 3, #6757.

those who would treacherously "wink the eye," that is, perhaps pinch or compress one or both eyes shut as a sign of contempt. In Prov 16:30 we have two facial gestures associated with the malevolent person as "one who winks the eyes" and "compresses the lips" (cf. §2.11). If winking or blinking is correct here, it may refer to some symbolic gesture denoting evil intent, but the Septuagint (LXX), the Greek translation of the OT, renders the expression by "fixing his gaze." If this is correct, the point may be that even when trying not to display any emotion (and remaining tightlipped), the evil person gives the game away as to his malevolent plans.[7] Prov 6:13 associates "winking the eyes" with "shuffling the feet" and "pointing the fingers" as the telltale signs of one sowing discord. Winking is an offensive gesture in contemporary Western Asia. This may also be the meaning of Prov 10:10: "Whoever winks the eye causes trouble, but the one who rebukes boldly makes peace" (NRSV; though the second line relies on a LXX reading where the Hebrew is more like: "and a babbling fool will come to ruin" [ESV]). Or the winking may be similar to our "turning a blind eye," avoiding a direct rebuke.[8] The proverbial "twinkling of an eye" indicating the rapidity of resurrection transformation, is based on either a rapid blinking movement, or a fleeting glance (1 Cor 15:52).

One of the prominent motifs of Scripture is the notion of spiritual insight and its opposite, spiritual blindness, using the imagery of sight or its absence. Moses laments, "But to this day the Lord has not given you a mind to understand, or eyes to see, or ears to hear" (Deut 29:4; cf. Isa 6:10; 44:18; Jer 5:21; Matt 13:15; Mark 8:18; Luke 19:42; John 12:40; Acts 28:27; Rom 11:8, 10; 2 Pet 1:9; 1 John 2:11; Rev 3:17). Isaiah informs us that it would be one of the tasks of the Servant "to open the eyes that are blind" (Isa 42:7; cf. Ps 19:8; Matt 9:30; 13:16; Luke 10:23; 24:31; Acts 26:18; Eph 1:18; Rev 3:18). Jesus' actions in restoring sight to the blind, as well as being compassionate acts towards the individuals, are pointers to this messianic role of restoring sight to Israel (e.g., Matt 11:5; 15:31; Mark 10:52; Luke 4:18; 7:21–22; 18:35–43; John 9:1–34).[9]

---

7. See Bryce, "Omen-Wisdom," 27.
8. Ibid., 25–26; Longman, *Proverbs*, 233–34.
9. See Hamm, "Sight to the Blind."

3.2 Eye Contact

Much can be communicated by various forms of eye contact or avoidance. Sometimes one is confronted with that which one does not wish to see; for example, "Surely there are mockers about me, and my eye dwells on their provocation" (Job 17:2). In general, however, looking is more intentional than seeing or catching sight of someone or something, and deliberately to focus one's visual attention is to make a statement with a range of significances depending on context. The deliberate action of watching, or gazing at someone or something (as distinct from simply glancing around and happening to catch sight of something), suggests interest, connection, engagement, and the like, whether positive or negative. The length of eye contact, combined with other facial expressions, can suggest a range of emotions and attitudes towards the object of attention, from delight to hostility, from apprehension to pity.

A look can be simply deictic, that is, it can serve to identify the referent of a remark, similar to a hand gesture. Joseph singled out Benjamin with a look and said to his other brothers, "Is this your youngest brother, of whom you spoke to me?" (Gen 43:29; cf. 33:5; Isa 40:26). When the crowd told Jesus, "Your mother and your brothers and sisters are outside, asking for you," his response involved casting his eyes about the room: "And looking at those who sat around him, he said, 'Here are my mother and my brothers!'" (Mark 3:32–34; cf. John 6:5).

Regular eye contact with one's conversation partner is normal (see e.g., Num 24:20, 21, where different groups are looked at and spoken to in turn) but when mention is explicitly made in a conversational context of the looking, we should see this as having some impact, reinforcing the verbal communication in some way. Jesus' initial response to the rich man who asked about eternal life and claimed to have kept the commandments was to give him a "searching look" (Mark 10:21).[10] Because we are then told that Jesus "loved" him (cf. §5.6), we understand this look not so much to be one of reproach, but one of tender compassion. In the ensuing discussion in which, given Jesus' comments about entering the kingdom of God, the disciples queried the possibility of salvation, we read, "But Jesus looked at them and said, 'For mortals it is impossible, but for God all things are possible'" (Mark 10:27; cf. Matt 19:26; Mark 8:33; Luke 6:20; 18:24; 20:17; John 1:42). A public speaker is more effective when maintaining eye contact

---

10. Swete, *Mark*, 225.

with the audience: "While Paul was looking intently at the council he said, 'Brothers, up to this day I have lived my life with a clear conscience before God'" (Acts 23:1). Occasionally a penetrating look alone is sufficient to elicit a reaction. When Elisha delivered his message to Hazael about Ben Hadad's recovery in 2 Kgs 8:10 (about which there is some uncertainty), "He fixed his gaze and stared at him, until he was ashamed. Then the man of God wept" (2 Kgs 8:11). Evidently Hazael was hoping for a different outcome. After Peter's denial, "the Lord turned and looked at Peter. Then Peter remembered the word of the Lord, how he had said to him, 'Before the cock crows today, you will deny me three times'" (Luke 22:61). When Jacob learned that there was food in Egypt, his question to his sons, "Why do you keep looking at one another?" (Gen 42:1), was a comment on their indecision and inaction.

To look fixedly or intently on something can suggest determination or commitment. A psalmist affirms, "My eyes are ever toward the LORD" (Ps 25:15). Of his enemies, a psalmist laments, "They track me down; now they surround me; they set their eyes to cast me to the ground" (Ps 17:11). The proverb advises, "Let your eyes look directly forward, and your gaze be straight before you" (Prov 4:25), that is, be resolute and not easily led astray. This is also the probable meaning of the description of Balaam as "the man whose eye is clear" (Num 24:3, 15 NRSV), or as Allegro puts it, "the unrelenting, or the grim-faced one."[11] The opposite is to look back as Lot's wife did, to her cost (Gen 19:26; cf. v. 17). Jesus declares, "No one who puts a hand to the plow and looks back is fit for the kingdom of God" (Luke 9:62).

The nuance of being under scrutiny or judgment can also be suggested by having eyes fixed on one: "For human ways are under the eyes of the LORD, and he examines all their paths" (Prov 5:21; cf. Gen 11:5; Exod 5:21; 2 Sam 16:12; 22:28; Job 14:3; 41:26; Pss 11:4; 14:2; 33:13; 39:13; 66:7; Amos 9:4; Zech 9:1; 12:4). In a slightly different idiom for discriminating justice, "A king who sits on the throne of judgment winnows all evil with his eyes" (Prov 20:8).

To fix one's gaze on something or someone can suggest admiration and desire: "Follow the inclination of your heart and the desire of your eyes, but know that for all these things God will bring you into judgment" (Eccl 11:9; cf. v. 10). Isaiah describes the Servant as one who "had no form or majesty that we should look at him" which is then paralleled by the fact that there was "nothing in his appearance that we should desire him" (Isa

---

11. Allegro, "Meaning."

53:2). One may look admiringly and be attracted by another in a wholesome way (Song 2:9; 3:11; 6:13; Ezek 24:16).[12] The acme of the Israelite elders' encounter with God at Sinai was when "they beheld God" (Exod 24:11). A number of psalmists long for and rejoice in such an experience of God couched in visual terms (Pss 27:4; 34:5; 42:2; 63:2), and the testimony of Jesus is: "Whoever has seen me has seen the Father" (John 14:9).

#3. A worshiper gazes in adoration at the deity. Note the enlarged eyes.
Abu Tempel: Tell Asmar. Sumerian, third millennium BC.
Drawn by Charlotte Whitehouse from Keel #411.

As well as wholesome admiration, looking can also be lustful or enticing, as when Potiphar's wife "cast her eyes on Joseph and said, 'Lie with me'" (Gen 39:7). Peter speaks of those who have "eyes full of adultery" (2 Pet 2:14; cf. Gen 3:6; Isa 3:16; Num 15:39; Deut 4:19; Ps 119:37; Ezek 20:7, 8; Matt 5:29; 18:9; Mark 9:47; 2 Pet 2:14; 1 John 2:16).

To have eyes on someone can express expectancy more generally. Bathsheba informs the ailing and inactive king David, "And now, my lord the king, the eyes of all Israel are on you, to tell them who shall sit on the

---

12. Cf. a lover's words from an Egyptian love song: "I kiss [her] before everyone, that they may see my love. Indeed it is she who captures my heart, when she looks at me, I am refreshed" (*Ostracon Gardiner 304* [*CoS*, 1:130]).

throne of my lord the king after him" (1 Kgs 1:20). After Jesus read from the scroll of Isaiah in the synagogue and sat down, "the eyes of all in the synagogue were fixed on him" because by taking up this position (cf. §4.5) he assumed the role of an expounder of the passage (Luke 4:20). The word used here has associations in Second Temple literature with gazing into heaven or at a supernatural phenomenon (cf. Acts 1:10; 7:25), so Luke may be hinting at a high Christology.

Looking to someone in authority, or to God (or the gods), can suggest confidence, dependency, or an appeal for help, mercy, or favor: "As the eyes of servants look to the hand of their master, as the eyes of a maid to the hand of her mistress, so our eyes look to the LORD our God, until he has mercy upon us" (Ps 123:2; cf. 2 Sam 22:42; Pss 25:15; 104:27; 141:8; 145:15; Isa 17:7–8; 31:1; Mic 7:7; cf. seeking the face, §2.7). Isaiah includes a criticism of the inhabitants of Jerusalem for their failure to acknowledge God as the architect of Jerusalem's defense system: "But you did not look to him who did it, or have regard for him who planned it long ago" (Isa 22:11). Of course such looking can be misdirected to idols (Ezek 6:9; 18:6, 12, 15; 20:7, 8, 24).

With God as the object of attention, the eyes are often said to be raised heavenward, so the gesture becomes one of prayer and the acknowledgement of divine sovereignty: "To you I lift up my eyes, O you who are enthroned in the heavens" (Ps 123:1; cf. Dan 4:34; Matt 14:19; Mark 6:41; 7:34; Luke 9:16; John 11:41; 17:1). Hezekiah laments, "Like a swallow or a crane I clamor, I moan like a dove. My eyes are weary with looking upward" (Isa 38:14).[13]

To turn one's eyes away, then, is to ignore something. Job is tired of God's relentless attention to him: "Will you not look away from me for a while?" (Job 7:19; cf. 14:6; Pss 10:11; 39:13; Isa 22:4). Paul told his Athenian audience that "God has overlooked the times of human ignorance" (Acts 17:30). Deliberate avoidance or disregard of one's obligations can be expressed by hiding one's eyes (Lev 20:4; cf. Prov 28:27), possibly in response to a bribe (1 Sam 12:3). God complains that the people "have disregarded my sabbaths [lit.: hidden their eyes . . .]" (Ezek 22:26), and God himself is said to hide his eyes from, that is, to disregard, the prayers of his faithless people (Isa 1:15). To cause one's eyes to dart back and forth is an indication of apprehension. When God speaks words of encouragement to his servant

---

13. Cf. a Ugaritic liturgy which prefaces a prayer with the words: "You shall lift your eyes to Baʻlu" (*Ugaritic Prayer for a City under Siege*, lines 26′–36′ [*CoS*, 1:284]).

Israel, "Do not fear, for I am with you, do not be afraid, for I am your God" (Isa 41:10; cf. v. 23), the word for "be afraid" is more literally "gaze about."

3.2.1 Attitudes and Emotions Expressed in the Eyes

Tenderness, pity, and favor can be displayed in the eyes, perhaps through the glint of a little extra moisture. The proverb declares, "The souls of the wicked desire evil; their neighbors find no mercy in their eyes" (Prov 21:10). People desired that their gods would look upon them, that is, grant favor. The mother of king Nabonidus of Babylon writes of how after a time of devastation, her prayers were answered: "Sin, the king of the gods, looked upon me. He called Nabunaid, my only son, my offspring, to kingship."[14] God declares through Isaiah, "But this is the one to whom I will look, to the humble and contrite in spirit, who trembles at my word" (Isa 66:2) but warns that God cannot be presumed upon to show pity in his eyes towards unfaithfulness (e.g., Ezek 5:11; 7:4, 9; 8:18; 9:10). When God does show pity or favor, it may be expressed via the idiom of looking down (from heaven), e.g., Deut 26:15, Ps 102:19; Lam 3:50. Such pity and concern for others may come to full expression in the shedding of tears (cf. §3.2.2).

In contrast with the rest of the ancient world, humility is a virtue in the Bible. It can be expressed with a downward cast of the eyes in the presence of others in contrast to haughty or raised eyes. Eliphaz mouths this platitude to Job: "When others are humiliated, you say it is pride; for he saves the humble [lit.: downcast of eyes]" (Job 22:29). The tax collector of Jesus' parable who stands in contrast to the proud Pharisee "would not even look up to heaven, but was beating his breast and saying, 'God, be merciful to me, a sinner!'" (Luke 18:13).

Eye idioms can be used to indicate vigilance, care, and protection. Jesus warned his disciples, "Watch out, and beware of the yeast of the Pharisees and Sadducees" (Matt 16:6; Mark 8:15). The apostle Paul urged the Corinthians, "So if you think you are standing, watch out that you do not fall" (1 Cor 10:12). As with the English idioms "look out for," "look after," "see to," and the like, vision language is used in biblical expressions for taking care, or attending to someone or something. Nebuchadnezzar instructs those holding Jeremiah, "Take him, look after him well [lit.: set eyes on him]" (Jer 39:12). God declares of his people, "I will set my eyes upon them for good" (Jer 24:6), and of the land we learn that "the eyes of the LORD

---

14. *The Adad-guppi Autobiography* (*CoS*, 1:478).

your God are always on it" (Deut 11:12). Solomon prays that God's "eyes may be open night and day" toward the temple (1 Kgs 8:29). Elisha informs the king of Israel, "Were it not that I have regard for Jehoshaphat the king of Judah, I would neither look at you nor see you" (2 Kgs 3:14; cf. Gen 4:4–5; 39:23; Exod 4:31; 5:9; Pss 32:8; 33:18; 34:15; 101:6; Prov 4:21; Ezra 5:5; Amos 5:22; Matt 27:24; 1 Pet 3:12). When Pilate washed his hands, he declared, "I am innocent of this man's blood; see to it yourselves" (Matt 27:24; cf. Acts 18:15; 1 Cor 16:10; Heb 8:5). When John fell down at the angel's feet to worship him, he was told, "You must not do that!" where the words are literally just "See not!" (Rev 19:10).

Another idiom involving the eye concerns generosity. According to the proverb, "Those who are generous [lit.: good of eye] are blessed, for they share their bread with the poor" (Prov 22:9). This association of the eye with generosity probably serves to explain the cryptic expression in Matt 6:22, "The eye is the lamp of the body. So, if your eye is healthy, your whole body will be full of light" (cf. Rom 12:8; 2 Cor 8:2; 9:11, 13). James reminds his readers that "God . . . gives to all generously and ungrudgingly" (Jas 1:5) where "generously" is an adverbial form of the word for "healthy" (eye). Less likely is the alternative explanation that the verse refers to single-minded devotion.

Just as a "healthy eye" is an idiom for generosity, so the "evil eye" is one that is envious or stingy. Moses entreats Israel, "Be careful that you do not entertain a mean thought, thinking, 'The seventh year, the year of remission, is near,' and therefore view your needy neighbor with hostility [lit.: do evil with your eye] and give nothing" (Deut 15:9). The proverb warns, "Do not eat the bread of the stingy [lit.: evil of eye]; do not desire their delicacies" (Prov 23:6). The generous landowner of Jesus' parable asks his grumbling laborers, "Am I not allowed to do what I choose with what belongs to me? Or are you envious [lit.: is your eye evil] because I am generous?" (Matt 20:15). Included in the list of sins which originate in the human heart is envy or an "evil eye" (Mark 7:22). A psalmist admits casting an envious eye at the prosperity of the wicked (Ps 73:3).

Closely related is contempt, which again is shown in the eyes. When Hagar saw that she was pregnant, "she looked with contempt on [lit.: despised with her eyes] her mistress" (Gen 16:4, 5), and when queen Vashti refused to accede to king Ahasuerus's request to display herself before the court, the king is advised, "This deed of the queen will be made known to all women, causing them to look with contempt on their husbands" (Esth 1:17; cf. 3:6).

Mockery or derision can also in part be expressed through the eyes. The proverb warns, "The eye that mocks a father and scorns to obey a mother will be pecked out by the ravens of the valley and eaten by the vultures" (Prov 30:17). The woman of the Song pleads, "Do not gaze at me because I am dark" (Song 1:6), meaning "Don't look down on me . . ." (Message).

Similarly, pride can be exhibited in "haughty eyes" or raised eyes (Pss 18:27; 101:5; Prov 6:17; 21:4; 30:13; Isa 2:11; 5:15; 10:12). God challenges Sennacherib: "Whom have you mocked and reviled? Against whom have you raised your voice and haughtily lifted your eyes? Against the Holy One of Israel!" (2 Kgs 19:22; cf. Isa 37:23).

Anger is another emotion which finds expression partly through a particular form of eye contact. This is possibly the meaning of Eliphaz's question to Job, "Why does your heart carry you away, and why do your eyes flash?" (Job 15:12). The word translated "flash" is obscure, but the following verse suggests that anger or hostility against God is what Job is accused of expressing (LXX has *thymos* = "indignation").[15] Job responds that God "has gnashed his teeth at me; my adversary sharpens his eyes against me" (Job 16:9) or as we might say, "looks daggers." Whatever the precise meaning, the verse reinforces the way that the "heart" (inner disposition) is reflected in the outward appearance. Jesus cast an angry look at those in the synagogue (perhaps at Capernaum) who watched him in order to find fault with his healing of the man with the withered hand (Mark 3:1-5).

Another form of looking with either positive or negative overtones, depending on the context, is the gloating look of triumph over one's enemies at their downfall: "For he has delivered me from every trouble, and my eye has looked in triumph on my enemies" (where NRSV has added "in triumph" to the regular word for "look, see," Ps 54:7; cf. Judg 16:27; Pss 22:17; 54:9; 59:10; 112:8; 118:7; Ezek 28:17; Mic 4:11; 7:10; Obad 12, 13).[16]

There is also the stare of astonishment or horror when the enormity of the sight which confronts the eye requires time for processing. Isaiah has a mock dirge over the king of Babylon: "Those who see you will stare at you, and ponder over you: 'Is this the man who made the earth tremble,

---

15. Other suggestions are: "Why have your eyes become dim?," "Why are your eyes so lofty?" and "Why are you rolling your eyes?"; see Pope, *Job*, 106-10; Gordis, *Job*, 161; Clines, *Job 1-20*, 342; Kotzé, "A Cognitive Linguistic Approach," 857.

16. See Emerton, "Looking."

who shook kingdoms?'" (Isa 14:16). Peter asked his astonished audience in Solomon's Portico after the healing of the lame man, "You Israelites, why do you wonder at this, or why do you stare at us, as though by our own power or piety we had made him walk?" (Acts 3:12).

3.2.2 Weeping

The shedding of tears receives prominent attention in the narrative accounts of laments and petitions of the Bible. In part weeping is a reflex response to strong emotional stimuli, and in part attachment behavior intended to produce a reaction of pity and care in others (1 Sam 1:8; John 20:13, 15), though if they are ill-disposed, the effect may be quite different (Ps 69:10).[17] The Bible's characters, both male and female, seem more prone to public exhibitions of grief and other emotions associated with crying than is customary in modern Western culture, where the expectations are that emotional expression, particularly in public, should be more restrained. In this they are similar to the depiction of the Homeric heroes who seem uninhibited about their public displays of grief.[18] We observe such people as Abraham (Gen 23:2), Esau (Gen 27:38), Jacob (Gen 37:34), Joseph (Gen 43:30), Hannah (1 Sam 1:8), David (1 Sam 20:41; 2 Sam 3:32; 18:33), Elisha (2 Kgs 8:11), Joash (2 Kgs 13:14), Hezekiah (2 Kgs 20:5), Nehemiah (Neh 1:4), Ezra (Ezra 10:6), Peter (Matt 26:75; Mark 14:72), Mary (John 20:11), Paul (Acts 20:31; Phil 3:18), and Jesus (Luke 19:41; John 11:35; Heb 5:7), all freely shedding tears.[19] In fact, of all the references to crying in Scripture, only twice is it children's tears that are shed (Exod 2:6; Job 17:5). In particular the psalmists frequently make mention of their own tears. These tears highlight the verbalized distress and (in some psalms) contrast with the joy upon being heard and answered (Pss 6:8; 30:5; 39:12; 42:3; 56:8; 116:8; 119:136; 126:5, 6). David Bentley Hart makes the point that while weeping on the part of the noble in the ancient world is tragic and sublime, the depiction of the tears of ordinary people such as Peter would normally be treated as a subject of mirth. The Gospel writers therefore represent "a profound shift in moral imagination and sensibility."[20]

---

17. See e.g., Bosworth, "Weeping."
18. Lateiner, *Sardonic Smile*, 69.
19. On Jesus' weeping, see Voorwinde, *Jesus' Emotions*, 182–84.
20. Bentley Hart, *The Story of Christianity*, 29.

Professional mourners or those "skilled in lamentation" were sometimes engaged (and still are in Western Asia) to carry on the display of grief at a funeral (Amos 5:16; cf. 2 Chr 35:25; Eccl 12:5; Jer 9:17–18; Matt 9:23; 11:17).

Weeping is closely associated with loud wailing (Gen 21:16; 27:38; Num 14:1; Judg 2:4; 21:2; 1 Sam 11:4; 24:16; 2 Sam 3:32; 13:36; Ezra 3:12; Job 2:12; Jer 31:15; Matt 2:18; Mark 5:38–39; Luke 8:52; Jas 5:1; Rev 18:9) which could be exhausting (1 Sam 30:4; Ps 6:6; Lam 2:18). We note the propensity of the biblical writers to use hyperbole in their description of copious tears; for example, "I am weary with my moaning; every night I flood my bed with tears; I drench my couch with my weeping" (Ps 6:6; cf. Pss 80:5; 102:9; Jer 9:1; Lam 2:18; 3:48; Mal 2:13). The abundant tears of the legendary grief-stricken Ugaritic hero Kirta are described very similarly.[21] A Hebrew idiom for overwhelming grief is to "exhaust one's eyes," that is, to run out of tears. A man of God prophesied to Eli, "The only one of you whom I shall not cut off from my altar shall be spared to weep out his eyes and grieve his heart; all the members of your household shall die by the sword" (1 Sam 2:33; cf. Lev 26:16; Deut 28:32, 65; 1 Sam 2:33; Job 11:20; 17:5; 31:16; Pss 69:3; 119:82, 123; Jer 14:6; Lam 4:17).[22] It has been suggested that the Hebrews, rather than seeing tears as a renewable resource, thought of them as the internal organs turning to water and welling up, taking at face value such laments as: "My eyes are spent with weeping; my stomach churns; my bile is poured out on the ground" (Lam 2:11).[23] A psalmist prays that God might record and preserve his tears in a skin bottle (Ps 56:8). Weeping can be associated with other grief gestures such as refusing to eat (1 Sam 1:7; 2 Sam 12:21; Neh 1:4; cf. §2.10), throwing dust on the head (Rev 18:19; cf. §2.4), shaving the head (Isa 22:12; cf. §2.1), and wearing sackcloth or tearing one's clothes (Gen 37:34; 2 Sam 3:31; 2 Kgs 22:19; Isa 15:3; cf. §4.11).

Primarily weeping signals grief at a loss or deprivation, present or anticipated (Gen 23:2; Num 11:4; 2 Sam 1:12; 3:32; 18:33; Ezra 3:12; Ps 137:1; Jas 5:1; Rev 5:4). Tears may accompany both the sadness of parting (Ruth 1:9; Acts 20:37) and the joy of reunion (Gen 33:4; 45:14; 46:29), or even a significant first meeting (Gen 27:38). Another motif of Scripture is that of tears of remorse or sorrow over one's own sin, or on behalf of the people:

---

21. *Kirta* i 26–31 (*CoS*, 1:333).
22. See Gruber, *Aspects*, 389–400.
23. Collins, "Physiology."

"While Ezra prayed and made confession, weeping and throwing himself down before the house of God, a very great assembly of men, women, and children gathered to him out of Israel; the people also wept bitterly" (Ezra 10:1, cf. v. 6; Jer 50:4; Matt 26:75; Mark 14:72; Luke 22:62). The glint of moisture to be seen in the tender pitying eye can overflow into expressions of tearful concern for others, for example in preaching or letter writing. Paul tells the Ephesian elders, "I did not cease night or day to warn everyone with tears" (Acts 20:31; cf. 2 Cor 2:4; Phil 3:18).

Though often involuntary, weeping can be controlled. Ezekiel is told to refrain from weeping on the death of his wife, as a communicative event (Ezek 24:16). As with other involuntary gestures, weeping can also be openly displayed or concealed. We note that Joseph withdrew to a private room so as not to let his tears be observed, then washed his face before returning to his brothers (Gen 43:31).[24] As with any other form of communication, weeping is subject to manipulative employment as when Samson's wife turned on the waterworks to wheedle the explanation of Samson's riddle out of him (Judg 14:16, 17).

Finally, comfort and the reversal of grief can be expressed as the wiping away of tears. When the new Jerusalem is revealed and God dwells with his people, "he will wipe every tear from their eyes. Death will be no more; mourning and crying and pain will be no more, for the first things have passed away" (Rev 21:4; cf. Isa 25:8; 65:19; 30:19; Rev 7:17).

---

24. See Yoo, "Why Does Joseph Wash His Face?" Yoo suggests Joseph may also be performing an Egyptian purification ritual to keep up the pretence.

4

The Neck, Torso, and Whole Body

4.1 The Neck and Shoulders

THE NECK AND SHOULDERS have several associations in Scripture including extremes of emotion, servitude, and the fragility of life. As with the head, the neck may stand for the whole person (Gen 17:14; 36:6).[1]

Necklaces might be worn either as an adornment (Song 1:10; 4:9; Ezek 16:11) or as a symbol of high office (Gen 41:42; Dan 5:7, 16, 29).[2] This is the background to the metaphorical treatment of abstract qualities such as wisdom and instruction, loyalty, and trustworthiness as a necklace (Prov 1:9; 3:3, 22; 6:21), and negatively to the necklace of pride (Ps 73:6).

To fall on another's neck is to hug or embrace them with a considerable display of emotion, notably in family reunions as when Joseph was reunited with his brother Benjamin (Gen 45:14; cf. 33:4; 46:29), or in Jesus' description of the father's welcome of his wayward son (Luke 15:20). Kissing the shoulders is a form of affectionate greeting in some parts of Western Asia today. Similarly it is a gesture of parting, as at Paul's leaving the Ephesian elders (Acts 20:37). This latter reference, which is literally "falling on Paul's neck," reinforces the extended family motif of the early church (cf. §2.11; §5.6).

The converse of falling on the neck is (lit.) to "turn the neck" in a display of indifference or contempt, as God charges Israel with doing to him (Jer 2:27). God then threatens to ignore his people in their distress by showing them the back of his neck, not his face (Jer 18:17; cf. 32:33; 2 Chr 29:6; cf. §4.3)

---

1. See the discussion in Gruber, "Many Faces", 252.

2. For royal necklaces, see *ANEP*, #378, #384, #394; *The Victory Stela of King Piye (Piankhy)*, 112 (CoS 2:49).

Another nuance of turning to present the back of the neck (often simply translated as "back") is that of shame and ignominy: "How Moab has turned his back in shame! So Moab has become a derision and a horror to all his neighbors" (Jer 48:39; cf. Ps 18:40).

The throat may become parched in times of grief or stress and its dryness can alert others to our state of mind: "My soul [throat] thirsts for God, for the living God" (Ps 42:2; cf. Lev 26:16; Deut 28:65; 1 Sam 2:33; Pss 63:1; 107:5; 143:6; Prov 25:25; Isa 29:8; 58:10; Jer 2:25; 31:25).[3] Perhaps in part because of the semantic range of Hebrew *nephesh* "throat, breath, life, soul" and Greek *pneuma* "breath, spirit," the thirst motif serves as a graphic depiction in Scripture of an inner spiritual need (Pss 42:2; 63:1; 143:6; Amos 8:11; Matt 5:6; John 4:13–14; 7:37; Rev 22:17; cf. §2.10).

The neck or throat then represents the vulnerability of human life.[4] A proverb suggests a knife to the throat as a drastic remedy for gluttony (Prov 23:2). The metaphor of being up to one's neck in water represents perilous situations (Pss 69:1; 124:4–5; Isa 8:8; 30:28; Lam 3:54; Jonah 2:5). Paul commends Priscilla and Aquila for risking their necks on his behalf (Rom 16:4). The word for "neck" is then frequently translated as "soul" in English versions: "You shall love the LORD your God with all your heart, and with all your soul, and with all your might" (Deut 6:5; cf. Gen 35:18; 1 Sam 1:15; 18:1; 1 Kgs 11:37; Job 30:16; Pss 13:2; 19:7; Isa 26:9).[5] For an oath gesture which may involve the neck or throat, cf. §5.9.

An idiom for pride or stubbornness, familiar also to English speakers, is the stiff or stretched neck which might be associated with a "hard heart" and often equates to willful disobedience to God's commands. God complains that his people "did not listen or incline their ear; they stiffened their necks and would not hear or receive instruction" (Jer 17:23; cf. Exod 32:9; Deut 10:16; 2 Chr 30:8; 36:13; Neh 9:16, 17, 29; Ps 75:5; Prov 29:1; Isa 3:16; 48:4; Jer 7:26; 19:15). In his defense, Stephen accuses his audience of the same stiff-necked attitude as their ancestors who resisted the Holy Spirit speaking through the prophets (Acts 7:51). The physiological background to the idiom would seem to be the tensioning of neck muscles so as to prevent the head from turning to listen to alternative points of view.

---

3. English translations do not generally recognize a reference to dryness of throat in some of these passages, but see Gruber, "Dryness of Throat."

4. On the association of the throat with the threat of death, see the Egyptian *Sinuhe* 21–24 (*CoS*, 1:78).

5. Staubli and Schroer, *Body Symbolism*, 56–67.

A common demonstration of the humiliating subjection of one's vanquished enemies was to place one's foot on their necks, a stance we find depicted in ancient scenes commemorating triumphs, such as a relief of Ramses II on a temple wall at Abu Simbel.⁶ This practice is represented in the Bible in Josh 10:24 when Joshua invited his commanders to place their feet on the necks of the five southern Canaanite kings, preparatory to killing them (cf. Pss 8:6; 18:38; 36:11; 47:3; 58:10; 68:30; 91:13).

#4. Pharaoh Ramses II triumphing over his enemy. Abu Simbel, Egypt, thirteenth century BC. Keel #404.

A variation is to place a hand on the neck of one's enemies, suggestive perhaps of a yoke (Gen 49:8). The frequently occurring metaphor of having one's neck in a yoke speaks of a burden, or of doing the bidding of

---

6. A liturgy of an Aramaic speaking community in Upper Egypt (third century BC) reads: "[Your foes] I shall destroy in front of you; your foot on their necks [you will place]" (*The Aramaic Text in Demotic Script*, col. vi [*CoS*, 1:313]).

another, like that of oxen plowing (1 Kgs 12:4–14).[7] This was a standard image of servitude to a foreign power. Jeremiah is instructed to make and wear a yoke as an acted prophecy urging submission to the sovereignty of Babylon (Jer 27:1–12; cf. Gen 27:40; 49:8; Lev 26:13; Deut 28:48; Isa 9:4; 10:27; 14:25; 52:2; Mic 2:3; Nah 1:13). Sin is described as a yoke around the neck (Lam 1:14), and elsewhere as enslaving those subject to it (John 8:34; Rom 6:16–20; 7:14, 25).

While submission to Christ can be expressed in the language of captivity and servitude (Rom 1:1; 2 Cor 10:5; Gal 1:10; Eph 6:6; Phil 1:1; Col 4:12; 2 Tim 2:24; Jas 1:1; 1 Pet 2:16), the yoke Jesus invites his disciples to take up is not burdensome but an easy one (Matt 11:29–30; cf. Lam 3:26–27 for a positive image of bearing the yoke of patient endurance, waiting for the Lord's deliverance).

In a debate in the early church regarding circumcision for gentiles, Peter likened requiring gentile submission to the Jewish law, epitomized by this rite, to an unbearable yoke (Acts 15:10; cf. Gal 5:1). Judaism adopted the image of the yoke as a positive one for submission to Torah.

Yoking can also suggest a willing alliance, particularly an illegitimate alliance such as Israel contracted with the Baal of Peor (Num 25:3, 5; Ps 106:23). In an image based on the prohibition of yoking together an ox and a donkey in a mismatch (Deut 22:10), Paul urges believers not to be unequally yoked with unbelievers (2 Cor 6:14).

There are several words for shoulders in Hebrew which partly overlap with words for neck. The shoulders (for both men and women) bore the brunt of burdens and hard work generally (Gen 21:14; 24:15; 49:15; Exod 12:34; Josh 4:5; Judg 9:48; 16:3; 1 Chr 15:15; Neh 3:5; Ps 81:6; Matt 23:4; Luke 15:5). This gives rise to the idiom where responsibility and authority can be said to rest on someone's shoulders: "For a child has been born for us, a son given to us; authority rests upon his shoulders" (Isa 9:6; cf. 22:22). Zephaniah envisages a reversal of the confusion of Babel, when everyone will serve God (lit.) "with one shoulder" (Zeph 3:9). An OT idiom for eagerness, or making an early start, makes use of a denominative verb derived from the word for "shoulder": "Absalom used to rise early and stand beside the road into the gate" (2 Sam 15:2; cf. Gen 19:2; 22:3; Exod 8:20; 9:13; 1 Sam 29:10; Ps 127:2; Isa 5:11). Turning the shoulder suggests an intention

---

7. In the Babylonian *Epic of Creation*, the gods complain, "Think of our burden, our eyes are pinched, Lift this unremitting yoke, let us sleep!" (Tablet 1, 122 [*CoS*, 1:392]).

to leave (1 Sam 10:9). As with the neck, "to turn a stubborn shoulder" indicates refusal to listen and obey (Neh 9:29; Zech 7:11).

4.2 The Chest or Breast

The chest or breast or bosom (and the same word is sometimes translated "embrace" or "lap") generally has warm and intimate associations such as that of husband and wife together (Deut 13:6; cf. Gen 16:5; Deut 28:56; 2 Sam 12:8; 1 Kgs 1:2; Mic 7:5) or a mother nursing a child, an image which speaks of sustenance and protection (Num 11:12; 1 Kgs 3:20). When Obed was born, "Naomi took the child and laid him in her bosom, and became his nurse" (Ruth 4:16; cf. 2 Sam 12:3; 1 Kgs 17:19). Though Naomi is the focus of the concluding scene of Ruth, with the reversal of her fortunes from death to life, it is not necessary to see this action of hers as constituting a formal adoption.[8] In a startling metaphor, the restored people of God are said to "suck the breasts of kings" (Isa 60:16). God is said to care for his people like a nursing mother (Isa 49:15; cf. Hos 11:3–4).

A different association is seen in the proverb, "The lot is cast into the lap, but the decision is the LORD's alone" (Prov 16:33). This gaming image would appear to be the source of the notion that the lap is the place one's destiny is determined or one is repaid for what one has done (Isa 65:6–7; Jer 32:18; Pss 79:12; 89:50).

To beat one's chest or breast is an indicator of humiliation and mourning. Isaiah summons the women of Jerusalem to "beat your breasts" in distress at the coming calamity (Isa 32:12; cf. Nah 2:7), and the characteristic LXX rendering of the verb *saphad*, generally translated "mourn" in English, suggests it has primary reference to the gesture of beating (that is, the breast: 2 Sam 1:12; Esth 4:3; Isa 22:12; Jer 4:8; Ezek 24:16, 23; Joel 2:12; Mic 1:8).[9] The Homeric epics similarly depict breast-beating (of women) as a sign of grief.[10] The tax collector of Jesus' parable beats his chest in a heartfelt prayer of penitence (Luke 18:13), and an often-overlooked detail of Luke's crucifixion account is that the crowds who witnessed the spectacle "returned home, beating their breasts" in sympathetic sorrow (Luke 23:48; cf. v. 27 where "breasts" is implied). Such a display of grief, still practiced in Western Asia, is more associated with women, so is an extreme gesture

---

8. Cf. Bush, *Ruth, Esther*, 258.
9. Cf. Gruber, *Aspects*, 436–49.
10. E.g., Homer, *Iliad* 18.50; Corbeill, *Nature Embodied*, 72.

when performed by men.¹¹ The chest would seem to be on the receiving end of such beating as the locus of the heart, the center of emotions such as grief (Gen 6:6; 1 Sam 1:8; Neh 2:2; Prov 14:13; Jer 8:18), as well as the source of evil (Gen 6:5; 8:21; Pss 12:2; 101:4; Prov 6:14; Jer 16:12; Zech 8:17; Matt 9:4; 15:19; Mark 7:21; Heb 3:12).¹²

Inflating the chest to give the impression that one is larger and more impressive gives rise to the idiom of being "puffed up" with pride or notions of self-importance. The church at Corinth needed reminding that "knowledge puffs up, but love builds up" (1 Cor 8:1; cf. 4:6, 18, 19; 5:2; 8:1; 13:4; Col 2:18).

4.3 The Back

To present one's back rather than one's face to something is to shun or ignore it. An Egyptian priest laments the state of his land: "Everybody alike is subjected to wrongs, (As for) reverence, backs are turned to it."¹³ Nehemiah similarly confesses to God that his people "cast your law behind their backs" (Neh 9:26). Unless fleeing an enemy (Exod 23:27; Josh 7:12; 2 Sam 22:41; Ps 18:40), deliberately to present one's back rather than one's face to another person can be insulting. Thus, the idolatrous worshipers of Ezekiel's time who were worshiping the sun in the temple forecourt pointedly had their back to the temple of the LORD as they faced the rising sun (Ezek 8:16). The LORD's judgment on Jeroboam through Ahijah was because "you . . . have thrust me behind your back" (1 Kgs 14:9). On the other hand, on being healed, Hezekiah thanks God, "for you have cast all my sins behind your back" (Isa 38:17).

Further instances of turning one's back are obscured in English translations, for a word now recognized to mean "turn the back" is a homonym of a word for "speak."¹⁴ So for NRSV "Even young children despise me; when I rise, they talk against me" (Job 19:18), read "Even young children despise me; when I rise, they turn their backs on me" (and similarly Gen 34:13; Pss 50:20; 75:5; 78:19; Song 5:6; Jer 31:20; cf. §4.1).

---

11. Bailey, *Through Peasant Eyes*, 153–54.
12. *Midrash Rabbah*, Eccl 7:2, 5.
13. *The Complaints of Khakheperreʿ-sonb* 12 (*CoS*, 1:105).
14. דבר III, in *DCH*.

4.4 The Loins

The word "loins" in English translations of the Bible renders a word referring to the lower abdomen and genital area (Gen 46:26; Exod 1:5; Jer 13:11; Heb 7:10). The same Hebrew and Greek words are also variously rendered "thigh," "hip," or "waist." Jeremiah describes a time of great distress as being like the agony of childbirth: "Ask now, and see, can a man bear a child? Why then do I see every man with his hands on his loins like a woman in labor? Why has every face turned pale?" (Jer 30:6).

A common idiom for being prepared for (masculine gendered) action is "gird up one's loins," that is, tuck in one's outer garment so as to be unrestricted for swift travel, battle, or other active movement and, by extension, to prepare for any activity.[15] The Akkadian *Marduk Prophecy* is prefaced with the words, "After I gird my loins, I will give my speech."[16] The Israelites were to eat the first Passover with their loins girded, ready for a hasty departure from Egypt (Exod 12:11; cf. 1 Kgs 18:46; 2 Kgs 3.21; 4:29; 9:1; Job 38:3; 40:7; Jer 1:17; Nah 2:1; Luke 12:35). Peter can speak (lit.) of "girding up the loins of your mind" (1 Pet 1:13), that is, "prepare your minds for action" (NRSV).

Abraham's instruction to his servant, "Put your hand under my thigh" (Gen 24:2; cf. 47:29) as he swore an oath, has occasioned a great deal of discussion.[17] Both passages where the expression is used are spoken by aging patriarchs and the oath involves matters relating to the future of the family's inheritance in the land, that is, the posterity issuing from Abraham's (and subsequently Jacob's) loins. The holding of the circumcised male member (for that is how Jewish tradition understands the practice), or at least placing the hand in the general region (as Viberg argues) may allude to the covenant sign (Gen 17:11–14), and/or may involve the patriarchal offspring (yet to issue from the loins) in the obligations entailed in the oath. A letter from southern Mesopotamia contains a reference to a somewhat parallel practice,[18] and a custom recorded in Saudi Arabia, while different in some respects, involves a sheikh or judge placing his hand near the genital organ of a man under questioning as an implied

---

15. Low, "Implications."
16. *The Marduk Prophecy* i (*CoS*, 1:480).
17. See e.g., Freedman, "Put Your Hand"; Smith, "Heel and Thigh," 468–69; Viberg, *Symbols of Law*, 45–51; Hugenberger, *Marriage*, 197; Hamilton, *Genesis 18–50*, 139.
18. Malul, "Touching."

threat to his posterity if he should fail to tell the truth.[19] There is also a suggestion that the enigmatic phrase which NRSV renders "the Fear of Isaac" (Gen 31:42, 53) ought to be "the thigh of Isaac" and so these verses would be further references to such a patriarchal oath.[20]

4.5 Sitting and Lying

While we may picture chairs when sitting is mentioned in the Bible, chairs were not a regular item of household furniture until relatively modern times. Apart from ceremonial seats (thrones) for persons of high rank (Exod 12:29; 2 Sam 19:8; 2 Chr 18:9; Ezek 23:41; Matt 19:28; Luke 22:30; Rev 4:2), people generally sat or squatted on the ground or a carpet or any object of a convenient height (Exod 17:12; Judg 5:10; 13:9; 1 Sam 2:8; Isa 47:1; Lam 2:10; Matt 28:2; John 4:6; 20:12). When David took up his position on his throne in the gateway (2 Kgs 19:8), it signaled to the people that the time of public mourning for Absalom was over, for a king vacates his throne during mourning to be one with his people (cf. Jonah 3:6).[21] When a suppliant approached an enthroned monarch, the suppliant would normally stand or fall to the ground, and not be invited to sit. Solomon's invitation to his mother to sit on a throne beside him to make representations on Adonijah's behalf indicates the exalted role of the queen mother within the royal household (1 Kgs 2:19). References to God sitting are to be understood not as references to his resting, but to his reigning: "He who sits in the heavens laughs; the LORD has them in derision" (Ps 2:4; cf. 1 Sam 4:4; 2 Sam 6:2; 2 Kgs 19:15; 1 Chr 13:6; Pss 9:7; 29:10; 99:1; Isa 37:16; 40:22). While some older translations of Ps 82:1 might lead us to picture God "standing" in the divine assembly, the word can mean "take one's place, be stationed," so we should probably understand God as being enthroned here also. To sit (on a throne) at the right hand of a king, or God, is to be granted a place of honor and authority (Ps 110:1; Matt 22:44; 26:64; Mark 12:36; 14:62; 16:19; Luke 22:69; Acts 2:34; Eph 1:20). We see the notion of the king seated at the god's

---

19. Barakat, "Arabic Gestures", 761, 784.

20. Malul, "More on *paḥad yiṣḥāq*"; פחד II, in *DOTTE*, 3 #7066. Another suggestion in the *DOTTE* entry is "the Protection of Isaac."

21. Even the high god ʾIlu vacated his throne to sit on the ground in a time of mourning in the Ugaritic epic *The Baʿlu Myth* vi 11–14 (*CoS*, 1:267); see Olyan, "Honor, Shame, and Covenant Relations," 208–11; Kruger, "Nonverbal Communication' in the Hebrew Bible," 155–57.

right hand represented, for example, in the statue of the enthroned Pharaoh Haremheb to the right of that of the god Horus.[22]

Sitting can communicate a range of possible intentions, depending on context. It can refer to inaction in contrast to the activity of others or one's own proposed activity (Num 32:6; 2 Kgs 7:3–4). To sit down with others can suggest readiness to confer or do business. In a Mesopotamian myth, "The great Anunnaki who decree destinies sat and conferred their counsel on the land."[23] Kings sit down to plan a battle (Luke 14:31). When Samuel learned that Jesse had one more son who was not present, he said, "Send and bring him; for we will not sit down until he comes here" (1 Sam 16:11). Boaz invited his relative and the elders of Bethlehem to sit down to discuss his proposal regarding Naomi's property (Ruth 4:1–2). Those who are blessed, according to Psalm 1, are those "who do not follow the advice of the wicked, or take the path that sinners tread, or sit in the seat of scoffers" (Ps 1:1; cf. §6.4; §6.5), where the sequence of walking ... standing ... sitting (the literal function words behind the translation) probably suggests a gradation of involvement just as the several words for evildoers increase in force (cf. Ps 26:4–5).[24] This may suggest a disturbing note to the astute reader of Luke 22:55 where, after learning that Peter had initially followed at a distance those who had arrested Jesus, we read that "Peter sat among them."

Judges performed their duty from a seated position. Pilate, for example, "sat on the judge's bench" (John 19:13; cf. Exod 18:13; Judg 4:5; Dan 7:10, 26; Joel 3:12; Matt 23:2; 27:19; Acts 23:3). Likewise teaching was typically conducted from a seated position. When Jesus read from the Isaiah scroll in the synagogue at Nazareth and then sat down, "the eyes of all in the synagogue were fixed on him" because they anticipated his exposition of the passage (Luke 4:20; cf. Matt 5:1; 13:1–2; 23:2; 24:3; 26:55; Mark 9:35; 13:3; Luke 5:3; John 8:2). Listeners also sat before a teacher, as Mary "who sat at the Lord's feet and listened to what he was saying" (Luke 10:39; cf. 2 Kgs 4:38; Ezek 33:31; Mark 3:32; Luke 2:46).

Sitting can also be a posture of worship in the OT. According to the Chronicler, who has a particular interest in cultic activity, David's response to Nathan's oracle was that he "sat before the LORD" to express his thankful response (1 Chr 17:16). A psalmist avers, "I shall sit [rather than

---

22. Keel, *Symbolism*, 353.
23. *Epic of Creation*, Tablet 1 (*CoS*, 1:453).
24. See, e.g., Longman, *Psalms*, 56.

NRSV's dwell] in the house of the LORD my whole life long" (Ps 23:6; cf. Judg 20:26; 21:2).

Sitting on the ground, or in dust and dirt, often in combination with other signs of grief (such as tearing one's clothing; §4.11), is frequently mentioned as a posture of mourning, as the exiles in Babylon employed at the memory of what they had lost (Ps 137:1; cf. Neh 1:4; Job 2:8, 13; Isa 47:1; Lam 2:10; Ezek 26:16; Jonah 3:6; Luke 10:13). A more dramatic exhibition of grief is to lie in the dirt or roll or wallow in it (2 Sam 12:16; 13:31; Esth 4:3; Isa 58:5; Jer 6:26; 25:34; Mic 1:10; Ezek 27:30). The Greek hero Achilles similarly sat in front of his ships, fasting and mourning for his friend Patroclus (*Iliad* 19.344-45), while king Priam rolled about in filth as a mourning gesture for his son Hector (*Iliad* 24.161-65). The reversal of the Israelite captives' fortunes is celebrated by Isaiah, "Shake yourself from the dust, rise up, O captive Jerusalem; loose the bonds from your neck, O captive daughter Zion!" (Isa 52:2).

Ordinary meals could be eaten while sitting, perhaps on a mat or cushions (or outdoors on the grass), or for more formal parties and banquets in the Hellenistic era, reclining on low couches around a low table (Matt 14:19; Mark 6:39; Luke 12:37; 14:7-11; John 6:10). At a banquet, reclining guests leaned on their left elbow with their feet away from the table.[25] A banquet was a social occasion which served to define social identity and where the observance of rank was considered important in the positioning of guests at the table, and provided an opportunity for followers of Jesus' teaching to demonstrate humility by taking a lower place (Luke 14:7-11; cf. 5:27-32; 7:36-50). Similarly James is presumably addressing a real tendency on the part of some to discriminate on the basis of wealth, using the differential treatment of those who come into the assembly: "[I]f you take notice of the one wearing the fine clothes and say, 'Have a seat here, please,' while to the one who is poor you say, 'Stand there,' or, 'Sit at my feet,' have you not made distinctions among yourselves, and become judges with evil thoughts?" (Jas 2:3-4).

To take to one's bed in the day when one ought to be active, as Ahab did when he failed to persuade Naboth to sell him his orchard (1 Kgs 21:4),

---

25. Some of the references to dining in the Gospels where "sitting" is mentioned in English translations are more strictly references to reclining in a banquet context; see Jeremias, *Eucharistic Words* 20-21; cf. a nineteenth-century description of a meal as guests of a bedouin sheikh in Tristram, *The Land of Israel*, 259-61. See also Louw and Nida, *Greek-English Lexicon*, 1:251-52; Willis, "Banquets."

indicates a troubled mind. Lying awake at night, or tossing and turning in bed, may also signify a depressed state (Job 7:4; Ps 102:7).[26]

4.6 Bowing, Kneeling, and Prostration

The Bible abounds in references to people bowing, kneeling, bending the knee, falling on their faces, prostrating themselves, and the like in displays of profound respect, reverence, or high level emotional response. Such displays are prevalent in the wider cultural context as evident from literary sources and iconography. A hymn in praise of the Mesopotamian sun god declares: "You heed, O Shamash, prayer, supplication, and blessing, obeisance, kneeling, whispered prayer, and prostration," suggesting there may have been subtle differences in the gestures mentioned but the same general effect.[27] It is a natural expression of social ranking for people to position themselves in such a way that the one of greater esteem is physically higher than others, and we have images from widespread regions of the ancient world such as Rome, Egypt, and Mesopotamia of people showing such physical deference before humans and deities or their symbols.[28] While in modern Western Asia the forms of deference have diminished in scale (a nod or lowering of the eyes may suffice), the concept of marking differences in social rank is still quite strong.

Quite a range of Hebrew and Greek words express these actions and it is not always easy to tell the extent of bodily movement intended. It would seem both from the word meanings in the Bible and the images we have that typically what is meant (with some variation) is dropping to the knees, drawing one knee back while bringing the other knee forward so as to facilitate getting up again.[29] The upper body is then free to bend, bringing the face low to or touching the ground, or to be upright with hands held forward or (for entreaty) clutching the legs of the one entreated. When praying for rain (Jas 5:17–18), Elijah "bowed himself down upon the earth and put his face between his knees" (1 Kgs 18:42), and in a unique expression, "Saul fell full length on the ground, filled with fear because of the

---

26. Kruger, "Depression," 192.
27. *The Shamash Hymn* 130 (*CoS*, 1:419).
28. Kneeling Syrians and Africans form the decoration for Amen-hotep's throne platform: *ANEP*, #4; cf. #46. For an image of a kneeling German prisoner (presumably originally before a triumphant Roman general) see Brilliant, *Gesture and Rank*, 74–75.
29. See #2.

words of Samuel" (1 Sam 28:20).³⁰ The verb "fall"—to one's knees (Luke 5:8), or on one's face (Gen 17:3), or the ground (Gen 44:14)—suggests some rapidity of action. A typical scene in ancient iconography depicts a procession before the monarch's throne with those further away approaching with arms raised, while those closer have already dropped to the ground.³¹ An Egyptian described his approach to the pharaoh:

> My forehead touched the ground between the sphinxes, and the royal children stood in the gateway to meet me. The courtiers who usher through the forecourt set me on the way to the audience-hall. I found his majesty on the great throne in a kiosk of gold. Stretched out on my belly, I did not know myself before him.³²

Naaman requests sympathetic understanding from Elisha: "when my master goes into the house of Rimmon to worship there, leaning on my arm, and I bow down in the house of Rimmon" (2 Kgs 5:18). While perhaps playing on an idiomatic designation of a trusted court official as one "on whose hand the king leaned" (2 Kgs 7:2; cf. v. 17; cf. §5.3), it is more likely here a literal reference, that is, the king needed assistance in getting down on his knees and up again and Naaman in getting down and up with him would be perceived as engaging in an act of homage. Whether such prostration is to be envisaged every time such language is used is not clear and many of the references to postures of obeisance are toned down in contemporary English translations, such that, for example, the unbeliever's anticipated response to Christian prophecy, when they (lit.) "fall on their face" becomes "bow down" (1 Cor 14:25 NRSV) or "fall to their knees" (NLT2).³³ Whereas we might be inclined to picture a single polite bow in greetings or farewells, a prolonged etiquette of bowing or prostration multiple times is probably often to be pictured. David prostrated himself before Jonathan three times (1 Sam 20:41), and Jacob did so seven times as he approached his estranged brother (Gen 33:3). A similar reference to a sevenfold (or twice sevenfold) bowing or falling at the feet of the sovereign is a standard deferential epistolary formula in the letters from Canaanite vassal kings (Amarna, Egypt) and the letters from Ugarit (Syria), suggesting that, were

---

30. For a Ugaritic parallel to the face between the knees, see *The Baʻlu Myth* i 19–29 (*CoS*, 1:246); Kruger, "On Non-verbal Communication in the Baal Epic," 60–63.

31. See #2, #5; Keel, *Symbolism*, 308–23; *ANEP*, #4, #5, #45,#46, #47; Gruber, *Aspects*, 182–291.

32. *Sinuhe* 249–53 (*CoS*, 1:81).

33. See חוה, השתחוה, in *TDOT*, 4:248–56.

the subjects present physically, they would perform this elaborate show of respect.³⁴ Jesus noted the scribes' and Pharisees' love of "elaborate greetings in the marketplaces" and we must picture these as not merely verbal exchanges, but physical demonstrations of deference (Matt 23:7; Mark 12:38; Luke 11:43 NET).³⁵ This also explains Jesus' instruction on commissioning his disciples for their mission: "Greet no one on the road" (Luke 10:4).

#5. Worshipers in various stages of prostration. Egyptian, sixteenth to eleventh century BC. Keel #412.

Falling to the ground or falling on the face can suggest that the subject is overwhelmed with awe or emotion. Abraham's varied reactions to hearing God's far-reaching commitments include falling on his face (Gen 17:3,

---

34. E.g., *Letter of Abdi-heba of Jerusalem* 1–4 (*CoS*, 3:237); *From an Official in Alashia to the King* 4–6 (*CoS*, 3:104).

35. See Windisch, ἀσπάζομαι, 498.

17; cf. Lev 9:24). Daniel's reaction to a frightening encounter is to fall on his face (Dan 8:17). Moses and Aaron fall on their faces in distress on learning of the people's desire to return to Egypt (Num 14:5; cf. 16:4; Josh 7:6, 10; Judg 13:20; 1 Chr 21:16; Ezek 1:28; 3:23; 9:8; 11:13; 43:3; 44:4; Dan 8:18; 10:9). Jesus' agonized prayer in the Garden of Gethsemane was from such a posture (Matt 26:39). Even the members of the constabulary who came to arrest Jesus in the Garden were temporarily overawed by his presence or his self-revelatory response, "I am he" (with its overtones of divine identity) so that "they stepped back and fell to the ground" (John 18:6). Sometimes it is not clear to interpreters whether an emotion such as grief or an attitude of worship (see below) is dominant in a given context. When Job "fell on the ground" in response to the news of the calamities that had befallen his family (Job 1:20), English translations mostly translate the next word "and worshiped" (as NRSV), but it would be better to understand the word here as a reference to physical posture, as does REB: "threw himself prostrate on the ground," and leave the reader to ponder the mix of emotions.

When a person bows or prostrates herself before another, or falls at the knees or feet of another, this serves first as an acknowledgement of the higher social rank of the other. *The (Israel) Stela of Merneptah* refers to rulers of the conquered nations prostrating themselves before the pharaoh and a relief from Nineveh shows subjects groveling at the feet of Ashurbanipal.[36] Similarly in the classical world we observe Phaedra in Seneca's play of the same name falling at the knees of Hippolytus.[37] In the scene of David's emotional parting from Jonathan referred to above, there may be elements of both respect to the royal heir and distress, when David "prostrated himself with his face to the ground. He bowed three times, and they kissed each other, and wept with each other" (1 Sam 20:41). A man knelt before Jesus to ask him, "Good Teacher, what must I do to inherit eternal life?" (Mark 10:17). In the case of the soldiers at the cross, their kneeling was of course in mock adoration (Matt 27:29; Mark 15:19). The gruesome account of the death of Sisera by the hand of the Israelite woman Jael uses language which is ironically suggestive of the obeisance of the Canaanite ruler, albeit in death: "He sank, he fell, he lay still at her feet; at her feet he sank, he fell; where he sank, there he fell dead" (Judg 5:27). Ruth's prostration before Boaz speaks both of their respective social ranks and Ruth's gratitude for Boaz's favorable treatment (Ruth 2:10).

---

36. See #6. Cf. *The (Israel) Stela of Merneptah* (*CoS*, 2:41).
37. Seneca, *Phaedra*, 666–71.

#6. Subjects of Ashurbanipal showing obeisance, including grasping his feet. Nineveh, seventh century BC. Keel #360a.

Such action frequently involves supplication or entreaty for the one of higher status to act on behalf of the petitioner. This might be accompanied by deferential language such as "your servant" (Gen 33:3–6; 43:28; Josh 5:11; 1 Sam 25:41; 2 Sam 9:6; 14:22). A captain of the Israelite army "fell on his knees before Elijah, and entreated him, 'O man of God, please let my life, and the life of these fifty servants of yours, be precious in your sight'" (2 Kgs 1:13). Though the Hittites had used deferential language to Abraham ("lord" and [lit.] "exalted of God": Gen 23:6), his bowing before them suggests that he did not wish to accept this status relative to them, so as to enable him legally to bargain for the purchase of a burial plot in perpetuity (Gen 23:7).[38] Jairus fell at Jesus' feet and urged him to come to his daughter (Luke 8:41; cf. 1 Sam 24:8; 25:23, 24, 41; 28:14; 2 Sam 14:4, 22, 33; 18:28; 24:20; 1 Kgs 1:23, 31; 18:7; 1 Chr 21:21; Esth 8:3; Dan 2:46; Mark 5:22; Luke 5:8, 12; 17:16; Rev 19:10; 22:8).

Bowing or prostrating oneself is not normal within a family context (cf. §5.6), so when we witness bowing to a relative, we ought to take notice of the special circumstances. Joseph's dreams, which suggested that his family would one day bow to him were considered outrageous (Gen 37:6–11). Jacob's elaborate bowing before his brother Esau, and his use of

---

38. Gruber, *Aspects*, 188–89.

master/servant language (Gen 33:3–8)—a "politeness strategy"—is due to their estrangement and Jacob's desire to curry favor.[39] The enigmatic verse Gen 47:31 is rendered by NRSV: "And he [Israel] said, 'Swear to me'; and he [Joseph] swore to him. Then Israel bowed himself on the head of his bed." The final words have been interpreted as a gesture (the nearest to prostration the invalid patriarch can manage)[40] directed towards God in thankfulness, but the LXX, followed by Heb 11:21, reads ". . . on the top of his staff." A variant explanation (since "staff" and "tribe" are the same word in Hebrew) is that because of Joseph's exalted status the bow of the dying Israel is to him, and that the final words ought to be translated "to the head of the tribe," that is, Israel is handing over the leadership of his extended family to Joseph and by gesture acknowledging this new role.[41] Moses is said to bow down and kiss his father-in-law who is a respected community leader (Exod 18:7; cf. 3:1), though the reference to bowing, rather than being a gesture in itself, may be rather "he bent over" (in order to kiss him).[42] Bathsheba "bowed and did obeisance" to her husband, King David (1 Kgs 1:16); in this case, as well as court etiquette which seems to apply even to the royal family (cf. 1 Kgs 1:31; 2 Sam 14:33), it is clear, even to the failing and generally unresponsive king, that Bathsheba has a request on her mind, so her bowing might also be seen as a politeness strategy towards achieving her goal. The one person to whom King Solomon perhaps bowed was his mother, who as queen mother occupied a revered position in the royal household (1 Kgs 2:19). However, in place of the Hebrew word translated "bowed" in this verse, the LXX has *ephilesen* which suggests it was translating a different Hebrew original which had "kissed," which would be a more customary filial greeting.[43]

Closely associated with gestures of obeisance is the offering of tribute to a monarch (or a token portion of it which is portable). Ancient images depict such tribute scenes in the form of a procession, with those behind carrying gifts, while those nearest the enthroned monarch have dropped

---

39. For the application of politeness theory to this passage, see Bridge, "The 'Slave' Is the 'Master.'"

40. Sarna, *Genesis*, 324.

41. Hoop, "Then Israel Bowed Himself"; Walton, *Genesis*, 709–10. Though Walton does not adopt the reading "to the head of the tribe," he does note the deferential tone Jacob adopts towards Joseph as the new head of the clan.

42. Gruber, *Aspects*, 307–8.

43. Ibid.

to the ground.⁴⁴ While English translations might not be clear, the magi presented their gifts to Jesus from a prostrate position (Matt 2:11). In John's vision of the heavenly throne room, "the twenty-four elders fall before the one who is seated on the throne and worship the one who lives forever and ever; they cast their crowns before the throne" (Rev 4:10; cf. Acts 4:35, 37; 5:2). It is possible to detect in Matthew's wording of the bringing to Jesus of those in need of healing an echo of the offering of tribute: "They put them at his feet, and he cured them" (Matt 15:30).⁴⁵

#7. *A tribute procession. Thebes, Egyptian, fifteenth century BC. Keel #408.*

To grasp the feet (or legs or knees) of another of necessity involves adopting a lowly posture in relation to the other and may accompany a petition. The Akkadian expression "to seize the feet" means "to do homage, obeisance."⁴⁶ A Hittite text envisages a suppliant grasping the knees of

---

44. *ANEP,* #45, #46, #47.

45. Hagner, *Matthew 14–28,* 445. Cf. the posture of the king of Heracleopolis "on his belly" as he brought tribute to the pharaoh: *The Victory Stela of King Piye* 55–56 (*CoS,* 2:46).

46. Oppenheim, "Idiomatic Accadian," 271.

temple officials in an attempt to persuade them to approve a variation to the accepted ritual.[47] Priam grasps Achilles' knees to implore him for the body of his son Hector (*Iliad* 24.476–79). The Shunammite woman grabs Elisha's feet (or legs) to indicate her deep distress at her son's death and to implore the prophet to do something (2 Kgs 4:27). A similar gesture, more in adoration than entreaty, is shown to the risen Jesus by his disciples as they "took hold of his feet, and worshiped him" (Matt 28:9). It is probable that Matthew intends us to see in this gesture an echo of the prostration before God to which the Psalms summon his worshipers (Pss 99:5; 132:7; cf. Rev 19:10). Homage might also be expressed through kissing the feet of the recipient of the homage (cf. §2.11).

An extension of the social use of gestures of obeisance and entreaty is the use of bowing or prostration in religious devotion and prayer. In the Ugaritic myth, Ba'lu reminds his messengers of the protocol to be observed in approaching the god of death: "At the feet of Môtu bow and fall, do homage and honor him."[48] Greeks and Romans sometimes adopted a kneeling posture in prayer.[49] Bowing or kneeling before God (that is, that which represents him, such as his sanctuary), is an acknowledgment of his deity and may include elements of thanksgiving or supplication. When the image of Dagon was found fallen face down in front of the Israelite ark, this would be interpreted as indicative of the Philistine god's submission to the Lord (1 Sam 5:3, 4). The Israelite congregation is summoned, "O come, let us worship and bow down, let us kneel before the Lord, our Maker!" (Ps 95:6; cf. Gen 24:26; Exod 4:31; 1 Sam 1:3; 15:25; 2 Chr 20:18; 22:27; 29:2; Pss 99:5; 132:7; Zech 14:17; Luke 4:8; 1 Cor 14:25; Rev 7:11; 11:16). The sight of Jesus being transfigured produced a response of adoration and fear from his disciples as they "fell to the ground [lit.: fell on their face] and were overcome by fear" (Matt 17:6; cf. Acts 22:7; 26:14). Bowing the knee would seem to be a recognized form of homage to other deities as well (1 Kgs 19:18; Rom 11:4), but the biblical writers entertain the expectation that every knee would one day bow in acknowledgement of the true God (Isa 45:23; Rom 14:11; Phil 2:10).

Prayer or petition may also involve getting to one's knees. Gideon "went to his knees before God in prayer" (Judg 7:15). Solomon "knelt with hands outstretched toward heaven" (1 Kgs 8:54; cf. 2 Chr 6:13; Ezra 9:5),

---

47. *Instructions to Priests and Temple Officials* 9 (CoS, 1:219).
48. *The Ba'lu Myth* viii 26–28 (CoS, 1:264).
49. Brilliant, *Gesture and Rank*, 15; Corbeill, *Nature Embodied*, 27.

THE NECK, TORSO, AND WHOLE BODY

and we may be intended to see in this dedicatory prayer a progression from a standing posture on Solomon's part when adoration was the focus (1 Kgs 8:22) to a kneeling posture for petition. Daniel knelt to pray three times a day (Dan 6:10), which those conspiring against him recognized as a posture of prayer (Dan 6:11). Jesus and the early church continued the practice of kneeling to pray (Luke 22:41; Acts 7:60; 9:40; 20:36; 21:5; Eph 3:14). The expression "bow the knee" (e.g., Isa 45:23) employs the same root as translated "feeble" when applied to knees (Job 4:4), suggesting one lacks the strength to stand erect so falls helpless before God. Full prostration was not the regular posture of prayer, however, particularly in NT times (cf. §6.4), so when we have references to falling to the ground, or on one's face, in prayer, we perceive a heightened emotional content to the prayer, as when Moses and Aaron pleaded with God not to destroy all Israel on account of the sin of Korah (Num 16:22), or when Jesus prayed in his anguish in the Garden of Gethsemane (Matt 26:39; Mark 14:35).

In both the OT and NT two of the regular words for worship have at their core references to a physical posture of deference. In the case of the Hebrew *hishtach^{a}wah*, the core meaning is the physical gesture of obeisance as described above. For the NT, there is some debate over the gesture originally involved in the word *proskyneo*, but its use to translate *hishtach^{a}wah* in the LXX suggests the NT writers may be using it with a similar force to the Hebrew word.[50] The same words may be used when humans are the object of such a show of respect or obeisance, e.g., one's captors (Isa 51:23), honored guests (Gen 18:2), kings or other high officials (1 Sam 2:36; Matt 2:2), as also when worshiping foreign gods (Num 25:2; 1 Kgs 16:31; 2 Chr 25:14; Zeph 1:5) or the LORD God (Exod 24:1; 1 Sam 15:25; 2 Kgs 17:36; Pss 22:27; 66:4; Isa 27:13; Matt 4:10; Luke 4:8; John 4:20–24; 12:20; Acts 8:27). Human and divine recipients of such attention may even occur together (1 Chr 29:20). As noted above, the significant physical activity involved in the worship gesture is evident in the OT in 2 Kgs 5:18 when Naaman requests Elisha for understanding when he inevitably bows, or prostrates himself, in the temple of Rimmon because he is physically supporting the king as he does likewise. In the letter to the church at Philadelphia, the church receives the assurance, "I will make those of the synagogue of Satan who say that they are Jews and are not, but are lying—I will make them come and bow down before your feet, and they will learn that I have loved you" (Rev 3:9). On the other hand, the pairing of "worship" with a separate

---

50. Gruber, *Aspects*, 244.

posture description such as "bowed [or fell] to the ground" or "knelt" suggests that the "worship" words of themselves, though perhaps never devoid of a suggestion of gesture, came to refer more to the inner attitude of respect or reverence (Exod 4:31; 12:27; 20:5; 34:8; Deut 5:9; 2 Sam 14:4; 14:22; 2 Kgs 4:37; Esth 3:2, 5; Matt 2:11; 4:9; 28:9; Mark 15:19; Acts 10:25; 1 Cor 14:25; Rev 4:10; 5:14; 7:11; 11:16).

Being bowed down or bent over is a mark of oppression, humiliation, or mourning.[51] A psalmist laments, "I went about as one who laments for a mother, bowed down and in mourning" (Ps 35:14; cf. 38:6; 145:14; 146:8; Isa 5:15; 21:3; 46:2; 51:23; 58:5; 65:12; Lam 2:10).

4.7 Dancing

Dancing, perhaps accompanied by singing and musical instruments (Exod 15:20; Judg 11:34; 1 Sam 18:6; 21:11; 29:5; 2 Sam 6:5; 1 Chr 13:8; Pss 149:3; 150:4; Jer 31:4; Matt 11:17; Luke 7:32; 15:25), is, among other things, a universal expression of joy and well-being. A psalmist rejoices, "You have turned my mourning into dancing" (Ps 30:11; cf. Eccl 3:4; Jer 31:13; Lam 5:15). The language used to describe David's dancing before the ark suggests that the whole body is involved, including facial expression and arm movements as well as leaping about (2 Sam 6:14–21; 1 Chr 15:29).

4.8 Trembling

Trembling is a natural indicator of fear, dismay or anguish. In the Babylonian *Epic of Creation*, following the slaughter of Tiamat, "the gods her allies, who had come to her aid, / They trembled, terrified, they ran in all directions."[52] On realizing that he had been deceived into giving his younger son Jacob the firstborn's blessing, "Isaac trembled violently" (Gen 27:33). The guards at Jesus' tomb shook with fear at the appearance of an angel (Matt 28:4). Paul came to Corinth "in fear and in much trembling" (1 Cor 2:3), perhaps in part discouraged by his preceding experience (Acts 17), in part as a response to the estimation of the Corinthians of his physical appearance (1 Cor 2:3), but perhaps most of all due to his high sense of responsibility to be true to the message entrusted to him (2 Cor 5:11; cf.

---

51. Cf. Kruger, "Depression," 190.
52. *Epic of Creation*, Tablet IV, 107–8 (*CoS*, 1:398).

Gen 42:28; Exod 15:14, 15; Deut 2:25; Judg 7:3; 1 Sam 4:13; 13:7; 14:15; 16:4; 21:1; 28:5; 2 Sam 17:2; 1 Kgs 1:49; Job 4:14; 21:6; Ps 55:5; Isa 19:16; 21:4; 32:11; 33:14; Ezek 26:16; 32:10; Dan 10:7; Mic 7:17; Mark 5:33; Luke 8:47; Heb 12:21).

A locus is sometimes given for the trembling: the lips (Hab 3:16), loins (Ps 69:23), knees (Nah 2:10), heart (Deut 28:65; 1 Sam 4:13; 28:5; Job 37:1), or (lit.) stomach (Hab 3:16). While the latter two at least might refer to a purely internal emotion, we ought not to rule out that a manifestation of trembling in the torso is intended. In each case a part may be mentioned for the whole. Likewise David's expression of grief over Absalom is translated in NRSV as "the king was deeply moved" (2 Sam 18:33), though the word implies a physical shaking.

While not to be sharply distinguished from dread, the fear of respect or reverence for one in authority, and above all for God or for his word, is sometimes said to be displayed in trembling. Haman observed that Mordecai "neither rose nor trembled before him" (Esth 5:9). The response of the Israelites to the manifestations of God's presence at Sinai, which included the trembling of the mountain itself (Exod 19:18), was to tremble (Exod 19:16; 20:18) A psalmist calls on the world's rulers to "serve the LORD with fear, with trembling" (Ps 2:11; cf. 96:9; 99:1; 119:120; Dan 6:26; 2 Cor 7:15; Eph 6:5; Phil 2:12). Prophetic words might at times encourage the troubled not to tremble, and at times provoke the complacent to tremble (Isa 32:11; Jer 30:10; 46:27; Mic 4:4). God undertakes to be favorable "to the humble and contrite in spirit, who trembles at my word" (Isa 66:2; cf. v. 5; Ezra 9:4;10:3). Blenkinsopp implies that the trembling in these verses is intended literally, referring to a devout eschatological sectarian group of "quakers."[53]

It may be that the phrase "fear and trembling" was sometimes used as a conventional expression of emotion, but lest we think none of the references to trembling involved any physical manifestation, there is one case in which a dual causation for the trembling is given—psychological and physiological: "All the people sat in the open square before the house of God, trembling because of this matter and because of the heavy rain" (Ezra 10:9).

---

53. Blenkinsopp, *Ezra-Nehemiah*, 178.

4.9 Self-laceration

One of the gestures of grief in ancient Western Asia was the cutting of one's flesh. In the Ugaritic myth, the god 'Ilu lacerates himself with a stone on learning of Ba'lu's death.[54] Though proscribed by the biblical writers, the OT bears testimony to the practice of this ritual of mourning and humiliation and its association with prophetic ecstasy. Jeremiah records the arrival in Jerusalem of a group of northern pilgrims: "Eighty men arrived from Shechem and Shiloh and Samaria, with their beards shaved and their clothes torn, and their bodies gashed, bringing grain offerings and incense to present at the temple of the LORD" (Jer 41:5; cf. Lev 19:28; 21:5; Deut 14:1; Jer 16:6; 47:5; 48:37; and perhaps 49:3).[55] Job's action of scraping his flesh while sitting in the dust mourning has been thought by some to reflect this custom (Job 2:8).[56] In Elijah's contest with the prophets of Baal, the latter cut themselves with swords in their frenzied attempts to arouse their god (1 Kgs 18:28), and Zech 13:4–6 may suggest that the wounds visible on some Israelite prophets had a similar cause.[57]

4.10 Bodily functions

Most societies observe taboos regarding the mention in polite society of such matters as urination, bowel movements, or menstruation. When they are mentioned, we note the distaste or revulsion intended. The references to those who urinate against a wall, (1 Sam 25:22, 34; 1 Kgs 14:10; 16:11; 21:21 2 Kgs 9:8), while they have "males" as their referent (NRSV), are intended in their contexts to evoke the bad odor of the urinal.[58] Elijah mocks Baal with what has long been understood by some as a crude reference to the god being on the toilet (1 Kgs 18:27),[59] and the lampooning of the Babylonian king Belshazzar: "His limbs gave way, and his knees knocked together" seems to refer to uncontrolled bowel movements in a highly shaming

---

54. *The Ba'lu Myth* vi ?–25 [sic] (*CoS*, 1:268); see Kruger, "On Non-verbal Communication in the Baal Epic," 64–66.

55. For the understanding of Jer 49:3 as a reference to gashing, see Kselman, "Wandering About," 275–76.

56. E.g., Pope, *Job*, 21.

57. For an Akkadian parallel to the action of the Baal prophets in 1 Kgs 18:28 see Roberts, "A New Parallel."

58. See Davies, *1 Kings*, 277.

59. Ibid., 342.

episode (Dan 5:6).[60] Jesus' healing of the woman who had been bleeding for twelve years restored her to normal social interactions of which she would have been long deprived (Mark 5:25-29; Luke 8:43-44).

4.11 Clothing

The clothes we wear can tell others a lot about us: our ethnicity, gender, social status, age, marital status, occupation, religion, and more might each at times find expression in how we dress. If this is true today, it was even more so in the strongly stratified societies which the biblical characters inhabited.[61] Gender differentiation is generally marked by distinctive clothing for men and women (Deut 22:5). Jesus highlighted the role clothing plays in social ranking when he asked the crowds concerning John the Baptist, "What then did you go out to see? Someone dressed in soft robes? Look, those who wear soft robes are in royal palaces" (Matt 11:8; cf. Luke 7:25). John had chosen to wear the rough clothing which was the prophet Elijah's trademark, and perhaps worn by other prophets (Matt 3:4; cf. 2 Kgs 1:8; Heb 11:37). High status people in most cultures have marked their status with more costly and elaborate clothing. Kings and queens in particular wore royal attire at least on significant occasions (1 Kgs 22:10; 2 Chr 18:9; Esth 5:1; 6:8; Isa 45:1; Zech 6:13; Matt 6:28-29; Luke 12:27; Acts 12:21), and even in battle a king could normally be identified by his clothing. King Jehoshaphat wore royal robes on the battlefield, whereas the king of Israel went in disguise, that is, without his customary royal garb, and the result was almost fatal for Jehoshaphat as the enemy targeted him, mistaking him for the king of Israel (1 Kgs 22:30; 2 Chr 18:29). A psalmist describes the robes of a princess as "gold-woven" and "many-colored" (or: "embroidered"; Ps 45:13-14). A particular type of veiling garment marked the social and sexual status of high-born virgins (2 Sam 13:18-19), while Joseph as the favorite son was given a garment that was also special in some way (Gen 37:3).[62]

In an era before synthetic dyes, the natural dye of the murex was highly prized and garments dyed with its purple were the preserve of royalty, high officials, and the wealthier classes (Judg 8:26; Esth 8:15; Prov 31:22; Jer 10:9; Lam 4:5; Dan 5:7; Luke 16:19; Rev 17:4; 18:12, 16). The soldiers at

---

60. See Brenner, "Who's Afraid?"
61. See Matthews, "Anthropology."
62. Dewrell, "How Tamar's Veil Became Joseph's Coat."

Jesus' crucifixion managed to find a purple cloak with which to mock Jesus' royal claims (Mark 15:17). Various items of clothing of distinctive character are mentioned in Scripture as marking out their wearers as wealthy or favored individuals (Isa 3:18–23; Gen 37:3; 2 Sam 13.18; Ezek 16:10). John draws attention to the fact that Jesus' tunic at his crucifixion was seamless (John 19:23). While a seamless tunic was not unusual, its mention (apart from the folly of dividing it and so fulfilling Ps 22:18) has sometimes been taken to have a symbolic reference, for example, to suggest priestly attire, but it is hard to demonstrate this.[63]

There were elements of Israelite dress which were to differentiate them from the surrounding nations, such as not mixing materials and the wearing of fringes on the corners of their garments (Lev 19:19; Num 15:38–39; Deut 22:12). The Pharisees, according to Matt 23:5, made their fringes larger than was customary in order to make a display of their piety.[64] While the early church consisted of men and women from all strata of society, in contrast with their pagan counterparts, wealthy Christians were not to flaunt their social distinctions, but to dress modestly (1 Tim 2:9; 1 Pet 3:3).

Different occasions and stages of life could be marked by different clothing. Brides and bridegrooms, as in many cultures, would be lavishly clothed and ornamented for their wedding (Isa 49:18; 61:10; Rev 21:2), and according to Jesus' parable, wedding guests were expected to wear special festive clothing (Matt 22:11–13). The father of the prodigal son kept a "best robe" for special occasions (Luke 15:22), and by clothing his son in it, made a statement regarding his rehabilitation into the family and community. At least in the period depicted in the Tamar story, widows customarily signaled their status with distinctive attire (Gen 38:14, 19).

In addition to royalty, distinctive clothing was associated with the priesthood (Exod 28:31–42), soldiers (2 Sam 20:8), and scribes (Luke 20:46), to name but a few occupational groups. Saul recognized a posthumous reappearance of Samuel in part from a description of his clothing (1 Sam 28:14). If an item of clothing were seen to carry something of the authority of its wearer, the transfer of the clothing to another could signify the transfer of that authority. Shebna, a royal official, was threatened with the removal of his robe and sash, and the investiture of another with them (Isa 22:15–21). Jonathan, the royal heir, gave David his cloak

---

63. See Beasley-Murray, *John*, 347–48; Lincoln, *John*, 475–76.

64. Fringed garments are known from other parts of the ancient world; see Stone, "Grasping the Fringe."

THE NECK, TORSO, AND WHOLE BODY

and other items in acknowledgement of David's divine anointing (1 Sam 18:4). David's remorse after stealthily removing a portion of Saul's cloak suggests more than that he regretted ruining a good garment. It betokened David's usurpation of royal authority (1 Sam 24:3–5; cf. 15:28; 1 Kgs 11:31), and Saul himself recognized the significance of the action (1 Sam 24:20).[65] This may be seen as the culmination of a series of events in which Saul is repeatedly divested of clothing and David repeatedly receives clothing.[66] The prophet Elijah threw his mantle over Elisha (1 Kgs 19:19) following his commission to anoint the younger man as his successor (v. 16).

In his extended clothing image, Paul likens aspects of the Christian experience to items of a soldier's attire and equipment, interwoven with elements of OT imagery, including the belt of truth, the breastplate of righteousness, the shield of faith, and the helmet of salvation (Eph 6:13–17).

Nakedness, though inherently nothing to be ashamed of (Gen 2:25), is, as a consequence of the disobedience in the Garden, from Gen 3 on considered shameful in the biblical texts (Gen 3:7, 10, 11; Exod 20:26; 47:3; Jer 13:26; Ezek 16:8; Mic 1:11; Nah 3:5; Rev 3:18). Mark's inclusion of a reference to a naked man fleeing from the Garden following the arrest of Jesus (Mark 14:52) makes sense as an allusion to the shame in the original Garden. The shame of the young man (Mark himself?) represents the shame of all of Jesus' followers who abandoned him. Some of the references to nakedness more strictly indicate being inadequately clothed rather than totally lacking clothing (2 Cor 11:27; Jas 2:15). Divesting oneself of one's normal clothing could be a sign of mourning (Mic 1:8). Isaiah was instructed to go naked for three years to portend the wretched state of the defeated Egyptians and Ethiopians as prisoners of war in the hands of the Assyrians (Isa 20:2–4).

Luke records the detail that the lynch mob who stoned Stephen laid their clothing at the feet of Saul (Acts 7:58). This not only introduces the major character of the second half of Acts but is probably an ironic reference, in that in getting ready for the physical action of stoning, it is the mob which is seen to be shamed by their relative nakedness rather than

---

65. Ibid., Part 2.

66. The hem of a garment could serve in Mesopotamia as a "signature," conveying the authority of its wearer. For an extended treatment of the narratological significance of the clothing motif in the Saul-David account, see Prouser, "Suited to the Throne."

the victim (as it is the *victim's* nakedness which is sometimes mentioned in such events).[67]

A pervasive motif of Scripture is the tearing of one's clothes in despair or grief, remorse or indignation, often in conjunction with putting on sackcloth (see below) or other signs of mourning. When Hezekiah heard the threatening words of the Assyrian Rabshakeh, "he tore his clothes, covered himself with sackcloth, and went into the house of the LORD" (2 Kgs 19:1; cf. Isa 36:22–37:1). A twist on the motif is found in 1 Kgs 11:29–32, which may involve tearing another's clothing. The prophet Ahijah met up with Jeroboam and he "had clothed himself with a new garment" and "Ahijah laid hold of the new garment he was wearing and tore it into twelve pieces." Though traditionally understood as Ahijah's new garment, the pronouns are ambiguous and there may be added dramatic effect if it is Jeroboam's new garment that the prophet grabs and rips to demonstrate the breakup of the united monarchy into its tribal constituents.[68] The grief will be that of the resulting kingdoms of Israel and Judah represented by the fragments of clothing. A similar practice is attested in Hellenistic times. Polemon (second century AD) gives the following account of a woman of Pamphylia who, on learning of the death of her daughter, "threw her veil from her, her head covering and her jewels, then she tore the front of her dress and stripped until she stood naked."[69] When Barnabas and Saul realized that the crowds at Lystra were about to venerate them as gods, they tore their clothes and rushed to put a stop to the idolatry (Acts 14:14; cf. Gen 37:29, 34; 44:13; Num 14:6; Josh 7:6; Judg 11:35; 2 Sam 1:11; 13:19; 13:31; 1 Kgs 21:27; 2 Kgs 5:7; 6:30; 11:14; 22:11; 2 Chr 23:13; 34:19; Ezra 9:3; Esth 4:1; Job 1:20; 2:12; Matt 26:65; Mark 14:63). Lepers were also to have their clothes torn as one indicator of their unclean status and social ostracism (Lev 13:45). Failure to tear one's clothes, when this is to be expected upon hearing something which should cause distress, is equally revealing as when Jehoiakim and his officials failed to respond positively to the prophetic message of Jeremiah being read to them (Jer 36:24).

Sackcloth, a coarse cloth usually made of goat's hair, marks its wearer as one in mourning or going through a time of crisis, humiliation, shame, or repentance. God announces through Amos a day of calamity when "I

---

67. Keener, *Acts*, 2:1458.
68. Chun, "Whose Cloak?"
69. *Physiognomy* 68 (Swain, *Seeing the Face*, 457).

will turn your feasts into mourning, and all your songs into lamentation; I will bring sackcloth on all loins, and baldness on every head; I will make it like the mourning for an only son, and the end of it like a bitter day" (Amos 8:10). A consequence of the wearing of sackcloth was the temporary suspension of social distinctions normally marked by dress. The mother of King Nabonidus of Babylon recalls that in a time of distress, "In order to appease the heart of my god and my goddess, I did not put on a garment of excellent wool, silver, gold, a fresh garment; I did not allow perfumes (or) fine oil to touch my body. I was clothed in a torn garment. My fabric was sackcloth."[70] On seeing the angel of the LORD wielding a drawn sword, "David and the elders, clothed in sackcloth, fell on their faces" (1 Chr 21:16). In his perplexity over Jeremiah's prophecy of a seventy-year exile, Daniel "turned to the LORD God, to seek an answer by prayer and supplication with fasting and sackcloth and ashes" (Dan 9:3; cf. Gen 37:34; Neh 9:1; 1 Kgs 21:27; 2 Kgs 6:30; Esth 4:1–4; Job 16:15; Pss 30:11; 35:13; 69:11; Isa 3:24; 22:12; 32:11; 37:2; 58:5; Jer 4:8; 6:26; 48:37; 49:3; Lam 2:10; Ezek 7:18; Joel 1:8, 13; Matt 11:21; Luke 10:13; Rev 11:3). According to 1 Kgs 20:31, the practice of wearing sackcloth extended beyond Israel's borders (cf. Isa 15:3; Jer 49:3; Ezek 27:31; Jonah 3:5, 6, 8).

To spread one's outer garments on the ground before an honored person, as the crowds did for Jesus on his entry into Jerusalem, is a strong gesture of respect (Matt 21:8; cf. 2 Kgs 9:13).

A quite different set of clothing gestures involves shaking out one's garments as a means of dissociation. Nehemiah informs us of a prophetic-type action he performed: "I also shook out the fold of my garment and said, 'So may God shake out everyone from house and from property who does not perform this promise. Thus may they be shaken out and emptied'" (Neh 5:13). The crowds who had listened to Paul up to a certain point had had enough and began "shouting, throwing off their cloaks, and tossing dust into the air" (Acts 22:23). The verb involved suggests quite a violent gesture of protest. When Paul faced opposition in the synagogue at Corinth, "in protest he shook the dust from his clothes and said to them, 'Your blood be on your own heads! I am innocent. From now on I will go to the gentiles'" (Acts 18:6; cf. shaking dust from the feet, §6.3).

Grabbing hold of the clothing of another, typically the hem or fringe of a garment, speaks of a desire to constrain the other person, to have them

---

70. *The Adad-guppi Autobiography* (*CoS*, 1:478); Kruger, "'Nonverbal Communication' in the Hebrew Bible," 155.

heed the request of a suppliant. In the Ugaritic myth, as 'Anatu implores Môtu to restore Ba'lu to her, "She seizes Môtu by the hem of his clothes, grasps [him] by the extremity of his garment."[71] On hearing the news of his rejection as king, Saul was desperate to have Samuel reconsider his refusal to go with Saul so that Saul might save face before the people: "As Samuel turned to go away, Saul caught hold of the hem of his robe, and it tore" (1 Sam 15:27; cf. Zech 8:23). While NRSV has supplied the subject "Saul" in this verse, there is some uncertainty (dating back to rabbinic discussions) as to who grasps whose hem, as the Hebrew only has pronouns, though NRSV is most probably correct. Kruger draws attention to the fact that Saul makes the same request of Samuel twice, once before and once after tearing the prophet's hem (1 Sam 15:24–31), that is, the gesture (which entails the king abasing himself before the prophet low enough to grasp Samuel's hem) was sufficient to persuade Samuel to relent.[72] A similar practice of grasping the hem in entreaty is attested elsewhere in ancient Western Asia.[73] With skillful *double entendre* the writer of Genesis portrays Potiphar's wife as the one urging Joseph to lie with her, not just by her cajoling words (Gen 39:7, 10), but by her gesture of grabbing his cloak, suggestive of a gesture of entreaty (Gen 39:12); Joseph escapes, however, leaving the cloak in her hand, suggestive of a legal rite of renunciation.[74] Because a garment is an extension of a person's body, even to touch a hem was tantamount to touching the person (cf. "Who touched my clothes?" [Mark 5:30] with "Who touched me?" [v. 31]). The sick who came to Jesus for healing "begged him that they might touch even the fringe of his cloak; and all who touched it were healed" (Matt 14:36; cf. 9:20–21; Mark 5:25–34; 6:56; Luke 8:44–47; Acts 19:12; cf. §5.6; §5.6.1).

When Ruth requested Boaz on the threshing floor, "Spread your cloak [or: hem] over your servant, for you are next-of-kin," she was (with *double entendre*) actually suggesting marriage using a well-understood expression (cf. Ezek 16:8).[75] This evokes the protection of a mother bird for her young, as in Deut 32:11, where the word for "wing" is the same

---

71. *The Ba'lu Myth* ii 4–37 (*CoS*, 1:270).

72. Kruger, "Symbolic Significance," 111; cf. Stone, "Grasping the Fringe," Part 1.

73. Greenstein, "To Grasp the Hem"; Kruger, "Symbolic Significance"; Kruger, "On Non-verbal Communication in the Baal Epic," 63–64.

74. Kruger, "'Nonverbal Communication' in the Hebrew Bible," 147–50. For a treatment of the motif of clothing in the Joseph narrative, see Matthews, "Anthropology," 28–36.

75. Kruger, "The Hem of the Garment"; Viberg, *Symbols of Law*, 136–44.

as the word for "hem." Probably to be related to this are the references to seeing or uncovering nakedness, that is, violations of the marriage bond (Gen 9:20–27; Lev 18:8; 20:11; Deut 27:20).[76]

There are a number of metaphors related to clothing as they give expression to that which pervades and characterizes a person. One can clothe oneself with all manner of abstract qualities such as vengeance, shame, compassion, kindness, humility, meekness, patience, or righteousness (Job 29:14; Pss 109:29; 132:9; Isa 59:17; 61:10; Col 3:12), or with the new self (Eph 4:24), or immortality, or the heavenly dwelling (1 Cor 15:54; 2 Cor 5:2), or even Christ (Gal 3:27).

---

76. Ibid., 139–41; Bergsma and Hahn, "Noah's Nakedness."

5

The Arms and Hands

HUMANS ARE BLESSED WITH arms and hands that we can shape and move in countless ways to express or accompany a huge array of meaningful acts of communication. The Bible refers to quite a few of these hand and arm gestures, whether as acts accompanying speech, as nonverbal communication events, or as idiomatic ways of referring to speech-acts which no longer involved an accompanying gesture.

Hands might be adorned with rings on the fingers. A signet ring served as an emblem of one's identity and (for those in office) of authority, so something precious and closely guarded (Hag 2:23). This underscores the strength of the gesture of removing it: "As I live, says the LORD, even if King Coniah son of Jehoiakim of Judah were the signet ring on my right hand, even from there I would tear you off" (Jer 22:24). For a king to hand over his ring to another is a strong affirmation of confidence: "Removing his signet ring from his hand, Pharaoh put it on Joseph's hand; he arrayed him in garments of fine linen, and put a gold chain around his neck" (Gen 41:42; cf. Esth 3:10; 8:2). The father in Jesus' parable ordered a ring to be placed on his wayward son's finger as a demonstration of his restoration (Luke 15:22).

Jesus' reported action of writing on the ground with his finger (John 8:1–11, found only in some manuscripts) has puzzled interpreters. He did this in the context of a dispute over the appropriate response to a woman caught in adultery. In the light of a late classical parallel, Botha wonders whether the act of writing conveys an added air of authority and a good case has been made for seeing this action as referencing God's action in writing the ten commandments with his finger (Exod 31:18; 32:15–16), and so making a subtle claim for Jesus' overriding authority in matters of law.[1]

---

1. Minear, "Writing on the Ground"; cf. Botha, "Exploring Gesture," 10; Keith, *The*

Another suggestion is that writing in the dust is an acted parable recalling the judgment of Jer 17:13: "all who forsake you will be put to shame. Those who turn away from you will be written in the dust" (NIV11).[2]

There is some evidence that hands might have been indelibly inscribed to mark ownership of slaves.[3] Isaiah may allude to this custom in describing the self-identification of the people of God: "Another will write on the hand, 'The LORD's'" (Isa 44:5), and John describes the martyrs as those who "had not worshiped the beast or its image and had not received its mark on their foreheads or their hands" (Rev 20:4). God reinforces the fact that he will not forget his people: "See, I have inscribed you on the palms of my hands" (Isa 49:16).

Words for hand and arm are used somewhat interchangeably or in parallel in some of the expressions and idioms of Scripture. A psalmist declares, "You have a mighty arm; strong is your hand, high your right hand" (Ps 89:13). A recurring expression is the phrase "a mighty hand and an outstretched arm" referring to God's power exercised on his people's behalf in the exodus, its culmination in the dedication of the temple, and in the new exodus (Deut 4:34; 5:15; 7:19; 9:29; 11:2; 26:8; 1 Kgs 8:41–42; 2 Kgs 17:36; 2 Chr 6:32; Ps 136:10–12; Jer 27:5; 32:17, 21; Ezek 20:33–34) but the epithets might also be reversed just as the situation is radically altered, as God declares, "I myself will fight against you with outstretched hand and mighty arm" (Jer 21:5). Some have seen in Jesus' outstretched arms on the cross a reminder of OT salvation imagery of God's outstretched arm, though the NT itself does not make anything of this.

The word most commonly translated "hand" in the OT includes the forearm, while another is more limited to the palm of the hand and yet another word refers to the whole arm up to the shoulder. The situation is complicated by the fact that the same vocabulary may be used to describe gestures with quite different significance. We might assume that for many of these the gestures themselves would have been distinguishable to an observer, though in some cases context alone might determine how a gesture is to be interpreted.[4] To "raise the hand," depending on the context, could mean to swear an oath (Gen 6:8); to bless (Lev 9:22); to rebel

---

Pericope Adulterae, 181–90.

2. Beasley-Murray, *John*, 146.
3. Clarke, *Commentary*, vol. 4 at Isa 44:5.
4. See Ackroyd, יד.

(2 Sam 18:28); to proceed (Isa 49:22); to surrender (Hab 3:10); to offer assistance (Ps 10:2); or (with plural "hands") to pray (Ps 28:2).

Sometimes the idiom involving the hand or arm has become so fossilized in the language that we do not necessarily picture the gesture at all. In Habakkuk's poetic description of God's mastery over creation and the forces of chaos, when the sun (NRSV), or perhaps the deep (NIV 11), "lifted its hands on high" (Hab 3:10), we are hardly to picture a celestial body or body of water with hands stretched out, though NIV's paraphrase "lifted its waves on high" loses the metaphor of surrender.

5.1 The Right and Left Hand

Since the majority of people are right-handed, societies adopt certain preferences and taboos associated with handedness. Many of the idioms discussed below may be expressed either with "hand" or (perhaps with added force) "right hand." The right hand particularly suggests dominance and power: "Your right hand, O Lord, glorious in power" (Exod 15:6; cf. Pss 17:7; 20:6; Matt 26:64; Mark 14:62; Luke 22:69). Notions of support and encouragement (see below) can also be expressed particularly with reference to the right hand—holding the right hand or simply being at the right side of one in need. The image of a courtroom advocate standing to the right of the plaintiff or accused may lie behind some references, while others envisage support in a military context (Pss 16:8; 18:35; 73:23; 109:31; 110:5; 121:5; Isa 41:13; 45:1; 63:12; Acts 3:7).

The right hand side is also the place of honor. In the Ugaritic myth, when the divine council wishes to fête the craftsman god, "A chair is prepared and they seat (him) at the right hand of Mighty Ba'lu."[5] To honor Bathsheba, Solomon "had a throne brought for the king's mother, and she sat on his right" (1 Kgs 2:19; cf. 1 Chr 6:39; Pss 45:9; 80:17). The depiction of the psalmist's "lord" seated at the right hand of God in Ps 110:1 gives rise to numerous references in the NT to Jesus (or the Son of Man) seated (or standing) at the right side of God (Matt 22:44; 26:64; Mark 12:36; 14:62; 16:19; Acts 2:33–34; 5:31; 7:55; Rom 8:34; Col 3:1; Heb 1:3; 8:1; 10:12; 12:2; 1 Pet 3:22). Egyptian statues of the pharaoh with a god typically depict the pharaoh seated at the right side of the god.

---

5. *The Ba'lu Myth* v 106–19 (*CoS*, 1:260).

THE ARMS AND HANDS

#8. Pharaoh Haremhab seated at the right hand of the god Horus. Egyptian, fourteenth century BC. Keel #353.

Most uses of "left" are in simple pairings with "right" to indicate both hands or sides (Gen 13:9; 1 Chr 12:2; Prov 3:16; Matt 6:3; 2 Cor 6:7). Since the right hand indicates dominance or prominence, the left hand may be associated with their correlatives. One passage where the symbolic value of right and left is clearly in evidence is when Jacob deliberately reversed the custom of primogeniture and crossed his hands over, unexpectedly laying his right hand on the head of Joseph's younger son Ephraim, and his left hand on the head of the older brother Manasseh (Gen 48:13–20). Qoheleth invokes this symbolism in his observation that "the heart of a wise person leads to his right, but the heart of a fool to his left" (Eccl 10:2). A moral force may also be read into God's words to Jonah, "And should I not be concerned about Nineveh, that great city, in which there are more than a hundred and twenty thousand persons who do not know their right hand from their left, and also many animals?" (Jonah 4:11).[6] Ehud, a Benjamite ("right-hander") was ironically left-handed (normally considered a disability), and used this to his advantage in his cloak and dagger assassination of Israel's oppressor Eglon (Judg 3:15; cf. 20:16; 1 Chr 12:2). Jesus teaches that the coming of the Son of Man will involve the separation of the nations into "sheep" and "goats" (Matt 25:33–34). The sheep are directed to the right and are said to inherit the kingdom.

5.2 Hand Signals

We can assume that a full range of hand gestures was used to signify such things as size and movement (advance, halt, get back, move to the right, etc.), particularly in situations requiring stealth or in battle where distance and tumult made verbal directions impracticable. We have occasional reference to such hand signals: "On a bare hill raise a signal; cry aloud to them; wave the hand for them to enter the gates of the nobles" (Isa 13:2); "Thus says the LORD God: 'Behold, I will lift up my hand to the nations, and raise my signal to the peoples; and they shall bring your sons in their arms, and your daughters shall be carried on their shoulders'" (Isa 49:22). While the verbs describing the hand movement are different in these two Isaiah passages and NRSV has translated the first as "wave," the contexts are similar and Milgrom has demonstrated that both should be rendered "raise."[7] Similarly in a fishing context, hand and arm signaling would be needed, as when Simon and his crew "signaled their partners in the other boat to come and help them" (Luke 5:7).

Hand gestures of course may also simply point to something as a gesture of identification.[8] The use of the word for hand to refer to a signpost (Ezek 21:19) is an echo of this deictic function of human hands. With an arm movement Jesus identified his disciples as his "mother and brothers" (Matt 12:49). When Zechariah found himself unable to speak, he improvised with gestures, no doubt including hand gestures (Luke 1:22), and

---

6. Wiseman adduces a Babylonian parallel for this use of left and right (Wiseman, "Jonah's Nineveh," 40); see also Simon, *Jonah*, 46.

7. Milgrom, "The Alleged Wave Offering." Possibly cf. also Isa 10:32 as referring to a military signal.

8. For the theory of deictic gesture, see Kendon, *Gesture*, 119–224.

when others wished to communicate with him, they too adopted gesture, as though Zechariah were also deaf (Luke 1:62). Their communication was enhanced by use of a writing tablet (v. 63).

A hand motion might also signal to others to be silent to enable one to have one's say as Peter did to the gathered believers on his release from prison (Acts 12:17). Paul held up his hand as he began his courtroom defense before Agrippa (Acts 26:1; cf. 13:16; 19:33; 21:40). The Roman orator Quintilian's textbook on classical rhetoric recommends that in public speaking "the right hand, at the moment when our speech begins, should be slightly extended ... with the most modest of gestures, as though waiting for the commencement."[9]

The hand over the mouth gesture, signaling silence, is discussed at §2.10.

5.3 The Hands and Arms at Work

The hands are considered the primary instruments in productive labor and skilled workmanship. Of the virtuous woman the proverb says, "She seeks wool and flax, and works with willing hands" (Prov 31:13), and the NT offers this ethical teaching: "Thieves must give up stealing; rather let them labor and work honestly with their own hands, so as to have something to share with the needy" (Eph 4:28; cf. Gen 5:29; 39:3; Deut 14:28-29; Ezra 5:8; Job 1:10; 10:3; 34:19; Ps 90:17; Prov 12:14; Eccl 5:6; 9:10; Song 7:1; Isa 19:25; Lam 4:2; Acts 20:34; 1 Cor 4:12; 1 Thess 4:11). The request to "withdraw your hand" (1 Sam 14:19) means to desist from doing something. A psalmist notes the incongruity of the fact that idols "have hands, but do not feel" (Ps 115:7). When the image of Dagon falls prostrate before the ark of the LORD, it is significant that not only its head but its hands are broken off, that is, Dagon is now seen to be powerless to act (1 Sam 5:4). Jesus' restoration of a man's withered hand would appear to be one of the carefully selected healing narratives with programmatic intent (Matt 12:10-13). By restoring the man's hand, Jesus restored his capacity for fully productive work and the man was able to stretch it out in a demonstration of strength (cf. §5.7). The Sabbath-day timing of the healing also drew attention to the cycle of work and satisfaction to which the Sabbath pointed. Queller has argued

---

9. Quintilian, *Institutio oratoria* 11.3.159. Botha ("Exploring Gesture," 12-13) goes somewhat beyond the evidence in seeing Paul as exactly following the best practice of the Roman orators.

for further significance, based on echoes of Exodus' language, whereby the restored hand, "stretched out" as was Moses' hand over the Red Sea (Exod 14:16), points to the restoration to wholeness of the body politic.[10]

The Egyptian hymn to the Sun-disk celebrates this god's creative power: "<Those on> earth come from your hand as you made them."[11] The Bible affirms that the cosmos is the work of God's hands (Pss 8:6; 28:5; 92:4; 102:25; Isa 45:12; 48:13; Heb 1:10), or even his fingers (Ps 8:3), and there is a thread running through Scripture which contrasts that which is made by human hands, and therefore subject to decay, with that which is not made by hands, and so eternal (Deut 4:28; Pss 115:4; 135:15; Isa 2:8; 37:19; Jer 1:16; 10:3, 9; 25:6–7; Hos 14:3; Mic 5:13; Mark 14:58; Acts 7:48; 19:26; 2 Cor 5:1; Heb 9:11, 24).

The arm may signify strength. Isaiah pictures the powerful arms of a blacksmith at work at the forge (Isa 44:12), and a psalmist likens his God-given inner strength to an archer bending a bronze bow (Ps 18:32–34). God is said to have a powerful arm, meaning he accomplishes what he purposes (Exod 15:16; Job 40:9; Pss 44:3; 89:10, 13; Isa 40:10; Luke 1:51; 1 Pet 5:6). A rare word, translated "descending blow" in Isa 30:30 (NRSV), is better understood as "strength": "The LORD will cause his majestic voice to be heard and display the strength of his arm."[12] The "hand of God" or "hand of the LORD" is used in a variety of expressions indicating God's activity in afflicting, protecting, nourishing, and exercising his providential rule (Exod 9:3; Josh 22:31; Judg 2:15; Ruth 1:13; 1 Sam 5:6, 11; 12:15; 2 Chr 30:12; Job 2:10; 19:21; 27:11; Eccl 2:24; 9:1; Acts 13:11; 1 Pet 5:6), and in particular can be a technical expression for prophetic inspiration or similar supernatural empowerment. When people heard the reports of Zechariah, the father of John the Baptist, regaining his speech, "all who heard them pondered them and said, 'What then will this child become?' For, indeed, the hand of the Lord was with him" (Luke 1:66; cf. 1 Kgs 18:46; Ezra 7:6; Ezek 1:3; 3:14, 22; 8:1; 33:22; 37:1; 40:1; Acts 11:21).[13]

To bare or reveal one's arm (remove it from any covering clothing and display it) is to make a show of strength, as a defensive or threatening gesture: "The LORD has bared his holy arm before the eyes of all the

---

10. Queller, "Stretch out Your Hand!"

11. *The Great Hymn to Aten* (*CoS*, 1:46).

12. Calabro, "Ritual Gestures," 57–59.

13. Cf. Roberts, "The Hand of Yahweh." Roberts adduces Mesopotamian parallels for the expression.

nations; and all the ends of the earth shall see the salvation of our God" (Isa 52:10; cf. Ps 74:11; Isa 30:30; 53:1; Ezek 4:7; John 12:38). The power of the arm is further emphasized when it is raised or stretched out in a gesture of defiance or domination, in readiness to strike or to reach out and rescue those in need. Israel came out of Egypt with a high hand, that is, defiantly (Exod 14:8; Num 33:3). God expressed his reluctance to wipe out his recalcitrant people because their enemies might triumphantly raise their hands on the misguided assumption that they were responsible for Israel's downfall (Deut 32:27).

To raise or reach out one's hand against another, perhaps with clenched fist or brandishing a weapon, real or imagined, can be a defiant or threatening gesture. A man explains to Joab why he did not harm Absalom: "Even if I felt in my hand the weight of a thousand pieces of silver, I would not raise my hand against the king's son; for in our hearing the king commanded you and Abishai and Ittai, saying: For my sake protect the young man Absalom!" (2 Sam 18:12). When we read that Moses lifted up his hand over the rock at Meribah (Num 20:11) we may think this is just the necessary prelude to striking the rock which ensues, though as Ka Leung Wong has demonstrated, the phrase alerts the reader to the fact that Moses is acting defiantly against God, part of the sin for which he is condemned to remain outside the promised land (cf. Exod 7:4–5, 19; Num 15:30; 33:3; Deut 32:27; Mic 5:9; 1 Kgs 11:26–27; Isa 19:16; 30:32).[14] For a subject people, or people in a treaty relationship, to raise the hand against the suzerain is to rebel or break the treaty (2 Sam 18:28; 20:21). Eliphaz speaks of those who "stretched out their hands against God, and bid defiance to the Almighty" (Job 15:25). Similar connotations were associated with the hand in Roman culture where a depiction of a hand served as a potent symbol for troops to rally around, and a coin with an image of a hand probably has the same significance of power and possession.[15] Isaiah 10:32 includes the words "he will shake [or: raise] his fist at the mount of daughter Zion" (NRSV). While this is generally interpreted as a hostile gesture on the part of the Assyrians towards Jerusalem, it could also be the action of God in claiming ownership and benevolent intention, and with a grouping of two Hebrew words together could read: "He raises his

---

14. Wong, "And Moses Raised His Hand"; cf. Labuschagne, "Meaning." A Lamashtu amulet for exorcising demons from the sick depicts figures with hands raised in a brandishing gesture: *ANEP*, #660.

15. Corbeill, *Nature Embodied*, 22; Brilliant, *Gesture and Rank*, 38.

hand to make Zion large."[16] The Jews who came to Lystra from Antioch and Iconium and incited the crowds against Paul and Barnabas did so (in part at least) by a shaking movement (that is, presumably of raised fists), according to the Western text (Acts 14:19).

God is frequently said to stretch out or raise his arm in judgment or deliverance, an idiom particularly associated with the exodus and found in association with such verbs as "destroy," "desolate," "break," "cut off," "divide," and "annihilate," targeting both enemy nations and God's faithless people, as well as words such as "redeem," "deliver," "salvation," and "victory" (Exod 3:19–20; 6:6; 7:5; Deut 4:34; 5:15; 7:19; 9:29; 11:2; 26:8; Pss 10:12; 44:3; 98:1; 136:12; Isa 5:25; 9:12, 17, 21; 10:4; 11:15; 14:26–27; 19:16; 23:11; 31:3; 26:11; 33:2; 51:5; 59:16; 63:5; Jer 6:12; 21:5; 32:17, 21; 51:25; Ezek 6:14; 14:9, 13; 16:27; 35:3; Mic 5:9; Zeph 1:4; 2:13; Zech 2:9, 13; Acts 4:30; 13:17).[17]

A large number of images from ancient Western Asia depict a god with upraised hand, perhaps clenched into a fist, or clutching a weapon, and often in contexts suggestive of combat (against humans, animals, or mythical creatures).[18] In Egyptian iconography, many of the representations of a raised arm of a deity are interpreted as having a protective function.[19] A threat against enemies and protection of one's allies are two sides of the same coin. After building an altar, and calling it "The Lord is my banner," Moses declares, "a hand upon the banner [or perhaps: throne] of the Lord! The Lord will have war with Amalek from generation to generation" (Exod 17:16).[20] The reference may be to Amalek's hand raised against God's throne, that is, a challenge to his sovereignty, or to Israelite hands placed on the altar as God's "banner" or "standard," a form of identification with him in his holy war.[21] A more legal context underlies the protestation of Job that he has not taken advantage of the vulnerable: "If I have raised my hand against the orphan, because I saw I had supporters at the gate [the place of legal transactions] ... " (Job 31:21).

---

16. Watts, *Isaiah 1–33*, 160–61.

17. Humbert, "Etendre la main."

18. E.g., *ANEP*, #481, #484, #485, #494, #496; for a detailed discussion of such "smiting god" images, see Calabro, "Ritual Gestures," 287–393.

19. Wilkinson, *Symbol and Magic*, 195–97.

20. Falk, "Gestures", 269.

21. The understanding of a reference to God's throne requires a small emendation to the text; see Durham, *Exodus*, 237.

The reverse of stretching out the arm is to withdraw it, removing a perceived threat, as when Job pleads with God, "Withdraw your hand far from me, and do not let dread of you terrify me" (Job 13:21). To be "short of hand" is to be deprived of power. God asks, "Is my hand shortened, that it cannot redeem? Or have I no power to deliver?" (Isa 50:2; cf. 2 Kgs 19:26; Isa 37:27). To "break the arm" of someone is then used as an idiom to indicate the destruction of their power and the removal of the threat they pose (Job 38:15; Pss 10:15; 37:17; Jer 48:25; Ezek 30:21–24).

Calabro draws attention to the contrast between those hand and arm gestures, like the ones above, which are performed at a distance and operate at a public and political level, and those which are more intimate and kin-based (or treaty-related, based on kinship analogies), these latter typically involving closer contact.[22] A Phoenician inscription speaks of King Kilamuwa holding by the hand a people bound to him by treaty and states that they regarded him "as an orphan regards his mother."[23] When Naomi urged her daughters-in-law to return to Moab, "Orpah kissed her mother-in-law, but Ruth clung to her" (Ruth 1:14). Some tender expressions involve God holding his people in his hand (Isa 49:2; 51:16; 62:3). In an extended treatment of his relationship with his servant Israel in which God identifies himself as his servant's "kinsman," he twice undertakes to hold them by the right hand (Isa 41:8–14). Jesus gives the assurance regarding his "sheep" that "no one will snatch them out of my hand" (John 10:28).

The notion of agency is frequently expressed in Scripture with "by the hand of . . . " (though translations may omit "the hand of": Gen 38:20; 1 Sam 11:7; 16:20; 2 Sam 10:2; 11:4; 1 Kgs 2:25; 2 Chr 23:18; Prov 26:6; Ezek 30:10, 12; Acts 2:23; 7:25, 35; 11:30; Gal 3:19). This is even the case when the hand cannot literally be involved, as when God speaks or commands (lit.) "by the hand of Moses" (Exod 9:35; Lev 8:36; 10:11; Num 4:37; 9:23; Josh 14:2; 20:2; 1 Kgs 8:53).

To strengthen one's own hands is to be more resolved, and to strengthen another's hands is to offer comfort, encouragement, or support—physical or moral. The mention of a court official "on whose hand the king leaned" (2 Kgs 7:2; cf. v. 17), has the ring of an idiomatic usage, suggesting a designation of a trusted adviser, though Naaman's description of his role as the one who supports the Syrian king "leaning on my arm" in the temple of Rimmon (2 Kgs 5:18), while perhaps playing on this idiomatic meaning, is more likely

---

22. Calabro, "When You Spread Your Palms."
23. *Kilamuwa*, 1, line 13; Calabro, "When You Spread Your Palms," 25.

a literal reference to the physical support the aging king needed (cf. §4.6). Eliphaz reminded Job of his former role as an encourager: "See, you have instructed many; you have strengthened the weak hands" (Job 4:3; cf. Judg 7:11; 9:24; 1 Sam 23:16; 2 Sam 2:7; 16:21; 2 Kgs 15:19; Ezra 6:22; Neh 6:9; Isa 51:18; Jer 23:14; Ezek 13:22; 22:14; 30:24, 25; Zech 8:9, 13).

Conversely, arms or hands that droop, perhaps coupled with wobbly knees, indicate inaction due to loss of courage or resolve. The Akkadian expression for laziness or negligence is to "drop one's arm."[24] The prophet Azariah encouraged King Asa and his people with these words: "But you, take courage! Do not let your hands be weak, for your work shall be rewarded" (2 Chr 15:7; cf. Josh 10:6; 2 Sam 4:1; 17:2; Ezra 4:4; Neh 6:9; Job 4:3; Isa 13:7; 35:3; Jer 6:24; 38:4; 47:3; 50:43; Ezek 21:7; Zeph 3:16). In his exhortation to discipline in the Christian life, the writer to the Hebrews urges his readers, "Therefore lift your drooping hands and strengthen your weak knees" (Heb 12:12).[25] Folded arms (which ought to be busily engaged) are the mark of foolish laziness (Prov 6:10; 10:4; 21:25; 24:33; Eccl 4:5; 10:18).

5.4 Good and Evil Hands

Hands have the capacity to do evil as well as good. Jesus provocatively teaches, "If your hand causes you to stumble, cut it off" (Mark 9:43; cf. Gen 4:11; 1 Sam 26:18; 2 Sam 4:11; 1 Chr 12:17; Job 16:17; Pss 7:3; 9:16; 28:4; Isa 59:6; Matt 5:30; 17:22; 18:8; Mark 14:41; Luke 22:21; 24:7; John 19:3; Acts 2:23; 7:41; 12:1; Rev 9:20). Isaiah condemns "pointing the finger" in parallel with false speech (Isa 58:9). Such a gesture is mentioned in both Babylonian law and omen texts, and constituted a slanderous accusation,[26] and a similar finger-pointing gesture is extremely offensive in an Arabic cultural context.[27] Proverbs links pointing with winking (cf. §3.1) and foot scraping (cf. §6.6) as the actions of a worthless person intent on causing trouble through lack of transparency (Prov 6:12–14).

The righteous person has (metaphorical) clean hands (Job 17:9) along with a pure heart (Ps 24:4). Symbolic washing of the hands is associated with the purity laws which are designed to point to a world free of sin and its consequences (Exod 30:19; Matt 15:2; Mark 7:3). Hand-washing then

24. Hempel, *Letters*, 167.
25. See Gruber, "Fear."
26. *ANET*, 171 (Hammurabi #132); Bryce, "Omen-Wisdom," 32–33.
27. Barakat, "Arabic Gestures," 773.

serves as a metaphor for demonstrating innocence or an inner cleansing from sin (Job 9:30; Pss 26:6; 73:13; Jas 4:8).[28] In line with their teacher's characteristic disdain for mere outward symbolism practiced at the expense of the inner reality, Jesus' disciples did not engage in ritual hand-washing before meals (Matt 15:2; Mark 7:2). Against the OT background (see particularly Deut 21:6–9), an ironic mention of hand-washing is Pilate's famous action in connection with the trial of Jesus.[29] By washing his hands, Pilate seeks to absolve himself of responsibility for the death of Jesus, while those who have brought accusations against Jesus take the guilt upon themselves (Matt 27:24–25).

5.5 Hands in Possession and Control, Generosity, and Meanness

To have or take hold of something in the hand is a natural expression of possession or control. Saul's servant (lit.) has in his hand (that is, his possession) a quarter of a shekel of silver (1 Sam 9:8). Ahimelech, the priest of Nob, does not have "under his hand" any ordinary bread for David's men to eat (1 Sam 21:4). Giving and receiving is then often expressed with reference to items passing from the hands of one party to the hands of another, even when the items "handed over," such as livestock, or real estate, or the universe, are too large or too numerous for hands literally to be involved (so idiomatic English translations might omit reference to hands: Gen 27:17; 30:35; 32:16; 39:8; Deut 3:8; 24:1, 3; 26:4; Josh 2:24; Judg 1:2; 1 Sam 10:4; 12:3–4; 21:3; 25:35; 2 Sam 8:1; 1 Kgs 11:31, 34–35; 15:18; 22:3; 2 Kgs 5:20; 13:25; Job 35:7; Isa 37:14; 40:2; Jer 20:5–6; 25:28; Ezek 10:7; Mal 2:13; John 3:35; 13:3). In a unique expression, Isaiah declares that "the hand of the LORD will rest on this mountain [Zion]" (Isa 25:10), perhaps including notions of divine presence, protection, and sovereignty.

Not accepting, then, can be expressed with reference to a hand gesture, such as turning back the hand. According to Ezekiel, one of the characteristics of a righteous person is that he "withholds [or: turns back] his hand from iniquity" (Ezek 18:17). Isaiah similarly pictures those "who wave away [lit: shake the palms of] a bribe instead of accepting it" (Isa 33:15).

---

28. Kruger, "Nonverbal Communication and Symbolic Gestures," 220. Kruger includes reference to a Ugaritic text where a symbolic hand-washing renders a person free of the legal consequences of his action.

29. See Wright, "Deuteronomy 21:1–9."

Closely aligned with possession, the notion of authority or control over things, or more commonly people (often through military victory), is often expressed by a reference to hands. A frequent expression in the OT is that of God blessing his people by giving their enemies into their hands, or, as a judgment, the reverse. God promises David, "I will give the Philistines into your hand" (1 Sam 23:4; cf. Exod 23:31; Num 21:2; Deut 1:27; 7:24; Josh 8:1; Judg 4:7; 1 Kgs 20:28; Jer 20:4; 21:5; 37:17; Ezek 16:39; 20:33-34; Matt 26:45; Mark 14:41; Luke 1:71, 74; 9:44; 24:7; John 3:35; 13:3). To place one's hand on the neck of one's enemies (the place of a yoke on oxen), as Judah is prophesied to do, is to assert one's power over them and hold them in subjection (Gen 49:8; cf. §4.1). God gave the animals (lit.) "into the hand" of humanity (Gen 9:2), that is, for humans to have custody and dominion over the animate creation. An Egyptian jailer committed all of the prisoners to Joseph's "hand" (Gen 39:2), and subsequently Potiphar gave responsibility for the management of his household into Joseph's "hand" (Gen 39:8). The medium at Endor, who had taken a great risk in summoning Samuel from the grave, said to Saul, "I have taken my life in my hand, and have listened to what you have said to me" (1 Sam 28:21). The angel with authority to bind Satan held in his hand the key to the bottomless pit (Rev 20:1). To lay a hand on someone, or to have them in your hand, is to wield power over them, or take them into custody. After Jesus' betrayal, "they came and laid hands on Jesus and arrested him" (Matt 26:50; cf. Judg 6:13; 8:6; 2 Sam 14:16; 2 Chr 30:6; Ps 139:5; Prov 6:3; Mark 14:46; Luke 20:19; 22:53; John 7:30, 44; 10:39; Acts 4:3; 5:18; 2 Cor 11:33). According to Luke, Jesus' last words were, "Father, into your hands I commend my spirit" (Luke 23:46).

To open one's hand, then, suggests generosity, the willingness to yield ownership or control. It is to God's hand that a psalmist looks for mercy, as servants look to their masters for provision of food (Ps 123:2).[30] God's open-handedness with his creation (Pss 104:28; 145:16) is to be emulated in his people's generosity to the needy (Deut 15:8, 11; Matt 6:3). The virtuous woman of Proverbs 31 "opens her hand to the poor and reaches out her hands to the needy" (Prov 31:20). The opposite is to shut one's hand through lack of concern for the poor (Deut 15:7).

---

30. This understanding of this verse suits the context better than that which sees servants looking to the hand of their master or mistress for gestures of command; see Allen, *Psalms 101-150*, 160.

5.6 Reaching, Touching, and Holding

A range of hand and arm movements indicates friendliness, support, and encouragement. To reach out to someone can be an overture of friendship and welcome. In a cylinder seal of Ur-Nammu, a seated god extends his right arm to an approaching worshiper in what has been interpreted as a token of welcome or acceptance of homage, though we might also see an initiative of a more formal nature, a pledge of commitment to the king (see below).[31] A Greek statue of Artemis depicts her with right arm raised.[32] In the Iliad, Achilles reaches out his arms to the ghost of his friend Patroclus.[33] The book of Proverbs pictures the personified Wisdom as extending her hand invitingly to an unresponsive audience (Prov 1:24; cf. 2 Sam 15:5). God patiently holds out his hands to his disobedient people, which could be interpreted as welcoming, or as entreating, or both (Isa 65:2; Rom 10:21).

#9. *The king is ushered into the presence of the deity. Cylinder seal of Ur-Nammu. Sumerian, twenty-first century BC. Drawn by Charlotte Whitehouse from Keel #272.*

31. See #9; cf. *ANEP*, #493.
32. Brilliant, *Gesture and Rank*, 16.
33. Homer, *Iliad*, 23.117–26.

Touching is a natural and universal mode of identification with an object or person and may sometimes suggest the notion of transference of some quality between persons and other persons or objects. Touching is subject to social norms, class distinctions, and gender differences, to a greater degree in comparison with other gestures, as to what forms of touch are appropriate, and what they might mean. In general, however, touching (as distinct from more forceful contact) suggests a desire to engage with others, cordial relations, or a level of intimacy.[34]

In the purity laws of the OT, anything that touches the altar, for example, is considered to be holy (Exod 29:37), and uncleanness is similarly communicated through touch (Lev 5:2–3). A person with certain skin conditions (traditionally "leprosy") had to live in isolation so that no physical contact was possible (Lev 13; Num 5:2). Likewise contact with death rendered one unclean (Num 19:11), and priests in particular were subject to restrictions in their contact with dead bodies so as to preserve their holiness (Lev 21:1–4). Even secondary touch could be considered effective. The priests responded to Haggai by declaring that something that makes contact with someone who had touched a dead body becomes unclean (Hag 2:13). Conversely, to come in contact with handkerchiefs or aprons which had touched Paul's skin was regarded as efficacious in healing and casting out evil spirits (Acts 19:22).

The laying of one's hand or hands on the head of a sacrificial victim before its slaughter or expulsion has been much discussed. At the very least, the hand gesture would appear to identify the sacrificial victim with the worshiper in some way (if not to act as a substitute), and in the case of the scapegoat at least, to symbolize the placement of the community's guilt upon the animal (Exod 29:10, 15; Lev 1:4; 3:2, 8, 13; 4:4, 15, 24, 29, 33; 16:21; 2 Chr 29:23).[35] Perhaps related is the laying of hands on the head of a person condemned to be stoned for blasphemy (Lev 24:14). This identifies the guilty party and perhaps absolves those who participate from any guilt which would otherwise attach to taking a life.[36]

The transfer of power or authority can be demonstrated by gestures involving touch. Jeremiah expresses the authority he has to speak on behalf

---

34. See Heslin and Alper, "Touch."

35. For discussion of the rationale of hand placement in the context of Israelite cultic practice, see van der Merwe, "The Laying on of Hands"; Wright, "Gesture"; Hartley, *Leviticus*, lvi–lxxii, 19–21; Dunn, *The Theology of Paul*, 220.

36. For a fuller discussion, see Wright, "Gesture," 435–36.

THE ARMS AND HANDS

of God, for example, as the result of God touching his mouth and putting his words in it (Jer 1:9; cf. Dan 10:16; cf. §2.10; §2.11; §5.6.1).

The touch of a hand, particularly by one in authority, can be an indication of encouragement and reassurance in a difficult or overwhelming situation (Dan 10:10; Matt 17:7; Rev 1:17). Ezra and Nehemiah speak of "the good hand of God" being upon them (Ezra 7:9; 8:18; Neh 2:8; cf. Luke 1:66; Acts 11:21), ensuring success in their missions.

To take someone by the hand or arm can be a natural gesture of comfort, support, and guidance and suggests metaphors of aid and encouragement for difficult tasks or daunting physical or metaphorical journeys. The blind and the intoxicated need to be led by the hand (Judg 16:26; Isa 51:17–18; Mark 8:23; Acts 9:8; 13:11; 22:11). Jesus grasps Peter by the hand when the disciple begins to sink under the water and appeals to Jesus for "salvation" (Matt 14:31), evoking such passages as Ps 69:1–2. A sin of Samaria ("Sodom") was that it "did not aid [lit.: grasp the hand of] the poor and needy" (Ezek 16:49). Through a military alliance, Assyria can be said to be "the strong arm of the children of Lot" (Ps 83:8). God takes his people by the hand to lead them on life's journey (Pss 73:23–24; 139:9–10; cf. §5.9). In an obscure reference, God's "hand was strong" upon Isaiah (Isa 8:11), which some have interpreted as imparting strength, but it could equally be a strong restraining hand, for the prophet is warned "not to walk in the way of this people." Zechariah 14:13 seems to contain two contradictory images, that of grasping the hand of another (in support) and that of a hand "raised against the hand of the other." But that is the point, for it describes a chaotic scene, "a great panic from the LORD." An Egyptian scene movingly depicts Pharaoh Akhenaton holding the arm of his queen as they mourn before their dead daughter.[37] A cylinder seal of Ur-Nammu shows a priest or minor deity leading a worshiper by the arm into the presence of a seated deity.[38] It is not easy to separate general expressions of support involving the hand from those making a more formal commitment or treaty (cf. §5.9).

Support is further demonstrated when the arms are used for lifting up and carrying. A shepherd gathering lambs in his arms suggests both gentleness and strength (Isa 40:11). God carries his people from birth to old age (Isa 46:3–4). In a tender image, Hosea pictures God as teaching his people Ephraim to walk as a toddler and picking them up in his arms (Hos 11:3). God upholds his people with his "everlasting arms" (Deut 33:27).

---

37. Keel, #68a.
38. Ibid., #272; Langdon, "Gesture", 533.

Psalm 91:12 (quoted in the temptation scene in Matt 4:6 and Luke 4:11) presents an image of angels carrying in their arms the one who finds refuge in the LORD. Jesus takes children into his arms as a prelude to blessing them (Mark 10:16; cf. Mark 9:36; Luke 2:28).

To take someone, generally either family members or children, into one's arms in an embrace is to show affection, to welcome them warmly, or bid them a fond farewell (Gen 29:13; 33:4; 48:10; 2 Kgs 4:16; Mark 10:16; Luke 2:28). Ruth's tight holding onto her mother-in-law indicates her devotion and her strong commitment to stay with her (Ruth 1:14). The father welcomes the prodigal son home with an embrace (Luke 15:20). The family gesture is extended to include the new family of Christian believers: the Ephesian elders tearfully embrace Paul at the news that they will not see him again (Acts 20:37; cf. §4.1), and the verb in Acts 21:1 suggests that some effort was required on the part of Paul's party to "tear themselves away." When a rich man asked Jesus concerning eternal life and claimed to have kept the commandments, we read, "Jesus, looking at him, loved him and said, 'You lack one thing; go, sell what you own, and give the money to the poor, and you will have treasure in heaven; then come, follow me'" (Mark 10:21). The word "loved" here probably refers to a physical gesture of affection, such as hugging or caressing.[39] The frequent reminders to Christians to greet one another most likely have in mind a hug, even when this is not possible physically, by correspondence (Matt 10:12; Rom 16:3–16; Phil 4:21; 1 Thess 5:26; 2 Tim 4:19; Heb 13:24), and the same verb is used for a farewell embrace (Mark 6:46; Luke 9:61; Acts 20:1).[40]

Embracing can of course also have a sexual overtone. The woman of the Song yearns, "O that his left hand were under my head, and that his right hand embraced me!" (Song 2:6; cf. Gen 16:5; Deut 13:6; Prov 4:8; 5:20).

A modified form of touching another person is to grasp their clothing (cf. §4.11).

Hands and arms are put to use in holding and carrying loads, though for heavy burdens the weight might be distributed by carrying them on the head and shoulders. Carrying heavy loads becomes a natural idiom for significant responsibilities. Moses was encouraged to appoint judges and elders to bear the burden with him (Exod 18:22; Num 11:17; Deut 1:12). Jesus criticized the Jewish religious authorities for the heavy loads

---

39. Gundry, *Mark*, 554.
40. See Windisch, ἀσπάζομαι, 497.

(unreasonable requirements) they laid on people (Luke 11:46). Christians are called on to "bear one another's burdens," that is, to show empathy and support more generally (Gal 6:2). Jesus physically carried his cross until he was no longer able (Matt 27:32; Luke 23:26; John 19:17). This added poignancy to the expression he had previously used of carrying one's cross (to execution) as a lesson in the ultimate self-denial to which he called his disciples (Matt 16:24; Mark 8:34; Luke 9:23; 14:27).

5.6.1 The Hands in Miracle Working

A particular trope in the Bible (an extension of the use of the hand and arm in demonstrations of power) is their use in acts of supernatural power such as healing. For these events the hands might either stretch out over or touch the target. Moses is called to stretch out his hand against the land of Egypt as a demonstration of his authority to initiate the plagues or control the waters of the Red Sea (Exod 9:22; 10:12, 21, 22; 14:16, 26, 27). When Moses raised his arm(s) above the battlefield with the Amalekites, Israel prevailed, and when it/they drooped, Israel faltered (Exod 17:11–12).[41] Joshua is summoned to stretch out his hand holding a javelin toward Ai as a foreboding of its capture and destruction (Josh 8:18). Naaman envisaged that Elisha would exercise his prophetic power by raising (rather than waving as NRSV) his hand, or fist, in a dramatic gesture over his skin disease (2 Kgs 5:11).[42] The expression suggests some aggression (against the disease) or perhaps some expectation of magic.

Physical contact might also be involved in healing. The most notable in terms of close physical contact is when the prophet Elisha "got up on the bed and lay upon the child, putting his mouth upon his mouth, his eyes upon his eyes, and his hands upon his hands; and while he lay bent over him, the flesh of the child became warm" (2 Kgs 4:34). As a prelude to healing a man with dropsy, Jesus took hold of him (Luke 14:4). Contact healing through the laying-on of hands was known also in Judaism in the Second Temple period.[43]

---

41. On the textual uncertainty whether it is "arm" (singular) or "arms" (plural), see Calabro, "Ritual Gestures," 59–62. If the plural is to be read, the gesture might be more obviously one of prayer (cf. §5.7).

42. See Milgrom, "The Alleged Wave Offering," 38.

43. See, e.g., Flusser, "Healing."

Those who witnessed Jesus' ministry remarked, "What deeds of power are being done by his hands!" (Mark 6:2), and apostolic healings are also said to be (lit.) "by the hands of the apostles" (Acts 5:12; cf. 19:11). References in the Gospels to Jesus' outstretched arm may be allusions to the OT image of God's arm outstretched in deliverance (Matt 8:3; Mark 1:41; Luke 5:13).

The use of touch in Jesus' healings is an application of the principle of identification and transference and could be initiated either by the healer or the one seeking healing. Touching was Jesus' characteristic accompanying gesture to his acts of power and it was the expectation of the crowds that Jesus' touch would bring healing. People brought a deaf man to Jesus, begging him to lay his hands on him, that is, to cure his deafness and lack of speech (Mark 7:32). Jesus touches (or is expected by others to touch) eyes, ears, tongue, and a dead body as well as unspecified areas of the body in his acts of deliverance and restoration of human wholeness (Matt 8:14-15; 9:18, 25, 29; 14:31; 20:34; Mark 1:31, 41; 5:22-23, 41; 6:5; 7:32-33; 8:22-25; 9:27; Luke 4:40; 5:13; 7:14; 8:54; 13:13; 22:51). The apostles and other believers similarly laid their hands on those in need of healing (Acts 5:12; 9:12, 17, 41; 14:3; 19:11; 28:8).

Others might also seek to touch Jesus with the expectation of healing (Matt 14:36; Mark 6:56). The accounts of the woman who was hemorrhaging for twelve years (Matt 9:20-22; Mark 5:25-34; Luke 8:43-48; cf. §4.11) make much of the woman's touching Jesus (the Markan account has the word "touch" four times). Jesus' question as to who it was who touched him seems not so much to be asked out of ignorance, but out of a desire that the woman make a public declaration of her identification with Jesus in this way. On this basis she is assured of her "salvation" (Mark 5:33-34).

Jesus' physical contact with "leprosy," with bodily fluids, and with death is particularly significant in view of the OT notions of uncleanness (Matt 8:2-3; Mark 1:40-41; 5:30; Luke 7:14; 8:46; cf. Lev 13:1-17; 15:19-33; 22:4-6; Num 19:13-16). The point would seem to be that through contact with Jesus, rather than impurity flowing to him, purity, and life-restoring power flow out to others. The clamor to have physical contact with Jesus, viewed against the background of the transference of guilt in OT sacrifice, might then suggest in hindsight to the reader of the Gospel accounts a theology of identification with Jesus in his death.

5.7 The Hands in Entreaty, Adoration, and Blessing

A natural gesture of entreaty or appeal for aid is to reach out in the direction of one who is in a position to offer support or assistance. Lamentations pictures a desolate Zion reaching out indiscriminately, "but there is no one to comfort her" (Lam 1:17). Jesus' request to the man with the withered hand, "stretch out your hand" (Matt 12:13; Mark 3:5; Luke 6:10) may suggest to the astute reader (if not to the man) a gestured request for healing, or perhaps even commitment (cf. §5.9), as well as facilitating a demonstration of the healing for all to see.

#10. *Desperate Libyan and Asiatics implore an official for food. Tomb of Horemheb. Sakkarah, Egyptian, fourteenth century BC. Keel #429.*

Extended hand movements are frequently associated with prayer (adoration and entreaty) and with blessing in Scripture. The raising of one's hands, or spreading out of one's palms (normally plural, but occasionally singular), as in many cultures, frequently accompanies praise (or blessing of a superior, particularly deity) or entreaty.[44] Prehistoric art from a wide variety of places shows human figures with hands held up in what is best understood from the contexts in which the artworks are found as

---

44. See Calabro, "When You Spread Your Palms."

gestures of adoration and prayer.[45] The Greek and Roman practice was to pray with arms extended in the direction of the gods in an adoration gesture.[46] The Adorans sculpture of Boidas, for example, depicts a young man praying, looking up, and with arms raised and palms turned half upwards and half inwards.[47] Bremmer considers the Greek gesture of upturned palms, free of weapons (a gesture associated with women in social interactions), to be one exhibiting diminution of status of a man before a god.[48] The practice is widely attested in Semitic texts. Esarhaddon, for example, raises his hands in prayer to the Assyrian gods, and the Ugaritic text *Kirta* describes the hero lifting his hands to heaven in prayer.[49]

The OT uses more than one word for hand and several verbs for raising or spreading out in expressions for prayer. A psalmist prays: "Let my prayer be counted as incense before you, and the lifting up of my hands as the evening sacrifice" (Ps 141:2; cf. Pss 28:2; 63:4; 134:2; Lam 2:19; 3:41). God's servants are called upon to lift up their hands to the holy place and bless, that is, praise, the LORD (Ps 134:2; cf. 63:4; Neh 8:6). Some of these reference to hand gestures may not be meant to be taken as describing a gesture, but read as idiomatic references to prayer. However, Isa 1:15 at least suggests a literal reference is intended: "When you stretch out your hands, I will hide my eyes from you; even though you make many prayers, I will not listen; your hands are full of blood." The writer of 1 Timothy calls on men to pray "lifting holy hands" (1 Tim 2:8), and this appears to be a literal reference suggesting that hand-raising was still a standard practice associated with prayer in the early church. In a metaphorical usage, a psalmist, in telling us that he reveres God's commandments, literally says he "lifts his hands" to them (Ps 119:48).

We cannot be sure of the precise positioning and movements of the hands in prayer. We have images of two-handed gestures of humans before deities, or symbols of deity such as the lotus and date palm, from Egypt and Western Asia with palms outward as well as palms inward. The majority of such images from the Levant and Egypt typically have standing or kneeling (never seated) figures facing the deity, with arms stretching forward with

---

45. See e.g., Maringer, "Adorants"; Hahnemann, "Nonverbal Behavior," 165.
46. Brilliant, *Gesture and Rank*, 15–17, 24; Corbeill, *Nature Embodied*, 26.
47. Brilliant, *Gesture and Rank*, 15.
48. Bremmer, "Walking," 22.
49. Fox, "Clapping Hands," 50; Frechette, *Mesopotamian Ritual-Prayers*; Gruber, *Aspects*, 50–89; *Kirta* iv 4–5 (*CoS*, 1:335).

elbows bent and with palms pointing up at about chin height.[50] As noted in the previous chapter, we are probably intended to picture a progression in some homage scenes. Those further away from the object of homage have arms raised, while those closer, having dropped to the ground, inevitably have their arms lower, though still not much below head height which is now close to the ground.[51] Other images depict those approaching a god or king with one or both hands raised but with palm facing sideways, or inwards and close to the face.[52] Some of these have a hand close to the mouth so as to suggest the self-deprecatory silence gesture (cf. §2.10). Langdon interprets these as capturing a moment of throwing a kiss (cf. §2.11).[53]

A possible descriptive clue in the Bible is the revolting image Isaiah presents of the humiliated Moab whose pathetic muck-filled hand gestures may be intended to echo those of a petitioner: "The Moabites shall be trodden down in their place as straw is trodden down in a dung-pit. Though they spread out their hands in the midst of it, as swimmers spread out their hands to swim, their pride will be laid low despite the struggle of their hands" (Isa 25:10–11), that is, arms are extended in front with fingers together and palms out. Whether movement of the arms up and down in prayer is also intended by this image is not clear. A sweeping movement of the hands may be implied by the verb in Ps 77:2 "my hand is stretched out [lit.: flows]" and a stretching out of hands (or palms) is the gesture in Ps 88:9 and again (with a different verb) in Exod 9:29, 33; 1 Kgs 8:22, 38, 54; 2 Chr 6:12–13, 29; Ezra 9:5; Pss 44:20; 143:6.[54] The suggestion that the word translated "spread out" in Exod 9:29, etc., above really means "to separate" and therefore implies a movement in which the palms are initially pressed or folded together then parted as they ascend, is attractive though difficult to maintain on lexicographical grounds.[55] Later Jewish practice was to have the hands crossed over the chest.[56] It is possible that behind the several expressions in Hebrew there was more than one type of hand gesture, sig-

---

50. For a thorough discussion of the iconography, see Calabro, "Ritual Gestures," 525–72.

51. See #5, #10; Keel, *Symbolism* 308–23; *ANEP*, #4, #5, #45, #46, #47.

52. For details of the iconography, see Calabro, "Ritual Gestures," 493–525, 572–84.

53. Langdon, "Gesture," 535, 544.

54. Other interpretations of Ps 77:2 are possible; see Calabro, "Ritual Gestures," 173–75.

55. See Burke, "Gesture"; *ANEP*, #18–19, #21, #23, #24, #431, #433, #435, #436.

56. Edersheim, *The Temple*, 156.

nifying different things, though the sharp distinction suggested by Gruber between supplicating and saluting gestures is difficult to maintain.[57]

As to the symbolism, does the display of empty palms suggest a desire for them to be filled (a begging gesture)?[58] Or is the action a symbolic offering of the petition or of the one praying?[59] Is the gesture akin to a gesture of surrender? (cf. §5.9)? Or do open hands invite scrutiny with a view to establishing one's innocence and hence the right to approach God (Ps 24:3–4; cf. Job 11:13–15; Isa 1:15)?[60] Tertullian's comment on the practice of prayer with which he was familiar lends support to the latter view: "We Christians offer up our prayers, with eyes lifted up to heaven, unfolded hands in token of our simplicity, and with uncovered heads."[61] The reality is probably that, whatever their origin, gestures such as raising hands are performed in accordance with custom and social expectations and can convey different elements of significance according to context.[62]

The idiom is so familiar that to "lift up your hands" or "spread out your palms" simply means to pray (Exod 9:29, 33; 1 Kgs 8:22, 38; Ezra 9:5; Job 11:13; Ps 143:6; Lam 3:41), and can be used to introduce direct or indirect speech for the content of the prayer (Jer 4:31; Lam 2:19). In a striking image, God himself is said to spread out his hands to his rebellious people (Isa 65:2), suggesting entreaty, or a welcoming gesture, or both.

The act of blessing (superior to inferior, cf. Heb 7:7) is typically signified by a hand gesture. The "Babylonian Noah" Utnapishtim and his wife are blessed by the god Enlil by a touch on the forehead as they kneel before him.[63] We have numerous examples from ancient art of people or gods raising their hand in what could be interpreted as a blessing or greeting gesture.[64] At the Israelite assembly following his ordination, "Aaron lifted his hands toward the people and blessed them" (Lev 9:22). Jesus' final gesture

---

57. Gruber, *Aspects*, 35–36; cf. Edersheim, *The Temple*, 156–57.

58. Gruber, *Aspects*, 36; Langdon, "Gesture," 542–43. Langdon regards the palms inwards and upwards as the original Semitic prayer gesture.

59. See Calabro, "When You Spread Your Palms."

60. See Clines, *Job 1–20*, 267–68.

61. Tertullian, *Apology* 30.4. For early Christian representations of the prayer posture with arms outstretched, see Giuentella, "Orans."

62. For a fuller listing of suggestions, see Calabro, "Ritual Gestures," 652–54.

63. *Gilgamesh* (CoS, 1:460).

64. *ANEP*, #460, #535, #537. See the thorough study of hand-raising in Mesopotamia as a formal respectful gesture of approach to the god, particularly as a prelude to petition: Frechette, *Mesopotamian Ritual-prayers*.

before his ascension, according to Luke, was to raise his hands in blessing his disciples (Luke 24:50). The blessing of children, as Israel's blessing of Ephraim and Manasseh (Gen 48:14), can involve the placing of a hand on the child's head. As noted above, if one hand is used, it would normally be the right hand. Jesus' blessing of the children brought to him involved laying his hands on them (Matt 19:13–15; Mark 10:13, 16; Luke 18:15). Prayer for blessing on individuals, or for them to receive the Spirit, may be accompanied by the laying on of hands (Acts 8:17, 18; 9:17, 19:6; Heb 6:2). This is closely related to the use of touch in healing (cf. §5.6.1) and the laying on of hands in commissioning (cf. §5.8).

5.8 The Hands in Commissioning

The laying on of hands in an act of commissioning for a task or office may be closely allied with the blessing gesture (cf. §5.7) or with the notion of the transference of power and authority (cf. §5.6).[65] Moses laid his hand on Joshua to indicate that he was passing on his leadership role to the younger man (Num 27:18–23; cf. Deut 34:9; Isa 22:21). The commissioning of people for positions of responsibility in the church may be accompanied by placing the hands on those commissioned (Acts 6:6; 13:3; 1 Tim 4:14; 2 Tim 1:6).[66] The advice given to Timothy not to be hasty in the laying on of hands has been interpreted as a gesture of restoration to fellowship of those who had been disciplined for some offense, but is most likely, in context, counseling caution in appointing church officials.[67] When the churches elected men to accompany Paul on his journey to take the collection to Jerusalem, the word used is lit. "stretch the hand," so may refer to an actual voting gesture (2 Cor 8:9), but the word can simply mean "appoint" without a vote, as when the apostles appointed elders in newly established churches (Acts 14:23).

An alternative expression for the consecration of priests in the OT is to "fill the hand" though what this originally signified is not clear. It may refer to pouring oil into the cupped hand (cf. Lev 14:15–29; cf. §2.5), or to empowerment for the priestly office (cf. §5.6), or may have its origins in the entitlement of a priest to some form of recompense for his labors (perhaps a portion of the sacrifice). Whatever the meaning, there is a striking

---

65. See Daube, *The New Testament and Rabbinic Judaism*, 224–46; Ferguson, "Jewish and Christian Ordination."
66. Parratt, "The Laying on of Hands."
67. Cf. Johnson, *First and Second Timothy*, 281.

expression in Jer 5:31, which is lit. "priests scrape out on their hands," best understood as a condemnation of priests for effectively undoing the "hand-filling" of their consecration by their behavior.[68] English translations may simply use words like "consecrate" or "ordain" where the Hebrew is more literally "fill the hand" (Exod 28:41; 29:9, 29, 33, 35; Lev 16:32; Judg 17:5, 12; 1 Kgs 13:33; 1 Chr 29:5; 2 Chr 13:9; Ezek 43:26). The latter verse, referring to the consecration of an altar, demonstrates that by Ezekiel's time the expression had lost any literal reference.

5.9 The Hands in Oaths and Pledges

Hand gestures are used in several solemn social and legal situations such as oaths and pledges. One form of oath is the adjuration found a number of times in the OT: "Thus will God [or: the gods] do . . . and thus will he [they] do in addition . . . ." Typically the adjuration is directed at the speaker ("to me": 2 Sam 3:35; 19:13; 1 Kgs 2:23; 20:10; 2 Kgs 6:31; Ruth 1:17; cf. 1 Sam 20:13; 2 Sam 3:9), or is unexpressed and probably implied (NRSV adds "to me": 1 Sam 14:44; 1 Kgs 19:2), but occasionally directed at another (1 Sam 3:17; 25:22). The deictic adverb "thus" is generally thought to refer to an accompanying action in which the oath-taker enacts a symbolic threat to life or well-being (generally his or her own), such as slitting the throat, the dire sanction one would anticipate in the event of non-fulfillment of the oath (cf. similar words used in Saul's threat in 1 Sam 11:7). An Akkadian phrase for taking an oath is "to touch the throat."[69] It is quite possible that the Hebrew expression became so formulaic that the gesture could be dropped and the form of words alone might suffice. It is not clear if references to swearing by the head might be a relic of such a gesture (Matt 5:36; cf. 1 Chr 12:19).[70]

Elsewhere the taking of an oath or making a pledge of commitment could be indicated by a reference to the raising of the hand. It is possible that in some instances the reference to hand-raising in oath-taking is the same threatening action as suggested in the adjuration formula above

---

68. Holladay, "The Priests."

69. In Tablet VI of the Babylonian *Epic of Creation* the gods pledge their allegiance to Marduk: "They made Marduk's destiny highest, they prostrated themselves. They laid upon themselves a curse (if they broke the oath), With water and oil they swore, they touched their throats" (*CoS*, 1:401); see Campbell, *Ruth*, 74; Sanders, "So May God Do!," 93; Ziegler, "So Shall God Do"; Conklin, *Oath Formulas*, 22-24, 84.

70. For the understanding of 1 Chr 12:19 as a reference to an oath, see Rogers, "The Use of ראש."

(e.g., raising the hand to the neck or head), or a vestige of it. But in other cases, it clearly has a different symbolism, directed towards a recipient, which in the Bible can be God, or the respectful variant, heaven. Viberg sees this as an extension of a more basic summoning function (Isa 13:2; Prov 1:24).[71] As such it is a performative gesture, saying "I hereby pledge ...." Abram assures the king of Sodom, "I have sworn [lit.: lifted my hand] to the LORD, God Most High, maker of heaven and earth, that I would not take a thread or a sandal-thong or anything that is yours" (Gen 14:22-23; cf. Deut 12:40; Rev 10:5-6). The symbolism may be that God is being invoked as witness or guarantor to the oath or covenant (even when God himself is the one swearing!: Exod 6:8; Num 14:30; Deut 32:40; Neh 9:15; Ps 106:26; Ezek 20:15, 28, 42; 36:7; 44:12; 47:14; cf. God swearing by himself: Gen 22:16; Exod 32:13; Isa 45:23; Jer 22:5; Heb 6:13).[72] Another possible interpretation is that the raised hand is extended to God as the other party, given that a physical handclasp (see below) is not possible as in some human pledges, though we should note that God can also be said to take people by the hand (cf. §5.6).[73] Hezekiah's summons to Israel to repent, "yield yourselves [lit.: give the hand] to the LORD" (2 Chr 30:8), suggests a pledge of commitment or covenant renewal. A gesture of hand-raising, with palm out, is found in numerous images from ancient Western Asia in contexts of expressions of commitment to a deity, such as temple scenes.[74] Unlike those images involving two hands raised (cf. §5.7), these may be performed by a superior (e.g., a deity or enthroned king) before an inferior, as well as inferior to superior. This fits well with the biblical image of God initiating covenantal commitments.

A reference to hand-raising might accompany a separate verb of swearing (Dan 12:7; Rev 10:5-6) or might be used alone to indicate swearing. English translations may use the word "swear" in the following passages, but the expression is lit. "raise the hand" and, as with raising the hands in prayer (cf. §5.7), reference to the gesture alone is sufficient to introduce the content of the oath without requiring a separate verb of swearing (Ps 106:26; Ezek 20:5-6, 15, 23, 28, 42; 47:14). In a few of the passages listed

71. Viberg, *Symbols of Law*, 31-32.
72. See Seely, "The Raised Hand."
73. Falk, "Gestures," 269.
74. Ibid.; *ANEP*, #132, #246, #325, #460, #609, #700; Calabro, "Ritual Gestures," 393-493, 636-51. Calabro interprets all instances of a one-hand palm-out gesture as signifying an oath or pledge, while allowing for a range of nuances such as an expression of sincerity, a transference of power, a decree and an invocation of deity.

above, we are perhaps to understand a *double entendre*. As well as serving as an oath formula in Ezek 20:5, God's raising his hand had the effect of "making myself known to them [Israel] in the land of Egypt." In Ezek 36:7, the raising of God's hand, as well as constituting an oath undertaking, has a nuance of threat against Israel's enemies (cf. LXX "I will raise my hand against the nations") who will suffer insults (using the same verb as in the idiom "raise my hand"; cf. Deut 32:39-40; Ezek 44:12-13).[75] Generally one hand (likely the right; cf. Deut 32:40 LXX) is used in such commitments, though once both hands are specified, when "the man clothed in linen, who was upstream, raised his right hand and his left hand toward heaven. And I heard him swear by the one who lives forever" (Dan 12:7), though it is possible that in this case prayer precedes or accompanies the swearing.[76] The phrase which is literally "to give the hand" is not explicit as to the nature of the gesture, though Gen 38:28 implies that reaching forward or upward is involved. On Solomon's accession, "all the leaders and the mighty warriors, and also all the sons of King David, pledged their allegiance [lit.: gave the hand] to King Solomon" (1 Chr 29:24; cf. Ezra 10:19; Ezek 17:18).[77] It is possible that the reference in Isa 56:5 to the LORD granting a "hand" to his faithful eunuchs means the initiation of a covenantal commitment (cf. v. 4), though NRSV is typical of modern interpretations in understanding this as a "monument."[78]

In some contexts, the raising of a hand or hands has the nuance of surrender. Two arms stretched out in front is still a gesture of surrender in Western Asia.[79] The people of Judah lament the fact that they have been forced to "give the hand" to Egypt and Assyria in submission to their foreign overlords in order to survive (Lam 5:6; cf. Jer 50:15). As noted above,

---

75. Johan Lust endeavors to show that in fact all of the hand-raising references which have been taken to refer to God's oath-taking are to be interpreted as indicating rather his intervention on behalf of or against others, though his arguments are not convincing (Lust, "For I Lift up My Hand"); cf. Calabro, "Ritual Gestures," 100–107.

76. See McGarry, "The Ambidextrous Angel." McGarry sees the two-handed gesture as based on a misunderstanding by the writer of Daniel of the Deuteronomy passage. However, a two-handed oath gesture is attested in a Phoenician inscription; see Calabro, "Ritual Gestures," 66–68; cf. Seely, "The Raised Hand of God," 411–12; Viberg, *Symbols of Law*, 25–26.

77. Strictly the expression in 1 Chr 29:24 is "gave the hand under," but the word "under" is best understood not as referring to a gestural element, but as indicating that the pledge was one of subordination.

78. Calabro, "Ritual Gestures," 168–73.

79. See Clines, *Job 1–20*, 267–68.

Habakkuk echoes the physical gesture of surrender in battle of raising both hands in his depiction of the surrender of creation to the Lord, "The sun [or: the deep] raised high its hands" (Hab 3:10).[80] It is possible that Ezra 10:19 has this nuance as well.[81] For NRSV: "They pledged themselves [lit.: gave their hand] to send away their wives" one might read: "They gave in (to Ezra) so as to send away their wives," though the reference to a "covenant" in v. 3 suggests that the notion of a pledge (to God) is uppermost. An obscure verse in Ps 68 is best understood as a reference to the surrender and offering of tribute by foreign powers to Israel's God: "Let bronze be brought from Egypt; let Ethiopia hasten to stretch out its hands to God" (Ps 68:31). The verb in this case stresses the rapidity of the hand movement.

Hands may come together in a handclasp to indicate or accompany an undertaking such as a pledge of loyalty or covenantal commitment.[82] A limestone relief from Nimrud (Iraq, ninth century BC) shows Shalmaneser III clasping the right hand of another monarch (the king of Babylon?) in what is interpreted as a gesture of alliance.[83] Likewise in Roman society an expression for closing a pact is "joining of the right hands."[84] While English translations may render some of the following by our more familiar gesture of "shaking hands," the idiom in Prov 6:1; 17:18; 22:26 and Job 17:3 is more lit. "strike the hand"; that is, the hands of the two parties may meet with some degree of force. Other expressions for making commitments are "give the hand" (Lam 5:6; Ezek 17:18), "join hands" (Exod 23:1), and "clasp hands" (lit.: "clap hands," Isa 2:6). We could deduce, then, that these refer to different stages of the gesture for making a commitment, such as putting up security for someone or agreeing on a trade deal: two parties might extend and strike right hands, continuing to hold them for a period. In 2 Kgs 10:15 Jehu invites Jehonadab to give him his hand. While a modern reader might read this as simply a friendly helping hand to assist Jehonadab to climb up into Jehu's chariot (and a *double entendre* is possible), Jehu is in reality soliciting by gesture a formal confirmation of the verbally expressed commitment.

80. This has also been understood as a hostile gesture; see Roberts, *Nahum*, 141, but the use of the plural "hands" would be unusual for this idiom and the context suggests that submission rather than aggression is the issue.

81. Viberg, *Symbols of Law*, 34.

82. For an extended treatment of the iconography of the handclasp, see Calabro, "Ritual Gestures," 584–611.

83. See #11.

84. Corbeill, *Nature Embodied*, 21; Brilliant, *Gesture and Rank*, 38.

#11. Two kings clasp hands in alliance. Assyrian, ninth century BC. Keel #123.

A psalmist accuses foreigners of deceitful dealing with their right hands (Ps 144:1), presumably a reference to dishonored commitments sealed with a handclasp. A proverb may allude to the handclasp gesture: "Be assured [lit.: hand to hand], the wicked will not go unpunished" (Prov 11:21). Where stretching out the hand is mentioned in the context of a compact or conspiracy, the image may be that of the hands of the two parties meeting, as when, according to Hosea, the king "stretched out his hand with mockers" (Hos 7:5), that is, joined in a conspiracy with the priests.

#12. Two men touch hands over what appear to be contract or treaty documents they are ratifying. Ras Shamra, fourteenth century BC. Keel #122.

It is against this background that we best understand the references to God taking his people or his anointed one by the hand. Through Jeremiah we learn of the new covenant: "It will not be like the covenant that I made with their ancestors when I took them by the hand to bring them out of the land of Egypt" (Jer 31:32; cf. Heb 8:9). Here "took them by the hand" followed by an infinitive of purpose, while not without overtones of guidance, is equivalent to "swore" or "made a commitment" (cf. Exod 13:11; Deut 7:8; Judg 2:1).[85] Kings liked to portray themselves as being held by the hand of their deity.[86] To be held by God's hand, then, is to be in a covenant or kinship-type alliance with him: "I am the LORD, I have called you in righteousness, I have taken you by the hand and kept you; I have given you as a covenant to the people, a light to the nations" (Isa 42:6). In particular, God pledges his commitment to his people at the exodus by a handclasp (or is simply said to hold them), undertakes to do so again in the new exodus, and pledges his commitment to faithful individuals (Pss 37:24; 41:12; 63:8; 73:23; 139:10; Isa 41:10, 13; 42:1, 6; 51:18). As the contexts for these references make clear, God's hand-holding is linked to election and its corollary, equipping for service. The wicked are specifically said to be denied God's hand (Job 8:20). All the more astonishing then is the undertaking the LORD makes with the Persian king Cyrus, "whose right hand I have grasped" to be the deliverer of his people (Isa 45:1).[87]

The clasping of hands, "the right hand of fellowship," is in the NT an expression of partnership in a gospel enterprise (Gal 2:9). Shaking (or clasping) of right hands is known in Greek and Etruscan iconography where, in contrast to bowing, it suggests social equality, and is used in greeting and farewelling as well as for the sealing of alliances.[88] The Christian right hand of fellowship may then combine elements of the classical friendship gesture and the Israelite (and wider) use of right hands in making commitments. We should note, however, that handshaking was not yet an everyday mode of greeting (cf. the holy kiss in the early church, §2.11), so its employment in the contexts Gal 2:9 envisages invests it with a more solemn significance. It speaks of equality, something Paul is keen to demonstrate in Galatians.

---

85. Calabro, "Ritual Gestures," 44–52.
86. E.g., *ANEP*, #541, #545.
87. Falk, "Gestures," 269.
88. Brilliant, *Gesture and Rank*, 18–19, 35–36; Stears, "Dead Women's Society," 126.

5.10 The Hand in Arbitration and Mediation

A further legal act involving the hand is that of an arbiter in a lawsuit, or mediator in a reconciliation process. Job laments that there is no arbiter/conciliator between God and himself "who might lay his hand on us both" (Job 9:33). Whether this gesture is pictured as demonstrating the authority of such a person or the reconciliation of the two parties is not clear.[89]

5.11 Clapping Hands in Celebration

Joy, exuberance, and celebration can be expressed by hand clapping. When Joash was crowned and anointed as king, the people "clapped their hands and shouted, 'Long live the king!'" (2 Kgs 11:12), and a psalmist urges all people to clap and shout to the LORD, "a great king over all the earth" (Ps 47:1, 2). While English translations may obscure the point, David's dancing before the LORD (2 Sam 6:14) involved hand clapping. In graphic images, even trees and rivers clap their hands in rejoicing over God's saving actions (Ps 98:8; Isa 55:12). Clapping as applause is also found in Sumerian royal hymns.[90]

5.12 The Hands in Grief, Derision, and Indignation

Various negative sentiments are also associated with clapping and other hand movements. Closely related to celebratory clapping, the gesture might sometimes be used as an expression of joy at another's downfall. The Ammonites maliciously clapped and stamped their feet at Israel's downfall (Ezek 25:6). Job envisages a personified storm lashing the wicked: "It claps its hands at them, and hisses at them" (Job 27:23; cf. Lam 2:15). Nahum pictures the response of those who witness the downfall of Assyria: "All who hear the news about you clap their hands over you" (Nah 3:19). While Rogland has argued for an interpretation of this verse which has people striking one another's hands in a pledge of united opposition to Assyria (cf. §5.9), the context suggests that Assyria is already mortally wounded, so the time for pledging opposition is past.[91] In Job 34:37, if the reading adopted by NRSV is correct, Job is accused of clapping in irreverent deri-

---

89. See Clines, *Job 1–20*, 243.
90. Fox, "Clapping Hands," 51.
91. Rogland, "Striking a Hand"; cf. Fox, "Clapping Hands," 55.

sion against God, though this interpretation is by no means certain.[92] A similar sentiment can be conveyed by shaking the fist. The prophet Zephaniah contemplates people's reaction to the devastation of Nineveh: "Everyone who passes by it hisses and shakes the fist" (Zeph 2:15) in a gesture of astonishment and scorn.

The hands may also be struck together in a display of indignation. Balak expressed his frustration with Balaam in this manner for his repeated failure to deliver the commissioned curse on Israel (Num 24:10; cf. Ezek 6:11; 21:14, 17; 22:13). A similar gesture is attested in Akkadian sources expressive of outrage. Esarhaddon reacts to his brothers' treachery with cries of woe, ripping his garments (§4.11), raging like a lion, and clapping his hands.[93] Finally Jeremiah envisages Ephraim displaying deep remorse and shame for its sins going back to its "youth" by slapping the thigh (Jer 31:19; cf. Ezek 21:12; cf. §6.1).

5.13 The Staff, Scepter, and Sword

The function of the hand can be extended with a staff, rod, or scepter, used for both ceremonial and practical purposes (for support or as a weapon: Lev 27:32; Num 22:27; Isa 10:24; Zech 8:4; Matt 10:10), or with a sword. One's staff was a very personal item, probably with identifying markings. Along with Judah's signet with its cord, his staff served to identify him as the man who had had intercourse with Tamar (Gen 38:18, 25). For rulers a staff or scepter was an emblem of authority (Gen 49:10; Num 24:17; Pss 45:6; 110:2; Ezek 19:11, 14; Amos 1:5, 8; Heb 1:8). In the Persian court the holding out of the royal scepter represented an invitation to approach the throne (Esth 4:11; 5:2; 8:4).[94] The tribal leaders of Israel had staffs representing their office, and Moses' and Aaron's staffs figure prominently in the acts of power performed in Egypt (Exod 4:3, 4, 17, 20; 7:9, 10, 17, 19, 20; 8:5, 6, 16, 17; 9:22–23; 10:12–13; 14:16; 17:9; Num 20:8, 11). God's rod and staff are reassuring emblems of his protection (Ps 23:4). Elisha gave his servant his staff to use in healing as a remote extension of the prophet's own hands (2 Kgs

---

92. See Tur-Sinai, *Job*, 488–89; for Job 34:37 *DCH* lists the word translated "claps" in this verse under five separate homophonous lemmas with very different meanings!

93. Fox, "Clapping Hands," 49–50.

94. See *ANEP*, #463 for an image of the Persian King Darius enthroned and holding a scepter.

4:29). To remove or break the staff of a ruler is a metaphor of destroying their power (Isa 14:5; Ps 89:44; Jer 48:17; Zech 10:11).

The act of drawing a sword is of course a potential threat. Joshua's sword stretched out against Ai was a ritual demonstration of that town's fate as one about to be taken in the holy war (Josh 8:18, 26). Ezekiel is instructed to prophesy against Israel, "Thus says the Lord: I am coming against you, and will draw my sword out of its sheath" (Ezek 21:3; cf. Exod 15:9; Ps 37:14; Ezek 30:25; 1 Chr 21:16).

6

The Legs and Feet

6.1 The Legs and Thighs

A NUMBER OF ASPECTS of nonverbal communication involve the legs, knees, and feet, and some idioms make reference to these body parts or to their functions.

Legs are normally a locus of strength and vigor, whereas "the legs of a disabled person hang limp," providing a point of comparison with the misuse of wisdom: "so does a proverb in the mouth of a fool" (Prov 26:7). In John's description of a mighty angel, the two features he singles out are his face and his legs which are "like pillars of fire" (Rev 10:1). The allusion may be to Exod 13:21, so suggestive of the powerful presence of God in the form of "a pillar of cloud by day" and "a pillar of fire by night." The idols of the nations are mocked because, though they have legs, they cannot walk (Ps 115:7; Jer 10:5). The following sections deal with the thighs, knees, and feet before considering the function of legs as a whole in standing, walking, running, and other movements.

The upper leg figures in a gesture of grief or shame associated with sober reflection and repentance. Ephraim acknowledges: "after I was discovered [or: became self-aware], I struck my thigh" (Jer 31:19). Ezekiel is told to strike the thigh in grief over the fate of his people (Ezek 21:12; cf. §5.12). In Arabic cultures, and indeed to some extent in the West, slapping the thigh can serve as a gesture of calling something to mind, particularly something one regrets.[1]

---

1. Barakat, "Arabic Gestures," 774; for Akkadian parallels see Gruber, *Aspects*, 380–84. The Akkadian text, *The Descent of Ishtar to the Underworld* 100 (*CoS*, 1:383), has Ereshkigal striking her thigh and biting her finger in response to an unwelcome proposition.

6.2 The Knees

Ordinarily we pay little attention to knees when persons are upright, though it is the muscles and ligaments attached to them that provide the strength for standing, walking, and running. When knees are weak or feeble they may droop, tremble, knock together, or "turn to water," betraying fear or shock (Job 4:4; Ps 109:24; Isa 35:3; Ezek 7:17; 21:7; Dan 5:6; Nah 2:10; Heb 12:12), and need to be strengthened with some form of encouragement. In the face of trying discipline, the writer to the Hebrews urges his readers, "Therefore lift your drooping hands and strengthen your weak knees, and make straight paths for your feet, so that what is lame may not be put out of joint, but rather be healed" (Heb 12:12).

To kneel or "bow the knee" in front of another is to acknowledge their position of authority and to indicate deference, adoration, or entreaty. Pharaoh had Joseph ride in the chariot of his second-in-command while the people were summoned to "bow the knee!" (Gen 41:43) in acknowledgement of Joseph's appointment to high office.[2] Because typically more than knees are involved in such deferential behavior, see §4.6 for a more detailed discussion of the postures involved.

Knees can have a tender association (cf. lap, §4.2) as a place for infants to be held by someone seated. Job laments, "Why were there knees to receive me, or breasts for me to suck?" (Job 3:12). While this could be a simple and natural indication of familial affection for a newborn, Viberg mounts a case for seeing a deeper significance in some of the references to newborns being placed on the knees. Paramount among these is Ruth 4:16 where Obed is placed on Naomi's knees. The declaration of the women, "A son has been born to Naomi" (Ruth 4:17), while not to be understood as signaling a formal adoption, serves to interpret the significance of the act in highlighting Obed's role in bringing about redemption, the reversal of Naomi's hopelessness in particular (cf. Gen 30:3; 48:5–12; 50:23; Isa 66:12).

---

2. The precise meaning and etymology of the word translated "bow the knee" here (possibly an Egyptian interjection) is uncertain, but as it shares the root letters of the Hebrew word for knee, it is likely that the Hebrew author intended to suggest an association with kneeling.

6.3 The Feet and Footwear

By NT times and probably long before, all but the poorest people wore some form of footwear when traveling, so (for those normally sandaled) to go about outdoors without footwear is to make a statement. Going barefoot is one of the outward signs of mourning (2 Sam 15:30; Mic 1:8). Ezekiel, who is forbidden to mourn, is told to wear his sandals (Ezek 24:17). Isaiah is instructed to go naked and barefoot as a prophetic sign concerning Egypt's fate at the hands of the Assyrians (Isa 20:2–4). Moses and Joshua are told to remove their footwear when approaching holy ground (Exod 3:5; Josh 5:15; Acts 7:33), and a similar custom prevails today in the Islamic world and parts of the Christian East. To wear sandals while at home eating a meal is abnormal and indicates readiness for a sudden departure, as at the first Passover (Exod 12:11). Priests performed their duties in the tabernacle and temple (sacred space) barefoot, perhaps with the symbolism that they are honored guests "at home" in God's dwelling or perhaps as an indication of submission (cf. barefoot prisoners of war).[3] Jesus sent out his disciples without (an extra pair of?) sandals (Luke 10:4; 22:35), that is, they were to be visibly without possessions (and see below for the foot as the marker of ownership and control).

To "set one's foot" on territory or other property can suggest ownership or dominion over that territory or property. The Akkadian phrase "lifting the foot" means releasing property to the ownership of another.[4] With regard to the land, Israel was promised, "Every place on which you set foot shall be yours" (Deut 11:24; cf. 1:36; 25; 28:65; Josh 1:3; Pss 8:6; 91:13). To place one's enemies under one's feet, or even to walk on them is to demonstrate their total subjection (Deut 33:29; Josh 10:24; 2 Sam 22:39; 1 Kgs 5:3; Pss 8:6; 36:11; 47:3; Isa 28:3; 41:2; 51:23; Lam 3:34; Mal 4:3; Mark 12:36; Rom 16:20; 1 Cor 15:25–28; Eph 1:22; Heb 2:8). A Hittite king requests a goddess, "Give me life, health, sons (and) daughters in the future . . . and put my enemies under my feet."[5] Pharaoh Thutmose III boasts, "Everyone on whom the sun shines is bound under my sandals," and the sandals recovered from the tomb of Tutankhamun depict the pharaoh's enemies, so that when wearing them in the afterlife he would be symbolically trampling

---

3. See Viberg, *Symbols of Law*, 162; Andersen, "Feet"; Davies, *A Royal Priesthood*, 105.

4. Lacheman, "Note."

5. Tsevat, "Two Old Testament Stories," 321.

on them.[6] As an enthroned monarch has his feet resting on a footstool (2 Chr 9:18), this item serves as a metaphor of that which is in subjection, such as the enemies of the divinely appointed king (Ps 110:1; Luke 20:43; Acts 2:35; Heb 1:13; 10:13).[7] The earth, Zion, the sanctuary, and the ark are all variously said to be God's footstool (1 Chr 28:2; Pss 99:5; 132:7; Isa 66:1; Lam 2:1; Matt 5:35; Acts 7:49).

Some customs involving the removal of a sandal, perhaps with the symbolism of the removal or transfer of power, are mentioned in Scripture. If a man refuses to marry his brother's widow, as expected in the law, she is to "pull his sandal off his foot, spit in his face, and declare, 'This is what is done to the man who does not build up his brother's house'" (Deut 25:9). A somewhat similar custom (though the details of the procedure and the nature of any legal connection remain obscure) lies behind the scene in Ruth 4, and is explained thus: "Now this was the custom in former times in Israel concerning redeeming and exchanging: to confirm a transaction, the one took off a sandal and gave it to the other; this was the manner of attesting in Israel" (Ruth 4:7).[8] In this case the transfer of sandals may have been reciprocal.

Another gesture involving feet or footwear was to "shake the dust off your feet" (Luke 9:5; cf. Matt 10:14; Mark 6:11; Luke 10:11; Acts 13:51) as one left an inhospitable or unresponsive place. It was Jewish practice to shake the dust from one's feet after leaving unclean gentile territory either as a judgment or as an indication that one had no further responsibility for the inhabitants of this region (cf. Acts 18:6; §4.11).[9] Opinions differ on the significance of God's sandal throwing in Ps 60:8 (= Ps 108:9): "Moab is my washbasin; on Edom I hurl my shoe." It is probably not so much a claim of ownership in this instance as a gesture of indifference or contempt to counter the pride of this enemy nation.

Providing the means to wash a guest's feet after a journey is the role of a good host (Gen 18:4; 19:2; 24:32; Luke 7:44). Actually to wash the feet of another is the role of a servant, but supremely demonstrated by Jesus as an example of a servant spirit (1 Sam 25:41; John 13:3-14).[10] John the Baptist

6. *The Gebel Barkal Stela of Thutmose III* 33-37a (*CoS*, 2:17); cf. Keel, #341.
7. *ANEP*, #28, #332, #371, #415-17, #463.
8. Cf. Carmichael, "A Ceremonial Crux"; Viberg, *Symbols of Law*, 145-65.
9. Keener, *Acts*, 2:2105-6; Strack and Billerbeck, *Kommentar*, 1:571.
10. Cf. the account of Odysseus's nurse washing his feet on his return from his adventures: Homer, *Odyssey*, 19:343-507.

declared himself not worthy to carry Jesus' sandals (Matt 3:11), or untie their thongs (as a prelude to washing his feet? John 1:27), both expressions of the most menial of tasks.

An idiom for treacherous behavior is to raise (lit.: enlarge) the heel, though whether based on a gesture involving the foot is not clear. The only biblical passage where the idiom occurs is Ps 41:9: "Even my bosom friend in whom I trusted, who ate of my bread, has lifted the heel against me" (and quoted in John 13:18). Another interpretation of the expression is ". . . he has woven slander," though the fact that the NT citation understands the expression as ". . . has raised his heel" suggests that at least in time there came to be an anatomical association with the idiom due to words of similar sound, and compare the play on words involved in the Jacob-Esau episode associating "heel" with Jacob's name and demonstrated character as a supplanter (Gen 25:26; 27:36).[11]

The gesture of kicking suggests rebellion or defiance. On the Damascus road, Saul heard a voice saying, "Saul, Saul, why are you persecuting me? It hurts you to kick against the goads" (Acts 26:14). Kicking against the goads was a proverbial Greek expression used, for example, by the tragedian Euripides (*Bacchae*, 794-95). There may be a reference in the Song of Moses to kicking in defiance, though the word is obscure: "Jeshurun [Israel] grew fat, and kicked" (Deut 32:15; cf. HCSB: "Then Jeshurun became fat and rebelled").

To be at the feet of someone is to adopt a lowly status, whether in a posture of obeisance (cf. §4.6) or adopting the position of a disciple in relation to a teacher (Luke 10:39; Acts 22:3). The woman who anointed Jesus' feet at a banquet approached him from behind, and by taking her position "at his feet" (Luke 7:38) already indicated her appraisal of Jesus as one to be honored. Several mentions have been made of this incident and, without a word being spoken, it is one of the most powerful statements made by someone to Jesus in the Gospels, telling of the woman's devotion and gratitude, and serving as a foil for the display of rudeness by the host.[12] Grasping the feet of another or kissing them is dealt with at §2.11; §4.6).

---

11. See עקב IV and גדל II, in *DCH*.
12. Bailey, *Through Peasant Eyes*, 6–10.

6.4 Rising and Standing

Readers of the English Bible, particularly older versions, will be struck by the number of references to persons "rising" before commencing an activity. While this might at times refer to standing up from a seated or lying position (Judg 3:20; 16:3; 2 Sam 11:2), it is a standard narrative device in Hebrew for indicating the commencement of a journey or a new action, e.g., "His servants arose, devised a conspiracy, and killed Joash" (2 Kgs 12:20). In Ezra 9:5, the physical movement initiated is downward: "At the evening sacrifice I got up from my fasting, with my garments and my mantle torn, and fell on my knees," so the function of the verb translated in NRSV as "got up" really means Ezra stopped doing one thing (fasting) and got ready or commenced another (praying) (cf. Gen 19:35; 1 Sam 25:41). In the NT, the standard word for rise is used for rising from the dead (Matt 11:5; 14:2; 27:63; John 5:2; Eph 5:14). For "rising early" cf. §4.1.

Rising can also have a hostile innuendo: "Cain rose up against his brother Abel, and killed him" (Gen 4:8; cf. Num 10:35; Deut 28:7; Judg 20:5; Ps 59:1; 86:14; 124:2; Jer 49:14; Mic 7:6; Matt 24:7; Mark 13:8; Luke 21:10). An "assailant" (Lam 3:62) is lit. "one who rises up." Sometimes, the hostility is in a judicial rather than physical context as when "the people of Nineveh will rise up at the judgment with this generation and condemn it" (Matt 12:41–42; Luke 11:31–32; cf. Matt 10:21).

While standing is, of course, an everyday occurrence in all sorts of contexts, there are some particular situations in the Bible in which standing takes on a distinctive character. When persons are said to stand still, in contrast with movement or activity, we may note the way their attention has been arrested, and are prepared for the heightened significance of any following action. When two blind men heard that Jesus was passing by, they called out and "Jesus stood still and called them, saying, 'What do you want me to do for you?'" (Matt 20:32; cf. Mark 10:49; Luke 18:40; Acts 9:7). When the risen Jesus asked the two disciples traveling to Emmaus, "What are you discussing with each other while you walk along?," we read: "they stood still, looking sad" (Luke 24:17); that is, Jesus' question stopped them in their tracks, so astonished were they that someone who had been in Jerusalem would not have heard of recent events there, and they would have to give expression of their grief to the as yet unrecognized Jesus. Likewise when the inclination would be for the tribe of Judah to take up arms, the Levite Jahaziel declares, "This battle is not for you to fight; take your position, stand still, and see the victory of the LORD on your behalf, O Judah and Jerusalem"

(2 Chr 20:17). People might also stand still as a mark of respect for the dead: "All those who came to the place where Asahel had fallen and died, stood still" (2 Sam 2:23).

Public speaking (as distinct from teaching; cf. §4.5) is typically done from a standing position, as when Paul stood to address the Areopagus (Acts 17:22). Even to address a question in a public gathering, one would first rise as did the lawyer who asked Jesus about inheriting eternal life (Luke 10:25; cf. Jer 7:2; 26:2; Acts 11:28; 13:16; 15:5, 7; 21:40; 23:9; 27:21).[13]

To cause someone to rise to a standing position after they have been overwhelmed and fallen to the ground is to restore them to full human dignity and perhaps prepare them to receive a commission or revelation, as Saul on the road to Damascus (Acts 26:16; cf. Josh 7:10; Ezek 1:28—2:1; Dan 10:9-11).

The language of standing, as with rising, can have military overtones of challenge or resistance. In the encounter of Israel with the Philistine champion, we read, "For forty days the Philistine came forward and took his stand, morning and evening" (1 Sam 17:16; cf. Num 22:22; Deut 7:24; 9:2; 11:25; Josh 1:5; 7:12, 13; Judg 2:14; 2 Sam 23:12; 2 Kgs 10:4; Pss 76:7; 147:17; Eccl 4:12; Dan 11:15; Eph 6:11-14). We note the aggressive stance of world leaders, first articulated by a psalmist (Ps 2:2) and echoed by the disciples in Acts 4:26: "The kings of the earth set themselves, and the rulers take counsel together, against the Lord and his anointed," and we note the outcome of this rebellion as the rulers eventually cry, "Who is able to stand?" (Rev 6:17; cf. Mal 3:2). There is a play on the meanings of the word "stand" in Exod 9:11: "The magicians could not stand before Moses because of the boils," meaning that the boils had debilitated them to the point where they could not stand up, and also that they lost the will to resist.

Standing then serves as a metaphor for the attainment and holding of a settled, secure position or receiving vindication. A psalmist is confident of his security in contrast with those whose trust is misplaced: "They will collapse and fall, but we shall rise and stand upright" (Ps 20:8), and believers in Christ stand firm on the basis of grace through faith (Rom 5:2; 14:4; 1 Cor 10:12; 15:1; 16:13; Gal 5:1; Phil 4:1; Col 4:12; 1 Thess 3:8; 2 Thess 2:15; 1 Pet 5:12).

Less deferential than bowing, standing up was a gesture of respect or greeting, particularly for others of equivalent or slightly higher social rank or seniority. An Egyptian text (with evident Asiatic influence) captures the

---

13. Bailey, *Through Peasant Eyes*, 35.

protocol operating in the divine realm: "The greater ones saw her; they stood up before her. The lesser ones saw her; they lay down on their bellies."[14] An Egyptian wisdom text advises, "Do not sit when another is standing, one who is older than you or greater than you in his rank."[15] The Homeric heroes Achilles and Patroclus rise to greet their guests (*Iliad* 9:192–94). Haman expected Mordecai to rise before him (Esth 5:9). Job looked back on the days when he was respected "and the aged rose up and stood" in his presence (Job 29:8; cf. Lev 19:32; Judg 3:20; Isa 49:7; Ezek 2:1).

To "stand before" one in authority, notably a king, particularly as he is envisaged seated on a throne in a royal court context, is a technical expression meaning to be in service to that one, to attend upon him. The queen of Sheba declared to Solomon, "Happy are these your servants, who continually attend [lit.: stand before] you and hear your wisdom!" (1 Kgs 10:8). The Jewish young men brought to the Babylonian court "were to be educated for three years, so that at the end of that time they could be stationed in the king's court [lit.: stand before the king]" (Dan 1:5; cf. Exod 18:13; 1 Sam 22:6; 2 Chr 10:8; 18:18; Jer 36:21; Acts 7:10).[16]

This same language is then used of the heavenly court. The prophet Micaiah claims, "I saw the LORD sitting on his throne, with all the host of heaven standing to the right and to the left of him" (2 Chr 18:18; cf. 1 Kgs 22:21; Job 1:6; 2:1; Jer 23:18, 22; Dan 7:10), and John claims to have seen "the seven angels who stand before God" (Rev 8:2; cf. Luke 1:19; Rev 7:9). The heavenly court imagery probably lies behind the descriptions of priests, levites, prophets, Rechabites, and apostles as those who "stand before the LORD" and (in contrast with those who teach) they are characteristically said to stand in the performance of their duties (Deut 10:8; 18:5, 7; 1 Kgs 17:1; 2 Chr 7:6; 20:19; 29:11; 30:27; 35:10; Jer 15:1; 19:14; 35:19; 2 Cor 2:17; Heb 10:11).

Standing is one of the postures of worship, public reading, or prayer in the Bible, as at the paradigmatic gathering of the whole people at Sinai (Exod 19:17; Lev 9:5; Deut 4:10, 11; 29:10; 1 Kgs 8:14; 2 Chr 29:26; Neh 9:3, 5; Ps 134:1; Jer 18:20; Luke 4:16). This is to be seen as an extension of the court posture of attendance upon the monarch as discussed above.[17] In

---

14. *The Legend of Astarte and the Tribute of the Sea*, col. 3 (*CoS* 1:35).

15. *Instruction of Any* 6.11-12 (*CoS*, 1:112).

16. The Akkadian equivalent, "to stand in the presence of," means "to do court service for"; Oppenheim, "Idiomatic Accadian," 258.

17. Cf. Edersheim, *The Temple*, 156; Ap Thomas, "Notes," 225-28; Gruber, *Aspects*, 154-55.

a Babylonian prayer to Marduk, the petitioner prays, "Let me stand before you always in prayer, supplication, and entreaty, / Let the fruitful peoples of a well-ordered land praise you."[18] While standing is not often mentioned in the OT as a posture specifically for prayer, Jesus presupposes a standing posture in his instructions on prayer (Mark 11:25), and (contrary to the kneeling posture sometimes imagined),[19] the tax collector in Jesus' comparison with the Pharisee at prayer was also standing (Luke 18:11–13; cf. 1 Sam 1:26; 1 Kgs 3:15; 8:22; 13:1; 19:11; 1 Chr 23:30; 2 Chr 5:14; 6:12; 7:6; 20:13, 19; Neh 8:5; 9:2; Ps 106:30; Jer 15:1; 28:5).

Those who appear before a judge, or a king, or elders functioning in a judicial capacity, or an informal self-appointed group of inquisitors stand in their presence. In making his defense before Agrippa, Paul declares, "And now I stand here on trial on account of my hope in the promise made by God to our ancestors" (Acts 26:6; cf. Num 27:2; 35:12; Deut 19:17; Josh 20:4; 1 Kgs 3:16; Zech 3:1; Matt 27:11; John 8:3; Acts 22:30; 25:10), and it will be standing room only at the last judgment, when "we will all stand before the judgment seat of God" (Rom 14:10). While sitting is the normal posture for a judge during a hearing (cf. §4.5), it would appear that a judge would stand preparatory to passing sentence (Matt 26:62; Mark 14:60), and God himself does so in his judicial capacity (Isa 3:13). It is likely that this is the significance of Stephen's description of Jesus "standing at the right hand of God." The point of altering the wording of Ps 110:1 ("Sit at my right hand") would be, as suggested by Coxhead, to make an allusion to the courtroom scene of Dan 7:10, 13–14, 26. It is the notion that Jesus is granted authority to execute judgment as Son of Man (cf. John 5:27) that provokes the crowd to fury.[20]

6.5 Walking and Running

Walking was of course the primary mode of travel in the ancient world. For those who could afford them, donkeys, mules, camels, horse-drawn chariots, and later horseback provided transport for longer distances, for military purposes or for high status ceremonial rides (Gen 22:3; 1 Sam 25:20; 2 Sam 13:29; 1 Kgs 1:38; 13:13; 2 Kgs 5:9; 9:17; Esth 6:9, Isa 21:7; Matt 21:7;

---

18. *Prayer to Marduk* 27–28 (*CoS*, 1:416).

19. See, e.g., the etching of the Pharisee and the Publican in the Temple by Gerard van Groeningen.

20. See Coxhead, "Significance."

John 12:14; Acts 8:28; 23:23). As an example of his frustrations with the world, Qoheleth observes, "I have seen slaves on horseback, and princes walking on foot like slaves" (Eccl 10:7), so (in an ideal world as Qoheleth would envisage it) walking in certain contexts does have a communicative role as a class identifier.

There are ways of walking for which English has a rich vocabulary: creeping, shuffling, strolling, ambling, sauntering, roaming, traipsing, striding, marching, and the like. Hebrew and Greek vocabularies are more limited in this respect and different modes of walking are more likely to be implied by context, but there are a couple of expressions we might note. The prophet Micah warns, "Therefore thus says the LORD: Now, I am devising against this family an evil from which you cannot remove your necks; and you shall not walk haughtily, for it will be an evil time" (Mic 2:3). Behind the metaphor is an image of people walking proudly erect with head held high. Isaiah likewise paints a picture of the women of Jerusalem who "walk with outstretched necks, glancing wantonly with their eyes, mincing along as they go, tinkling with their feet" (Isa 3:16), that is, wearing jangling anklets and drawing attention to themselves, perhaps in the manner of a prostitute, as they promenade around Jerusalem (cf. Isa 3:18).[21]

The converse is the stooped walk of humility: "The descendants of those who oppressed you shall come bending low to you" (Isa 60:14), which gives rise to the metaphorical: "He has told you, O mortal, what is good; and what does the LORD require of you but to do justice, and to love kindness, and to walk humbly with your God?" (Mic 6:8). Mourners would also walk with bowed head: "I went about as one who laments for a mother, bowed down and in mourning" (Ps 35:14).

As well as for undertaking journeys from A to B, walking might be apparently aimless. Israel's time in the wilderness was one of wandering (Num 32:13; 2 Kgs 21:8). Barré has demonstrated that walking about or wandering is a motif of depression in the Bible and other texts of Western Asia. When Ahab heard Elijah's words of prophetic condemnation, "he tore his clothes and put sackcloth over his bare flesh; he fasted, lay in the sackcloth, and went about dejectedly" (1 Kgs 21:27). The word translated "dejectedly" in NRSV is perhaps more accurately "slowly," so "straggled about" might be close to the meaning.[22] Other examples indicative of a

---

21. Greek writers also drew attention to women walking in what they considered the manner of a courtesan; see Bremmer, "Walking," 21.

22. Kruger, "Depression," 191.

depressed state (some involving a fresh understanding of the meaning of the verb as indicating aimless movement) are Gen 24:63; Judg 11:37; Job 12:24; 30:28; Pss 34:14; 38:6; 42:9; 43:2; 55:2; 107:40; Isa 15:3; Jer 49:3; Lam 3:19; and Amos 8:12.[23]

One can also walk back and forth deliberately to cover large amounts of territory, so presumably with a more determined stride. When the LORD asked the Satan, "'Where have you come from?' Satan answered the LORD, 'From going to and fro on the earth, and from walking up and down on it'" (Job 1:7). While this is variously interpreted, the verb translated "going to and fro" here suggests purposeful traversing of territory on a mission or in a quest for something (cf. Num 11:8; 2 Sam 24:8; Jer 5:1; Amos 8:12), and the form of the verb translated "walking up and down" can similarly suggest purposeful movement (Gen 13:17; Josh 18:4, 8; 2 Sam 7:6; Esth 2:11; Zech 1:10–11). One might also, like the Pharisees, promenade about in order to be seen, presumably with a slow gait (Luke 20:46).

There is then the interesting case of Gen 3:8: "They heard the sound of the LORD God walking in the garden at the time of the evening breeze, and the man and his wife hid themselves from the presence of the LORD God among the trees of the garden." This traditional English rendering suggests God was out for a pleasant evening stroll, but it is more likely that his activity suggested an inspectorial visit of his domain, which is what provokes the couple's fear.[24]

Another mode of walking is the processional walk or march. A psalmist reflects a ritual of walking around the altar as the culmination of his pilgrimage (Ps 26:6). The altar represents the presence of God, and the circumnavigation of it a form of identification with the altar and so with God. The march of the Israelites around the walls of Jericho spoke volumes to its inhabitants about their besieged and perilous condition and was designed to instill fear (Josh 6:15).

Walking provides commonplace metaphors for both life experience (including those parts of the journey over which we have no control) and lifestyle, with a focus on moral choices and religious commitment. Our life experience may take us to places we might not choose: "Even though I walk through the darkest valley, I fear no evil" (Ps 23:4; cf. Job 29:3; Pss 42:10; 84:8; Isa 50:10; John 8:12; 12:35).

---

23. See Barré, "Wandering About."
24. Kline, *Images*, 97–98.

Much of the walk idiom in the Bible concerns how we conduct ourselves. God commanded Abram: "Walk before me, and be blameless" (Gen 17:1), and there is a constant summons to Israel to walk in God's ways, or his law, or in faithfulness, or righteously, or in the light (Deut 13:5; Josh 22:5; Judg 2:22; 1 Kgs 2:4; 6:12; 8:61; Ps 26:3; Isa 2:5; 33:15; Jer 7:23). The NT perpetuates the image with its call to walk in newness of life, or in the Spirit, or by faith, or in the light, or the truth, or God's commandments (John 8:12; 12:35; Rom 6:4; 8:4; 2 Cor 5:7; 1 John 1:7; 2:6; 2 John 4, 6).

A commonplace metaphor for a trouble-free experience or for righteous living is walking in a direct line. In a Mesopotamian theodicy, the righteous sufferer is assured: "The path is straight for you, mercy is granted you."[25] In the context of moral instruction, a supervisor recounts something of his educational experience, recalling his teacher who "kept me on the straight line. He opened my mouth to all the words; he showed me the (wisest) counsels."[26] The exiles in Babylon are assured: "I will let them walk by brooks of water, in a straight path in which they shall not stumble" (Jer 31:9), and the writer to the Hebrews encourages his readers: "Make straight paths for your feet, so that what is lame may not be put out of joint, but rather be healed" (Heb 12:13; cf. Ps 107:7; Prov 14:2; 15:21; Jer 31:9; Mic 2:7; Acts 13:10; 2 Pet 2:15). To deviate from walking in a direct path is to turn to the right or the left (literal: Num 20:17; Deut 2:27; 2 Sam 2:19; metaphorical: Deut 5:32; 17:11, 20; 28:14; Josh 1:7; 2 Sam 14:19; 2 Kgs 22:2; 2 Chr 34:2; Prov 4:27; Heb 12:13). Jesus warns his disciples not to let anyone lead them astray (Matt 24:4; Mark 13:5; cf. Heb 3:10; Jas 5:19–20; 1 Pet 2:25; 2 Pet 2:15). This notion of diverting from a straight course is a pervasive ethical metaphor in many cultures. The Egyptian *Instruction of Merikare* warns of the consequence for "one who strays from god's path."[27] The English word "perverse," applied to behavior, is from Latin *perversus* "turned aside."

Following or going after leaders, human or divine, is a prevalent motif of Scripture. In an era when not only did military commanders physically lead their troops, but also prophets and teachers led their disciples when out walking, to follow a leader was more than a metaphor (Judg 9:4, 49; 1 Sam 13:7, 15; 25:27; 1 Kgs 1:35, 40; 19:20; 20:19; Mark 10:32; Acts 5:36). God led his people through the wilderness and in the holy war by means of the cloudy fiery pillar and the ark as symbols of his presence (Exod 13:21;

---

25. *Dialogue between a Man and His God* viii (CoS, 1:485).
26. *The Dialogue between a Supervisor and a Scribe* (CoS 1:590–91).
27. *CoS*, 1:63.

Josh 3:3). Jesus called people to follow him (Matt 4:19; 8:1, 22, 23; 9:9; 10:38; 12:15; 14:13; John 1:38; 21:19), and this had both literal and metaphorical significance. The idea of following can then be wholly metaphorical, and following God (or going "after" God), or avoiding following other gods, then becomes a standard expression for covenant faithfulness. Elijah challenged the people of Israel, "How long will you go limping with two different opinions? If the LORD is God, follow him; but if Baal, then follow him" (1 Kgs 18:21; cf. Num 14:43; 32:11, 12, 15; Deut 4:3; 6:14; 7:4; 8:19; 11:28; 13:2, 4; 28:14; Josh 14:8; Judg 2:12, 19; 1 Sam 12:20; 1 Kgs 11:5, 10; 14:8; Jer 3:19; Zeph 1:6; 1 Tim 5:15; 1 Pet 2:21; 2 Pet 2:15; Rev 14:4). Most graphically, we have the idiom in 1 Pet 2:21: "For to this you have been called, because Christ also suffered for you, leaving you an example, so that you should follow in his steps."

Running in contrast with walking can indicate urgency as when escape is necessary (Gen 16:6; Judg 7:21; John 10:12), or an emergency needs to be averted (Num 16:47), when a message needs to be delivered without delay (Num 11:27; 1 Sam 4:12; 2 Sam 18:19–27; Jer 51:31), or in situations of excitement (Gen 24:29; 29:13; 33:4; Matt 28:8; Mark 9:15; Acts 12:14). Competitive running was not unknown in the world of the OT (Jer 12:5), though the NT reflects the higher profile of the Hellenistic athletic games, and running becomes a metaphor for striving and endurance: "Do you not know that in a race the runners all compete, but only one receives the prize? Run in such a way that you may win it" (1 Cor 9:24, cf. v. 26; Gal 2:2; 5:7; Phil 2:16; Heb 12:1).

Servants might run or be expected to run in the performance of their masters' wishes or to show their eagerness to please. Elisha sent his servant Gehazi running to meet the Shunammite woman to inquire after her well-being (2 Kgs 4:26; cf. 1 Sam 3:5; 20:36; 1 Kgs 19:20; Acts 12:14). The running slave is a common motif of Roman comedy.[28] To run ahead of an official is to make a show of the importance of that official. In his maneuvering to take the throne, "Absalom got himself a chariot and horses, and fifty men to run ahead of him" (2 Sam 15:1; cf. 1 Sam 8:11; 1 Kgs 1:5; 18:46).

People of standing or seniority in society do not generally run, this being rather undignified, so when they do we note the heightened sense of urgency or joy at a reunion for example. As a good host, Abraham runs to attend to his unexpected visitors (Gen 18:2, 7). Peter and John, on hearing of the empty

---

28. Corbeill, *Nature Embodied*, 117.

tomb, run to investigate (Luke 24:12; John 20:4). The father of Jesus' parable runs to embrace his wayward son on his return home (Luke 15:20).[29]

Finally, to run to and fro indicates desperation. Amos tells of a coming time when there will be a famine of the word of God: "They shall wander from sea to sea, and from north to east; they shall run to and fro, seeking the word of the LORD, but they shall not find it" (Amos 8:12; cf. Jer 49:3; Dan 12:4).

6.6 Leaping, Stamping, Staggering, Limping, and Scraping

Leaping is a characteristic activity of young animals like calves or deer (Ps 29:6; Isa 35:6) but may be performed by people to express joyful enthusiasm or exuberance, as when the lover of the Song comes "leaping upon the mountains, bounding over the hills" (Song 2:8), or when king David leapt about uninhibitedly before the ark (2 Sam 6:16; 1 Chr 15:29; cf. Mal 4:2). David's confidence in his God-given ability is expressed hyperbolically as an ability to "leap over a wall" (2 Sam 22:30; Ps 18:29). When a lame man was healed at the Beautiful Gate through the agency of Peter and John, "jumping up, he stood and began to walk, and he entered the temple with them, walking and leaping and praising God" (Acts 3:8). From the way Luke profiles this incident, it has been regarded as a fulfillment of Isa 35:6 ("then the lame shall leap like a deer), symbolizing the transition of Israel from lameness to praise.[30] In Jesus' teaching, paradoxically his disciples are exhorted, when they experience persecution, to "Rejoice in that day and leap for joy, for surely your reward is great in heaven" (Luke 6:23).

Stamping the feet is found only at Ezek 6:11 and 25:6. In the former it accompanies clapping the hands (cf. §5.12), which in context suggests an expression of grief and anger at Israel's deserved fate. Ezek 25:6 is an oracle directed against the Ammonites for clapping and stamping their feet against Israel. The implication is that the Ammonites are performing gestures of gloating and mock grief.

Staggering or reeling is the erratic movement of someone struggling with a heavy load (Lam 5:13) or more commonly one under the influence of alcohol, either literally (Isa 28:7), or as an image for someone in confusion or distress, as in Isaiah's graphic image of the Egyptians: "The LORD has poured into them a spirit of confusion; and they have made Egypt stagger

---

29. Bailey, *Poet and Peasant*, 181.
30. Hamm, "Acts 3:1–10."

in all its doings as a drunkard staggers around in vomit" (Isa 19:14; cf. Job 12:25; Isa 24:20; 28:7; 29:9; Jer 25:16; Hab 2:16).

The frantic activity of the prophets of Baal around his altar as they called on their god to hear them is sometimes translated "limping" (1 Kgs 18:26), though perhaps an ungainly lurching movement is closer to the intended picture. This same verb is used metaphorically in Elijah's challenge to the Israelites, "How long will you go limping with two different opinions? If the LORD is God, follow him; but if Baal, then follow him" (1 Kgs 18:21).

If walking straight is an image of regular progression in life, particularly with moral rectitude, then to stumble, slip, or falter is to think or behave inappropriately or to meet with trouble. A psalmist declares, "My steps have held fast to your paths; my feet have not slipped" (Ps 17:5; cf. Deut 32:35; 2 Sam 22:37; Pss 18:36; 73:2, 18; Prov 3:23; 24:17; Isa 3:8; 59:10; 63:13; Jer 6:15, 21; 8:12; 18:15, 23; 20:11; 31:9; Ezek 33:12; Hos 14:9; Matt 18:8-9; Luke 17:2; John 11:9-10; Rom 9:32-33; 1 Pet 2:8; 2 Pet 1:10).

Finally, a proverb regards a foot movement as a telltale sign of one intent on causing trouble: "winking the eyes, shuffling [or: scraping] the feet, pointing the fingers, with perverted mind devising evil, continually sowing discord" (Prov 6:13-14; cf. §3.1; §5.4). We cannot be certain of the precise foot movement intended, and in any case it is an impressionistic composite portrait of one whose external characteristics betray the inner character flaw of a "scoundrel and a villain" (v. 12).

6.7 Proxemics

As noted in the Introduction, how close or far apart people position themselves in relation to each other as they stand or move (proxemics) has communicative value. Jacob's elaborate tactic in dividing his family into groups and keeping some distance between them as they approached his brother Esau is an indication of Jacob's level of apprehension, but in turn they each "drew near" as required by the act of entreaty (Gen 33:1-7; cf. Gen 18:23; 44:18; 2 Kgs 5:13).

When Elijah "called" (rather than "spoke") to the widow of Zarephath (1 Kgs 17:10), it suggests (by the implied volume of the utterance) that he kept an acceptable distance (public distance) from an unaccompanied woman rather than intrude upon her social or personal space.[31] To "come close" often signals that a significant discussion is to ensue, perhaps one

---

31. Davies, *1 Kings*, 322.

requiring a major decision, as when Elijah called on the people to desist from their compromise with Baalism, or summoned them to come close as he repaired the Lord's altar (1 Kgs 18:21, 30; cf. Gen 18:23; 27:21; 45:4; Josh 21:1; 1 Sam 14:38; 1 Kgs 20:22, 28; 2 Kgs 2:5; 5:13; Jer 42:1; Isa 41:1, 50:8; Joel 4:9; Luke 18:40; 24:15). More generally, expressions of physical proximity or aloofness serve as a gauge of the level of affinity or estrangement of two parties. According to the proverb, "a true friend sticks closer than one's nearest kin" (Prov 18:24), and when two people "walk together" we assume it is by agreement (Amos 3:3). Job laments the shunning and contempt he now experiences in contrast with the high regard in which he was once held: "They abhor me, they keep aloof from me; they do not hesitate to spit at the sight of me" (Job 30:10; cf. 2 Sam 18:13; Ps 38:11).

In Jesus' comparison of the Pharisee and the tax collector, the Pharisee's "standing by himself" suggests that he positioned himself aloof from other worshipers either in order to be noticed, or to avoid defilement under the stringent pharisaic code of purity.[32] There is also possibly a *double entendre* as the Pharisee's prayer could be read as being offered "to himself."[33] On the other hand, the tax collector, "standing far off" (Luke 18:10–14), wished to be inconspicuous out of a sense of shame or humility (though he is noticed and remarked upon by the Pharisee). While both men endeavor to put some distance between themselves and the congregation, the context makes clear it is for diametrically opposite reasons. The one considers the congregation unworthy of his association with it; the other considers himself to be the unworthy one.

The Parable of the Good Samaritan relies on our understanding of the attitude of the priest and the levite when they "passed by on the other side," and of the Samaritan who "came near" the unconscious man on the road to Jericho (Luke 10:31–33). In the case of the priest we know that by Jewish oral law concerning priestly defilement, he would have kept at least four cubits away from the man in order to avoid contamination with what gave every indication of being a dead body.[34] The action of the father of the prodigal in spotting and running to his son "while he was still far off" (Luke 15:20) speaks volumes of the father's never-ceasing vigilance and love.

The story of Ruth can be viewed from the perspective of proxemics. Ruth, a Moabitess, movingly pledges not to be separated from her

32. Bailey, *Through Peasant Eyes*, 142–56.
33. Plummer, *Luke*, 416.
34. Bailey, *Through Peasant Eyes*, 45.

mother-in-law Naomi even in death (Ruth 1:16–17). Coming with her to Naomi's home town of Bethlehem with few prospects, she gleans for food, alone "behind the reapers" (2:3), but is soon invited to "keep close" to Boaz's servant girls (2:8), then to "come here" to join in the communal meal, sitting "beside the reapers" (2:14). Boaz turns out to be a relative (lit.: close one) of her mother-in-law (2:20), and Ruth's dealings with him rapidly progress from lying "at his feet" on the threshing floor (3:8) to the point when, shortly thereafter, they "came together" in marriage (4:13).[35]

The proxemics of Jesus in relation to his disciples in his final hours are informative. Entering the Garden with the eleven, he soon leaves most of them, taking with him his inner circle of Peter, James, and John. He then leaves these three, going on further to pray alone, and returns three times to find them asleep (Matt 26:36–46; Mark 14:32–42; cf. Luke 22:40–46). Jesus' repeated physical removal from his disciples while he undergoes this agonized time of testing contrasts with the disciples' total passivity and weakness, a prelude to their abandonment of him, and underscores the fact that Jesus must experience this "cup" alone. Shortly after, as Jesus breathed his last, "all his acquaintances, including the women who had followed him from Galilee, stood at a distance, watching these things" (Luke 23:49; cf. Matt 27:55; Mark 15:40).

Relationships with God can be expressed by an extension of the near–far dynamic of human relationships. A psalmist laments what he perceives as God's inaccessibility: "Why, O LORD, do you stand far off?" (Ps 10:1; cf. Pss 22:1, 11, 19; 31:22; 35:22; 38:21; 71:12; Jer 23:23). Moses is drawn to the burning bush, but is warned to "come no closer" upon the ground made holy by God's presence (Exod 3:5). The Sinai encounter of God with Israel has a complex set of proxemic tensions as Israel is instructed to keep at a safe distance from God while Moses and others approach him by degrees (Exod 19; 24; 34).[36] Through the symbolism of Israel's worship, priests are those who "draw near" to God (Lev 9:7; Ezek 43:19), which points to the reality that "The LORD is near to all who call on him, to all who call on him in truth" (Ps 145:18), while believers are assured, "But now in Christ Jesus you who once were far off have been brought near by the blood of Christ" (Eph 2:13; cf. Jas 4:8).

---

35. Cf. Kruger, "'Nonverbal Communication' in the Hebrew Bible," 157–60.
36. See Davies, *A Royal Priesthood*, 103–37.

7

Conclusion

THE FOREGOING CHAPTERS HAVE outlined something of the rich tapestry of nonverbal communication described or alluded to in the Bible. It is to be hoped that this discussion has gone some way towards redressing the relative neglect of this topic by general readers of the Bible and the limited attention it has been given by many scholars. Much of the Western tradition of Bible reading and exegesis has focussed on its verbal and propositional content—the things said by its characters, the observations of its narrators, poets and prophets, the teachings of Jesus and the theological and ethical discourse of the apostles. There has been a suspicion that gesture and posture are second-rate conveyers of meaning. As Kruger remarks, "The term 'nonverbal communication,' which is mostly used to denote this manner of communication, reflects our 'logocentric' bias."[1]

One of the important aspects of biblical research of the past couple of generations has been the application of literary approaches to the study of the Bible. Among other things, this has led to a focus on dialogue and a recognition of its significance for highlighting the message of the biblical texts.[2] Slower to make an impact on biblical studies have been the advances in the social scientific study of nonverbal communication, though, as noted throughout, there is a growing number of specialist studies in this area.

As the designation "nonverbal communication" implies, gestures, postures, and the like convey meaning. There are no wasted references to gesture in the Bible. We have noted that gestures are frequently depicted as accompaniments of speech. Speakers may rise to speak, raise a hand, look at their listeners, pause for a response, show their reactions in their faces, or fall to the ground with expressions of dismay, adoration, or entreaty.

1. Kruger, "'Nonverbal Communication' in the Hebrew Bible," 142.
2. See e.g., Alter, *Art*, 63–87; Berlin, *Poetics*, 64–72; Bar-Efrat, *Narrative Art*, 64–77.

CONCLUSION

Sometimes, such actions may serve to give an interpretive context for speech, steering us away from possible misinterpretation of what is said.[3] When Jephthah meets his daughter after his rash vow, we might be inclined to interpret his words to her, "You have brought me very low; you have become the cause of great trouble to me" (Judg 11:35), as words of blame, but his act of tearing his clothes suggests we need to read them as words of bitter grief. When Obadiah encounters Elijah on the road and asks, "Is it you, my lord Elijah?" (1 Kgs 18:7), we know he is not having trouble recognizing the senior prophet. Obadiah's action of falling down before him tells the reader to interpret his words as those of relief, bordering on disbelief, at seeing the prophet who has been long absent from the kingdom and much needed to bring an end to the drought. Elijah's words to the prophets of Baal, "Surely he is a god" (1 Kgs 18:27) are to be read in the light of the information supplied to the reader that this was said in mockery, so perhaps indicated to the listeners by tone of voice (cf. 2 Sam 6:20; Mark 7:9). The action of Saul in tearing the hem of Samuel's robe (1 Sam 15:27), far from annoying him, is what persuades Samuel to accede to Saul's repeated request which he has previously refused (cf. §4.11). The gesture tells Samuel (and the reader) that Saul's words are now to be understood as being uttered with a sincere humility. We might also detect in the prophet Micaiah's words to the king of Israel a tongue-in-cheek tone or facial expression as he mimicked the advice of the other prophets (1 Kgs 22:15–16). The king, at least, seems to have picked up the communicative dissonance between the words uttered and the prophet's real intended message.

Sometimes a gesture alone speaks volumes. A penetrating look may be all that is needed to provoke a response. Some actions, such as laughter or weeping, throwing dust on one's head, tearing one's clothes, or even failing to do so when this would be expected, function *in lieu* of words to convey a mood, a response to a situation, and hence, perhaps, an insight into character.

Some gestures are performative: that is, they effect a change, perhaps legal or relational. Just as in a modern auction, to raise a hand in an oath-taking context was to make a binding commitment. Less familiar to us would be the functions of placing a hand under the thigh, or removing and transferring a sandal. A scepter held out or withheld could signal the difference between life and death.

---

3. On the semantic interaction of gesture and speech, see Friedman, "Modification."

The foregoing study has not been insensitive to the fact that not all of the references to body movement, even in narrative, are necessarily photo-realistic. Writers are at liberty to interpret and portray their characters, even historical characters, according to literary conventions. If we know that God does not literally raise his hand or make his face shine, we might hesitate before insisting that all references to the gestures of human characters must be so understood. Presumably vassal rulers did not actually prostrate themselves multiple times in the act of writing a letter to their suzerain, so some narrative references to prostration may also be taken as a literary convention. Do all references to trembling denote involuntary physical shaking? Perhaps not. Descriptions of nonverbal behavior may be included to indicate the affective or performative intent of the action described (swearing, being favorably disposed, holding in high regard, being apprehensive). Many gesture references have become idioms, though unlike some scholars such as Gruber, I have not felt it important (or even possible) to sort out in each case exactly which references are intended literally.

We are also conscious that only a small percentage of the gestures and body language which may be assumed to be present in any conversation can be recorded via the medium of text. Written language is not subtle enough to convey the range of degrees of smiling, for example, or how high one lifts one's head, or the duration of a handclasp. It will not always be clear from the vocabulary employed whether a look is a mere glance, a penetrating scrutiny, a disdainful glare, or an admiring gaze, but context will generally narrow the possibilities down considerably. On the other hand, as noted in the Introduction, the biblical writers have selected for us those gestures they deem significant for an understanding of the encounter and, in their economy of language, have left us to picture others.

There can be deliberate dissimulation in nonverbal language as with verbal—David feigning madness (1 Sam 21:13), Amnon faking illness (2 Sam 13:6), or the "wise woman" of Tekoa who, at Joab's prompting, pretended to be in mourning (2 Sam 14:2-4). Israel's prophets denounce the people's sham show of repentance (e.g., Jer 3:10), and the apostle Paul speaks of those "who boast in outward appearance [lit.: in face] and not in the heart" (2 Cor 5:12). Body language, like spoken language, may be ignored, as when people fail to take notice of God's raised hand (Isa 26:11). It is also susceptible to ambiguity and misinterpretation. Job's friends wag their heads in sympathy, but Job chooses to interpret this as mockery (Job

16:4).[4] When Haman petitioned queen Esther for his life, his act of throwing himself on the couch as an act of supplication was interpreted as a sexual assault (Esth 7:7-8). More work remains to be done on the possible instances of *double entendre* in gesture description.

Though many of the metaphors and idioms of Scripture, used in all of its genres, have their origin in body language, the bulk of the examples in the foregoing study are drawn from the narrative portions of Scripture. Relevant information is lost if we ignore the rubrics surrounding dialogue. By paying attention to descriptions of bodies, their placement, their dress, their gestures—even at times their silence and lack of action—our reading of the Bible takes on new dimensions. The Bible's characters are not presented as third-rate actors, delivering their lines deadpan. They can speak with passion, beating their breasts, ripping their clothes, sobbing their hearts out, tearing their hair out, or sinking to their knees to grasp the feet of one whom they adore, or whom they hope will attend to their pleas. At times they are lost for words and at times they choke back their tears. Some put on airs; others care little for their dignity. Some just want to cover their heads in shame or grief, or shrink off into a corner.

What is more, just as in the Bible God deigns to communicate with humans in human language, so his emotions and inner thoughts are characterized through the idioms of human body language. God can be near or far off, can sit or stand, smile, bare a threatening arm, breathe out, whistle, laugh, display a face inflamed with anger, gnash his teeth, and avert or direct his gaze where he wills. He can walk about, and toss off his sandals, and rest his feet on his footstool. He can take people by the hand, lift them up in his arms, and press them to his cheek. Such language serves the theological purpose of presenting God as both transcendent and immanent: as one to be feared, and yet as one with whom humans can be in a close relationship.

While much of the gesture description in the Bible is culturally specific, a great deal is common to humanity and (as with linguistic expressions) we can, through immersion in the text and comparative study of literature and iconography, learn to read the less familiar ones. As we do so, the actions of the characters serve as a mirror in which we may see ourselves. Even though we might express our attitudes and emotions in a different idiom, we enter into their joys and sorrows, their fear and shame, and contemplate our own responses to the complex situations in which we find ourselves.

4. See Clines, *Job 1–20*, 379.

We might also discern a parenetic value in gesture description in the Bible. By recording the physical reactions of the participants in a dialogue, the writers are subtly telling their readers how they *ought* to feel. Death is an ugly intrusion into a world created "good," and (whether or not we rip our t-shirts or drop to the floor) the writers would expect us to respond to the pain and grief of the human condition. We may not tear out the hair of those who violate God's laws as Nehemiah did, but it ought to distress us when those who claim to be the people of God sit loose to his standards of behavior. Paul's injunction, "Let your gentleness be known to everyone" (Phil 4:5) is presumably also, in part at least, to be demonstrated through our nonverbal responses.

There are also ways in which the biblical writers subvert their prevailing culture. One of the functions of nonverbal communication in any culture is the marking and maintaining of social distinctions (gender, class, office, ethnicity, etc.). While not all such distinctions are abolished by any means, there are subtle ways in which the distinctions of rank, for example, begin to be leveled out. Followers of Jesus are not to be concerned with the protocols of observing social status, or flaunting their wealth, or privileging it in others, or making a show of their piety in order to gain respect. Jesus' injunction to his disciples not to spend time in the customary greetings of those they encounter on their mission journey (Luke 10:4) suggests that kingdom proclamation takes precedence over social convention. The "holy kiss," enjoined upon members of the early church, extended what was primarily a family greeting to the new family of believers and in the process subverted the bowing etiquette (which served to reinforce rank) still operating in the wider society. Society's marginalized are enfolded into the community of faith, not least through gesture. Paul urges a Christian slave owner, "Welcome [your runaway slave] as you would welcome me" (Philem 17; cf. §4.6; §5.6 for the gestural character of welcoming).

Another function of nonverbal communication is the marking of liminal stages in life. Marriage, for example, has its markers of dress, festive eating, and movement as the bride is led to the bridegroom's house. Formal periods of mourning, likewise, could be marked by removal of status-specific clothing and donning mourning garments, lack of grooming, the application of dust, and in the case of a monarch, vacating the throne, which is then followed by a reversal of these markers and a reintegration into normal life (e.g., 2 Sam 12).[5]

---

5. Kruger, "'Nonverbal Communication' in the Hebrew Bible," 156–57.

CONCLUSION

Do the biblical writers make use of idiosyncratic patterns of gesture as a means of characterization? The Bible is not generally regarded as strong on overt character development, so we may not expect to see marked differences in the portrayal of its *personae* based on gesture or body language.[6] Some people are naturally more demonstrative than others. Michal thought that David was being embarrassingly exhibitionist in his dancing (2 Sam 6:16), but this is more a comment on how she felt he ought to behave as king. It is possible that Joseph is consciously depicted as more emotional than others. Though his emotions on recognizing his brothers are initially hidden from them, the reader is made aware of his secret weeping on more than one occasion (Gen 42:24; 43:30), and after his self-disclosure, twice we are told that as he wept he "fell on the neck" of a family member (not a common expression), first his brother Benjamin, and later his father. In the latter case the word neck is repeated as, after falling on his father's neck, the weeping is again said to be "on his neck" and for "a good while" (Gen 45:14; 46:29). However, it is equally possible that the lavish tears and gestures described are the author's way of drawing our attention to the highly emotional situation rather than an observation regarding the personalities of the characters. Apart from a few instances such as these where we may detect a heightened employment of body language, we do not observe in the written text much in the way of the subtle variations in gesture (analogous to idiolect in speech) which humans naturally exhibit. A rare instance where a direct comparison is made regarding the intensity of emotional display is when David and Jonathan part company and we are told that David's weeping was the more intense (1 Sam 20:41).

Finally, as the public reading or "performance" of Scripture was from the beginning a primary mode of its reception, and perhaps much of it was written with this in mind (Exod 24:7; Deut 31:11; Josh 8:34–35; 2 Kgs 22:8–10; 23:2; 2 Chr 34:18; 34:30; Ezra 4:18, 23; Neh 8:3, 8, 18; 9:3; 13:1; Jer 36:5–23; 51:61, 63; Luke 4:16; Acts 13:15, 27; 15:21; 2 Cor 3:14; Col 4:16; 1 Thess 5:27; 1 Tim 4:13; Rev 22:18),[7] we are hardly to imagine this reading being done robotically. Nonverbal cues in the text may function as rubrics for the reader or performer, so that when the text indicates that

---

6. For biblical characterization in general, see Alter, *Art*, 114–130; Bar-Efrat, *Narrative Art*, 47–92.

7. By "performance" I am not necessarily implying delivery from memory; for performance criticism and ancient reading practice see, e.g., Rhoads, "Performance Criticism"; Johnson and Parker, *Ancient Literacies*; Hurtado, "Oral Fixation"; Nässelqvist, *Public Reading*.

someone looked up as they spoke (Mark 7:34; 8:24; Luke 19:5; John 11:41; John 17:1), we expect an accomplished reader to raise her head in delivering the content of the speech. To read the words of mocking lament over Jerusalem, "Is this the city that was called the perfection of beauty, the joy of all the earth?" without the indicated shaking of the head (Lam 2:15), would be an impoverished reading. We might similarly expect the anger (Gen 30:2; Matt 26:8; Mark 3:5; 10:14; Luke 14:21), or amazement (Matt 9:33; 13:54; Mark 10:26; Luke 8:25; Acts 9:21), or fear (Gen 27:33; Matt 27:54; Acts 10:4; 24:25) identified in the speaker to be reflected in the facial expression and tone of voice of the skilled reader.

Much more remains to be said on the topic of nonverbal communication in the Bible, but it is to be hoped that this general survey will stimulate further reflection and lead to an enhanced appreciation of its literary subtlety and the profundity of its message.

Bibliography

Aldrete, Gregory S. *Gestures and Acclamations in Ancient Rome*. Baltimore: Johns Hopkins University Press, 1999.
Allegro, John M. "The Meaning of the Phrase *šeṯūm hā 'ayin* in Num 24:3, 15." *VT* 3 (1953) 78–79.
Allen, Leslie C. *Psalms 101–150*. WBC. Waco, TX: Word, 1983.
Alter, Robert. *The Art of Biblical Narrative*. New York: Basic, 1981.
Andersen, Francis I. "Feet in Ancient Times." *Buried History* 35, no. 2 (1999) 9–20.
Andersen, Francis I., and David Noel Freedman. *Hosea: A New Translation with Introduction and Commentary*. AB. Garden City, NY: Doubleday, 1980.
Ap Thomas, D. R. "Notes on Some Terms Relating to Prayer." *VT* 6 (1956) 225–41.
Babut, Jean-Marc. *Idiomatic Expressions of the Hebrew Bible: Their Meaning and Translation through Componential Analysis*. North Richland Hills, TX: BIBAL, 2003.
Bailey, Kenneth E. *Paul through Mediterranean Eyes: Cultural Studies in 1 Corinthians*. Downers Grove, IL: IVP Academic, 2011.
———. *Poet and Peasant: A Literary Cultural Approach to the Parables in Luke*. Grand Rapids: Eerdmans, 1975.
———. *Through Peasant Eyes: More Lucan Parables, Their Culture and Style*. Grand Rapids: Eerdmans, 1980.
Bar-Efrat, Shimon. *Narrative Art in the Bible*. Rev. ed. London: T. & T. Clark, 2004.
Barakat, Robert A. "Arabic Gestures." *Journal of Popular Culture* 6 (1973) 749–87.
Barré, Michael L. "'Wandering About' as a Topos of Depression in Ancient Near Eastern Literature and in the Bible." *JNES* 60 (2001) 177–87.
Beasley-Murray, George R. *John*. WBC. Waco, TX: Word, 1987.
Bentley Hart, David. *The Story of Christianity: A History of 2,000 Years of the Christian Faith*. London: Quercus, 2009.
Bergsma, John Sietze, and Scott Walker Hahn. "Noah's Nakedness and the Curse on Canaan (Genesis 9:20–27)." *JBL* 124 (2005) 25–40.
Berlin, Adele. *Poetics and Interpretation of Biblical Narrative*. Winona Lake, IN: Eisenbrauns, 1994.
Blenkinsopp, J. *Ezra-Nehemiah: A Commentary*. OTL. Philadelphia: Westminster, 1988.
Block, Daniel I. *The Book of Ezekiel, Chapters 1–24*. NICOT. Grand Rapids: Eerdmans, 1997.
Bosworth, David A. "Weeping in the Psalms." *VT* 63 (2013) 36–46.

BIBLIOGRAPHY

Botha, J. Eugene. "Exploring Gesture and Nonverbal Communication in the Bible and the Ancient World: Some Initial Observations." *Neotestamentica* 30 (1996) 1–19.

Bremmer, Jan. "Walking, Standing, and Sitting in Ancient Greek Culture." In *A Cultural History of Gesture*, edited by Jan Bremmer and Herman Roodenburg, 15–35. Ithaca, NY: Cornell University Press, 1992.

Brenner, Athalya. "Who's Afraid of Feminist Criticism? Who's Afraid of Biblical Humour? The Case of the Obtuse Foreign Ruler in the Hebrew Bible." In *Prophets and Daniel*, edited by Athalya Brenner, 228–44. A Feminist Companion to the Bible [Second Series]. Sheffield, UK: Sheffield Academic Press, 2001.

Bridge, Edward J. "The 'Slave' Is the 'Master': Jacob's Servile Language to Esau in Genesis 33.1–17." *JSOT* 39 (2014) 263–78.

Brilliant, Richard. *Gesture and Rank in Roman Art: The Use of Gestures to Denote Status in Roman Sculpture and Coinage*. Memoirs of the Connecticut Academy of Arts and Sciences 14 (1963).

Bryce, Glendon E. "Omen-Wisdom in Ancient Israel." *JBL* 94 (1975) 19–37.

Burke, David. "Gesture." In *The International Standard Bible Encyclopedia*, edited by Geoffrey W. Bromiley, 2:449–57. Grand Rapids: Eerdmans, 1982.

Bush, Frederic W. *Ruth, Esther*. WBC. Dallas, TX: Word, 1996.

Cairns, Douglas, ed. *Body Language in the Greek and Roman Worlds*. Swansea: Classical Press of Wales, 2005.

Calabro, David Michael. "Ritual Gestures of Lifting, Extending, and Clasping the Hand(s) in Northwest Semitic Literature and Iconography." PhD diss., University of Chicago, 2014.

———. "'When You Spread Your Palms, I Will Hide My Eyes': The Symbolism of Body Gestures in Isaiah." *Studia Antiqua* 9 (2011) 16–32.

Campbell, Edward F. *Ruth: A New Translation with Introduction, Notes, and Commentary*. AB. London: Doubleday, 1973.

Carmichael, Calum M. "A Ceremonial Crux: Removing a Man's Sandal as a Female Gesture of Contempt." *JBL* 96 (1977) 321–36.

Cheung, Alex T. M. "The Priest as the Redeemed Man: A Biblical-theological Study of the Priesthood." *JETS* 29 (1986) 265–75.

Chun, S. Min. "Whose Cloak Did Ahijah Seize and Tear? A Note on 1 Kings xi 29–30." *VT* 56 (2006) 268–74.

Clark, Christina A., et al., eds. *Kinesis: The Ancient Depiction of Gesture, Motion, and Emotion; Essays for Donald Lateiner*. Ann Arbor, MI: University of Michigan Press, 2015.

Clarke, Adam. *The Holy Bible Containing the Old and New Testament with a Commentary and Critical Notes*. Rev. ed. by Thornley Smith. London: Ward, Lock & Co., no date.

Clines, David J. A. *Job 1–20*. WBC. Dallas, TX: Word, 1989.

Cohen, Jeffrey M. "An Unrecognized Connotation of *nśq peh* with Special Reference to Three Biblical Occurrences." *VT* 32 (1982) 416–24.

Collins, T. "The Physiology of Tears in the Old Testament." *CBQ* 33 (1971) Part I, 18–38; Part II, 185–97.

Conklin, Blane. *Oath Formulas in Biblical Hebrew*. Winona Lake, IN: Eisenbrauns, 2011.

Corbeill, Anthony. *Nature Embodied: Gesture in Ancient Rome*. Princeton: Princeton University Press, 2004.

Cotterell, Peter, and Max Turner. *Linguistics and Biblical Interpretation*. London: SPCK, 1989.

Coxhead, Steven. "The Significance of Jesus Standing in Acts 7:55–56." http://berithroad.blogspot.com.au/2010/04/jesus-standing-in-acts-7-55-56.html.

Darwin, Charles. *The Expression of the Emotions in Man and Animals*. London: John Murray, 1872.

Daube, David. *The New Testament and Rabbinic Judaism*. London: Athlone, 1956.

Davies, Glenys. "The Significance of the Handshake Motif in Classical Funerary Art." *American Journal of Archaeology* 89 (1985) 627–40.

Davies, John A. *A Royal Priesthood: Literary and Intertextual Perspectives on an Image of Israel in Exodus 19:6*. JSOTS 395. London: T. & T. Clark International, 2004.

———. *A Study Commentary on 1 Kings*. EP Study Commentary. Faverdale North, UK: EP, 2012.

Day, John N. "'Coals of Fire' in Romans 12:19–20." *Bibliotheca Sacra* 160 (2003) 414–20.

Dewald, Carolyn, and Rachel Kitzinger. "Speaking Silences in Herodotus and Sophocles." In *Kinesis: The Ancient Depiction of Gesture, Motion, and Emotion; Essays for Donald Lateiner*, edited by Christina A. Clark et al., 86–102. Ann Arbor, MI: University of Michigan Press, 2015.

Dewrell, Heath. "How Tamar's Veil Became Joseph's Coat." *Biblica* 97 (2016) 161–73.

Dhorme, Edouard. *L'emploi métaphorique des noms de parties du corps en hébreu et en akkadien*. Paris: Librairie Victor Lecoffre, 1923.

Doidge, Norman. *The Brain's Way of Healing: Remarkable Discoveries and Recoveries from the Frontiers of Neuroplasticity*. Melbourne: Scribe, 2015.

Draffkorn Kilmer, Anne. "Symbolic Gestures in Akkadian Contracts from Alalakh and Ugarit." *JAOS* 94 (1974) 177–83.

Dunn, J. D. G. *The Theology of Paul the Apostle*. Grand Rapids: Eerdmans, 1998.

Durham, John I. *Exodus*. WBC. Waco, TX: Word, 1987.

Edersheim, Alfred. *The Temple: Its Ministry and Services as They Were at the Time of Jesus Christ*. Grand Rapids: Eerdmans, 1958.

Emerton, J. A. "Looking on One's Enemies." *VT* 51 (2001) 186–96.

Evans, Craig A. *Mark 8:27—16:20*. WBC. Nashville: Thomas Nelson, 2001.

Falk, Ze'ev W. "Gestures Expressing Affirmation." *Journal of Semitic Studies* 4 (1959) 268–69.

Fee, Gordon D. *The First Epistle to the Corinthians*. NICNT. Grand Rapids: Eerdmans, 1987.

Ferguson, Everett. "Jewish and Christian Ordination: Some Observations." *HTR* 56 (1963) 13–19.

Finley, T. J. "'The Apple of His Eye' (*bābat 'ênô*) in Zechariah ii 12." *VT* 38 (1988) 337–38.

Fleming, Daniel E. "Anointing." In *Dictionary of the Old Testament Historical Books*, edited by Bill T. Arnold and H. G. M. Williamson, 32–36. Leicester, UK: Inter-Varsity, 2005.

———. "The Biblical Tradition of Anointing Priests." *JBL* 117 (1998) 401–14.

Flusser, D. "Healing through the Laying-on of Hands in a Dead Sea Scroll." *IEJ* 7 (1957) 107–8.

Foreman, Benjamin A. "Strike the Tongue: Silencing the Prophet in Jeremiah 18:18b." *VT* 59 (2009) 653–57.

Fox, Nili S. "Clapping Hands as a Gesture of Anguish and Anger in Mesopotamia and in Israel." *JANES* 23 (1995) 49–60.

Frechette, Christopher G. *Mesopotamian Ritual-Prayers of "Hand-Lifting" (Akkadian Suillas): An Investigation of Function in Light of the Idiomatic Meaning of the Rubric*. AOAT 379. Münster: Ugarit-Verlag, 2012.

Freedman, R. D. "'Put Your Hand under My Thigh'—The Patriarchal Oath." *Biblical Archaeology Review* 2 (1976) 3–4, 42.

Friebel, Kelvin G. *Jeremiah's and Ezekiel's Sign-Acts: Rhetorical Nonverbal Communication.* Sheffield, UK: Sheffield Academic Press, 1999.

Friedman, Howard S. "The Modification of Word Meaning by Nonverbal Cues." In *Nonverbal Communication Today*, edited by Mary Ritchie Key, 57–67. Berlin: Mouton, 1982.

Frye, J. K. *FIND: Frye's Index to Nonverbal Data.* Duluth: University of Minnesota, 1980.

Garland, David E. *1 Corinthians.* Grand Rapids: Baker Academic, 2003.

Gillmayr-Bucher, Susanne. "Body Images in the Psalms." *JSOT* 83 (2004) 301–26.

Giuentella, A. M. "Orans." In *Encyclopedia of Ancient Christianity*, edited by Angelo di Berardino, 972–73. Downers Grove, IL: IVP Academic, 2014.

Glazov, Gregory Yuri. "The Significance of the 'Hand on the Mouth' Gesture in Job xl 4." *VT* 52 (2002) 30–41.

Gordis, Robert. *The Book of Job: Commentary, New Translation and Special Studies.* New York: Jewish Theological Seminary, 1978.

Gorman, F. H. *The Ideology of Ritual: Space, Time and Status in the Priestly Theology.* JSOTS 91. Sheffield, UK: Sheffield Academic Press, 1990.

Graf, Fritz. "Gestures and Conventions: The Gestures of Roman Actors and Orators." In *A Cultural History of Gesture*, edited by J. Bremmer and J. Roodenburg, 36–58. Ithaca, NY: Cornell University Press, 1986.

Greenberg, Moshe. "On Ezekiel's Dumbness." *JBL* 77 (1958) 101–5.

Greenstein, Edward L. "'To Grasp the Hem' in Ugaritic Literature." *VT* 32 (1982) 217–18.

Grice, E. P. "Meaning." *Philosophical Review* 66 (1957) 377–88.

Griffin, Jeffery D. "An Investigation of Idiomatic Expressions in the Hebrew Bible with a Case Study of Anatomical Idioms." PhD diss., Mid-America Baptist Theological Seminary, 1998.

Gruber, Mayer I. *Aspects of Nonverbal Communication in the Ancient Near East.* 2 vols. Rome: Biblical Institute, 1980.

———. "Fear, Anxiety and Reverence in Akkadian, Biblical Hebrew and Other Northwest Semitic Languages." *VT* 40 (1990) 411–22.

———. "Hebrew *daʾăbôn nepeš* 'Dryness of Throat': From Symptom to Literary Convention." *VT* 37 (1987) 365–69.

———. "The Many Faces of Hebrew נשא פנים 'Lift up the face.'" *ZAW* 95 (1983) 252–60.

Gundry, Robert H. *Mark: A Commentary on His Apology for the Cross.* Grand Rapids: Eerdmans, 1993.

Hagelia, Hallgard. "Meal on Mount Zion: Does Isa 25:6–8 Describe a Covenant Meal?" *Svensk Exegetisk Årsbok* 68 (2003) 73–95.

Hagner, Donald A. *Matthew 14–28.* WBC. Dallas, TX: Word, 1995.

Hahnemann, Carolin. "Nonverbal Behavior in Seneca's Phaedra." In *Kinesis: The Ancient Depiction of Gesture, Motion, and Emotion; Essays for Donald Lateiner* edited by Christina A. Clark et al., 160–72. Ann Arbor, MI: University of Michigan Press, 2015.

Hamilton, Victor P. *The Book of Genesis, Chapters 18–50.* NICOT. Grand Rapids: Eerdmans, 1995.

Hamm, Dennis. "Acts 3:1–10: The Healing of the Temple Beggar as Lucan Theology." *Biblica* 67 (1986) 304–19.

———. "Sight to the Blind: Vision as Metaphor in Luke." *Biblica* 67 (1986) 457–77.

Haran, Menahem. *Temples and Temple Service in Ancient Israel.* Oxford: Clarendon, 1978.

Hartley, John E. *Leviticus*. WBC. Dallas, TX: Word, 1992.
Hempel, Wolfgang. *Letters to the King of Mari: A New Translation, with Historical Introduction, Notes, and Commentary*. Winona Lake, IN: Eisenbrauns, 2003.
Heslin, Richard, and Tari Alper. "Touch: A Bonding Gesture." In *Nonverbal Interaction*, edited by John M. Wiemann and Randall P. Harrison, 47–75. Beverly Hills: Sage, 1983.
Holladay, William Lee. "'The Priests Scrape out on Their Hands,' Jeremiah V 31." *VT* 15 (1965) 111–13.
Hoop, Raymond de. "'Then Israel Bowed Himself . . .' (Genesis 47.31)." *JSOT* 28 (2004) 467–80.
Hugenberger, Gordon P. *Marriage as a Covenant: Biblical Law and Ethics as Developed from Malachi*. VT Supplement 52. Leiden: Brill, 1994.
Humbert, Paul. "'Etendre la main' (Note de lexicographie hébraïque)." *VT* 12 (1962) 383–85.
Hupka, R. B., et al. "Anger, Envy, Fear, and Jealousy as Felt in the Body: A Five-Nation Study." *Cross-Cultural Research* 30 (1996) 243–64.
Hurtado, Larry W. "Oral Fixation and New Testament Studies." *NTS* 60 (2014) 321–40.
Jenson, Philip Peter. *Graded Holiness: A Key to the Priestly Conception of the World*. JSOTS 106. Sheffield, UK: JSOT, 1992.
Jeremias, Joachim. *The Eucharistic Words of Jesus*. Oxford: Blackwell, 1955.
Johnson, Luke Timothy. *The First and Second Letters to Timothy: A New Translation with Introduction and Commentary*. Anchor Yale Bible. New Haven: Yale University Press, 2001.
Johnson, William A., and Holt N. Parker, eds. *Ancient Literacies: The Culture of Reading in Greece and Rome*. Oxford: Oxford University Press, 2009.
Keel, Othmar. *The Song of Songs*. Minneapolis: Fortress, 1994.
———. *The Symbolism of the Biblical World: Ancient Near Eastern Iconography and the Book of Psalms*. New York: Seabury, 1978.
Keener, Craig S. *Acts: An Exegetical Commentary*. Baker Exegetical Commentary on the New Testament. Grand Rapids: Baker Academic, 2012.
———. "Head Coverings." In *Dictionary of New Testament Background*, edited by Craig A. Evans and Stanley E. Porter, 442–47. Downers Grove, IL: InterVarsity, 2000.
Keith, Chris. *The Pericope Adulterae, the Gospel of John, and the Literacy of Jesus*. Leiden: Brill, 2014.
Kendon, Adam. *Gesture: Visible Action as Utterance*. Cambridge: Cambridge University Press, 2004.
Kio, Stephen Hre. "What Does 'You Will Heap Burning Coals upon His Head' Mean in Romans 12.20?" *BT* 51 (2000) 418–24.
Klassen, William. "Coals of Fire: Sign of Repentance or Revenge?" *NTS* 9 (1963) 337–50.
Kline, Meredith G. *Images of the Spirit*. Grand Rapids: Baker, 1980.
Kotzé, Zacharias. "A Cognitive Linguistic Approach to the Emotion of Anger in the Old Testament." *Theological Studies* 60 (2004) 843–63.
Kruger, Paul A. "Depression in the Hebrew Bible: An Update." *JNES* 64 (2005) 187–92.
———. "The Hem of the Garment in Marriage: The Meaning of the Symbolic Gesture in Ruth 3:9 and Ezek 16:8." *JNSL* 12 (1984) 79–86.
———. "Nonverbal Communication and Symbolic Gestures in the Psalms." *BT* 45 (1994) 213–22.

———. "'Nonverbal Communication' in the Hebrew Bible: A Few Comments." *JNSL* 24 (1998) 141–64.

———. "On Non-verbal Communication in the Baal Epic." *Journal for Semitics* 1 (1989) 54–69.

———. "The Symbolic Significance of the Hem (*kānāf*) in 1 Samuel 15:27." In *Text and Context: Old Testament and Semitic Studies for F. C. Fensham*, edited by W. Claassen, 105–16. JSOTS 48. Sheffield, UK: JSOT, 1988.

Kselman, John S. "'Wandering About' and Depression: More Examples." *JNES* 61 (2002) 275–77.

Labuschagne, C. J. "The Meaning of *beyād rāmā* in the Old Testament." In *Von Kanaan bis Kerala. Fs. J. P. M. van der Ploeg*, edited by W. S. Delsman et al., 143–48. AOAT 211. Kevelaer: Butzon & Bercker, 1982.

Lacheman, E. R. "Note on Ruth 4:7, 8." *JBL* 56 (1937) 53–56.

Lambert, David. "Fasting as a Penitential Rite: A Biblical Phenomenon?" *HTR* 96 (2003) 477–512.

Langdon, Stephen. "Gesture in Sumerian and Babylonian Prayer: A Study in Assyrian and Babylonian Archaeology." *Journal of the Royal Asiatic Society* 1919, 531–56.

Lateiner, Donald. *Sardonic Smile: Nonverbal Behavior in Homeric Epic*. Ann Arbor: University of Michigan Press, 1995.

Levine, B. A. "Silence, Sound, and the Phenomenology of Mourning in Biblical Israel." *JANES* 22 (1993) 89–106.

Limburg, James. *Jonah: A Commentary*. OTL. Louisville: Westminster / John Knox, 1993.

Lincoln, Andrew T. *The Gospel according to Saint John*. Black's New Testament Commentaries. London: Continuum, 2005.

Longman, Tremper III. *Proverbs*. Baker Commentary on the Old Testament Wisdom and Psalms. Grand Rapids: Baker Academic, 2006.

———. *Psalms*. Tyndale Old Testament Commentary. Downers Grove, IL: Inter-Varsity, 2014.

Louw, Johannes P., and Eugene A. Nida. *Greek–English Lexicon of the New Testament Based on Semantic Domains*. New York: United Bible Societies, 1988.

Low, Katherine. "Implications Surrounding Girding the Loins in Light of Gender, Body, and Power." *JSOT* 36 (2011) 3–30.

Lübbe, J. C. "Idioms in the Old Testament." *Journal for Semitics* 11 (2002) 45–63.

Lundbom, Jack R. *The Hebrew Prophets: An Introduction*. Minneapolis: Fortress, 2010.

Lust, Johan. "For I Lift up My Hand to Heaven and Swear." In *Studies in Deuteronomy in Honour of C. J. Labuschagne on the Occasion of His 65th Birthday*, edited by F. García Martínez et al., 155–64. Leiden: Brill, 1994.

Lynch, Matthew J. "Neglected Physical Dimensions of 'Shame' Terminology in the Hebrew Bible." *Biblica* 91 (2010) 499–517.

Malul, Meir. "More on *paḥad yiṣḥāq* (Genesis xxxi 42, 53) and the Oath by the Thigh." *VT* 35 (1985) 192–200.

———. "Touching the Sexual Organs as an Oath Ceremony in an Akkadian Letter." *VT* 37 (1987) 491–92.

Maringer, Johannes. "Adorants in Prehistoric Art: Prehistoric Attitudes and Gestures of Prayer." *Numen* 26 (1979) 215–30.

Martens, John W. "Burning Questions in Romans 12:20: What Is the Meaning and Purpose of 'Coals of Fire'?" *CBQ* 76 (2014) 291–305.

Matthews, Victor H. "The Anthropology of Clothing in the Joseph Narrative." *JSOT* 65 (1995) 25–36.

———. *More Than Meets the Ear: Discovering the Hidden Contexts of Old Testament Conversations*. Grand Rapids Eerdmans, 2008.

McCree, Walter T. "The Covenant Meal in the Old Testament." *JBL* 45 (1926) 120–28.

McGarry, Eugene P. "The Ambidextrous Angel (Daniel 12:7 and Deuteronomy 32:40): Inner-Biblical Exegesis and Textual Criticism in Counterpoint." *JBL* 124 (2005) 211–28.

McNeill, D. *Hand and Mind: What Gestures Reveal about Thought*. Chicago: University of Chicago Press, 1992.

Mettinger, Tryggve N. D. *King and Messiah: The Civil and Sacral Legitimation of the Israelite Kings*. Lund: Gleerup, 1976.

Milgrom, Jacob. "The Alleged Wave Offering in Israel and in the Ancient Near East." *IEJ* 22 (1972) 33–38.

———. *Leviticus 1–16: A New Translation with Introduction and Commentary*. AB. Garden City, NY: Doubleday, 1991.

———. *Leviticus 17–22: A New Translation with Introduction and Commentary*. AB. Garden City, NY: Doubleday, 2000.

———. *Leviticus 23–27: A New Translation with Introduction and Commentary*. AB. Garden City, NY: Doubleday, 2001.

———. *Studies in Cultic Theology and Terminology*. Leiden: Brill, 1983.

Minear, Paul S. "Writing on the Ground: The Puzzle in John 8:1–11." *Horizons in Biblical Theology* 13 (1991) 23–37.

Nässelqvist, Daniel. *Public Reading in Early Christianity: Lectors, Manuscripts, and Sound in the Oral Delivery of John 1–4*. Leiden: Brill, 2016.

Newell, B. Lynne. "Job: Repentant or Rebellious?" *Westminster Theological Journal* 46 (1984) 298–316.

Olyan, Saul M. "Honor, Shame, and Covenant Relations in Ancient Israel and Its Environment." *JBL* 115 (1996) 201–18.

———. "What Do Shaving Rites Accomplish and What Do They Signal in Biblical Ritual Contexts?" *JBL* 117 (1998) 611–22.

Oppenheim, A. Leo. "Idiomatic Accadian (Lexicographical Researches)." *JAOS* 61 (1941) 251–71.

Pace, Sharon. *Daniel*. Smyth & Helwys Bible Commentary. Macon, GA: Smyth & Helwys, 2009.

Parratt, J. K. "The Laying on of Hands in the New Testament: A Re-examination in the Light of the Hebrew Terminology." *Expository Times* 80 (1969) 210–14.

Plummer, Alfred. *A Critical and Exegetical Commentary on the Gospel according to S. Luke*. International Critical Commentary. Edinburgh: T. & T. Clark, 1896.

Plutchik, R. *The Psychology and Biology of Emotion*. New York: HarperCollins College, 1994.

Pope, Marvin H. *Job: Introduction, Translation, and Notes*. 3rd ed. AB. Garden City, NY: Doubleday, 1973.

Porter, Stanley E. "Paul of Tarsus and His Letters." In *Handbook of Classical Rhetoric in the Hellenistic Period: 330 B.C.–A.D. 400*, edited by Stanley E. Porter, 533–85. Boston: Brill Academic, 1997.

Prouser, Ora Horn. "Suited to the Throne: The Symbolic Use of Clothing in the David and Saul Narratives." *JSOT* 77 (1996) 27–37.

Queller, Kurt. "'Stretch Out Your Hand!' Echo and Metalepsis in Mark's Sabbath Healing Controversy." *JBL* 129 (2010) 737–58.

Rhoads, David. "Performance Criticism: An Emerging Methodology in Second Testament Studies." *Biblical Theology Bulletin* 36 (2006) 118–33, 164–84.

Roberts, J. J. M. "The Hand of Yahweh." *VT* 21 (1971) 244–51.

———. *Nahum, Habakkuk, and Zephaniah: A Commentary*. OTL. Louisville: Westminster / John Knox, 1991.

———. "A New Parallel to 1 Kings 18:28–29." *JBL* 89 (1970) 76–77.

Robinson, Ira. "*běpetaḥ ʿênayim* in Genesis 38:14." *JBL* 96 (1977) 569.

Rogers, Virgil M. "The Use of ראש in an Oath." *JBL* 74 (1955) 272.

Rogland, Max. "'Striking a Hand' (*tqʿ kp*) in Biblical Hebrew." *VT* 51 (2001) 107–9.

Saggs, H. W. F. "The Branch to the Nose." *Journal of Theological Studies* n.s. 11 (1960) 318–29.

Sanders, Paul. "So May God Do to Me!" *Biblica* 85 (2004) 91–98.

Sarna, Nahum M. *Genesis: The Traditional Hebrew Text with the New JPS Translation—Commentary*. The JPS Torah Commentary. Philadelphia: Jewish Publication Society, 1989.

Schroer, Silvia, and Thomas Staubli. *Body Symbolism in the Bible*. Translated by Linda M. Maloney. Collegeville, MN: Liturgical, 2001.

Seely, David Rolph. "The Raised Hand of God as an Oath Gesture." In *Fortunate the Eyes That See: Essays in Honor of David Noel Freedman in Celebration of His Seventieth Birthday*, edited by Astrid B. Beck et al., 411–21. Grand Rapids: Eerdmans, 1995.

Shi, Wenhua. *Paul's Message of the Cross as Body Language*. WUNT. Tübingen: Mohr Siebeck, 2008.

Simon, Uriel. *Jonah: The Traditional Hebrew Text with the New JPS Translation*. The JPS Bible Commentary. Philadelphia: Jewish Publication Society, 1999.

Smith, Mark S. "The Heart and Innards in Israelite Emotional Expressions: Notes from Anthropology and Psychobiology." *JBL* 117 (1998) 427–36.

Smith, S. H. "'Heel' and 'Thigh': The Concept of Sexuality in the Jacob–Esau Narratives." *VT* 40 (1990) 464–73.

Stears, Karen. "Dead Women's Society." In *Time, Tradition and Society in Greek Archaeology: Bridging the "Great Divide,"* edited by Nigel Spencer, 109–31. New York: Routledge, 1995.

Stevenson, Gregory M. "Conceptual Background to Golden Crown Imagery in the Apocalypse of John (4:4, 10; 14:14)." *JBL* 114 (1995) 257–72.

Stone, G. R. "Grasping the Fringe." *Buried History* 31 (1995) Part 1, 4–20; Part 2, 36–47.

Strack, Hermann L., and Paul Billerbeck. *Kommentar zum Neuen Testament aus Talmud und Midrasch*. 8th ed. 6 vols. Munich: Beck, 1982.

Swain, Simon, ed. *Seeing the Face, Seeing the Soul: Polemon's Physiognomy from Classical Antiquity to Medieval Islam*. Oxford: Oxford University Press, 2007.

Swete, Henry Barclay. *The Gospel according to St Mark: The Greek Text with Introduction, Notes and Indices*. London: Macmillan, 1913.

Tate, Marvin E. *Psalms 51–100*. WBC. Dallas, TX: Word, 1990.

Thomas, Keith. "Introduction." In *A Cultural History of Gesture*, edited by Jan Bremmer and Herman Roodenburg, 1–14. Ithaca, NY: Cornell University Press, 1992.

Tilford, Nicole L. *Sensing World, Sensing Wisdom: The Cognitive Foundation of Biblical Metaphors*. Atlanta: SBL, 2017.

Tristram, H. B. *The Land of Israel: A Journal of Travels in Palestine, Undertaken with Special Reference to Its Physical Character*. 3rd rev. ed. London: SPCK, 1876.

BIBLIOGRAPHY

Tsevat, Matitiatu. "Two Old Testament Stories and Their Hittite Analogues." *JAOS* 103 (1983) 321–26.

Tur-Sinai, N. H. *The Book of Job*. Rev. ed. Jerusalem: Kiryath Sepher, 1967.

Van Den Heever, Cornelius Marthinus. "Idioms in Biblical Hebrew: Towards Their Identification and Classification with Special Reference to 1 and 2 Samuel." PhD diss., Stellenbosch University, 2013.

van der Merwe, B. J. "The Laying on of Hands in the Old Testament." In *New Light on Some Old Testament Problems: Papers Read at 5th Meeting Held at the University of South Africa, Pretoria, 30 January–2 February 1962*, 34–43. Pretoria: Die Ou Testamentiese Werkgemeenkap in Suid-Afrika, 1962.

VanGemeren, Willem A., ed. *New International Dictionary of Old Testament Theology and Exegesis*. 5 vols. Grand Rapids: Zondervan, 1997.

Vaux, Roland de. *Ancient Israel: 1. Social Institutions*. New York: McGraw-Hill, 1965.

Viberg, Åke. *Symbols of Law: A Contextual Analysis of Legal Symbolic Acts in the Old Testament*. Stockholm: Almqvist and Wiksell, 1992.

Voorwinde, Stephen. *Jesus' Emotions in the Fourth Gospel*. The Library of New Testament Studies. London: T. & T. Clark, 2005.

Walton, John H. *Genesis*. NIV Application Commentary. Grand Rapids: Zondervan, 2001.

Warren-Rothlin, Andy L. "Body Idioms and the Psalms." In *Interpreting the Psalms*, edited by David Firth and Philip S. Johnston, 195–212. Downers Grove, IL: IVP Academic, 2005.

Watts, John D. W. *Isaiah 1–33*. WBC. Waco, TX: Word, 1985.

Watts, R. E. "The Meaning of ʿālāw yiqpᵉṣûmᵉlākîm pîhem in Isaiah lii 15." *VT* 40 (1990) 327–35.

Welborn, Laurence L. *Paul, the Fool of Christ: A Study of 1 Corinthians 1–4 in the Comic-philosophic Tradition*. The Library of New Testament Studies. London: T. & T. Clark, 2005.

Wharton, Tim. *Pragmatics and Non-Verbal Communication*. Cambridge: Cambridge University Press, 2009.

Wiemann, John M., and Randall P. Harrison, ed. *Nonverbal Interaction*. Beverly Hills: Sage, 1983.

Wilkinson, Richard H. *Symbol and Magic in Egyptian Art*. London: Thames and Hudson, 1994.

Willis, W. L. "Banquets." In *Dictionary of New Testament Background*, edited by Craig A. Evans and Stanley E. Porter, 143–46. Downers Grove, IL: InterVarsity, 2000.

Wilson, Robert R. "An Interpretation of Ezekiel's Dumbness." *VT* 22 (1972) 91–104.

Windisch, Hans. "ἀσπάζομαι." In *TDNT*, 1:496–502.

Wiseman, Donald J. "Jonah's Nineveh." *Tyndale Bulletin* 30 (1979) 29–52.

Wong, Ka Leung. "'And Moses Raised His Hand' in Numbers 20:11." *Biblica* 89 (2008) 397–400.

Wright, D. P. "Deuteronomy 21:1–9 as a Rite of Elimination." *CBQ* 49 (1987) 387–403.

———. "The Gesture of Hand Placement in the Hebrew Bible and in Hittite Literature." *JAOS* 106 (1986) 433–46.

Wright, N. T. *Paul and the Faithfulness of God*. Christian Origins and the Question of God 4. Minneapolis: Fortress, 2013.

Yoo, Philip Y. "Why Does Joseph Wash His Face?" *JSOT* 38 (2013) 3–14.

Ziegler, Yael. "'So Shall God Do . . .': Variations of an Oath Formula and Its Literary Meaning." *JBL* 126 (2007) 59–81.

Subject Index

acceptance, 22, 31, 40, 107, 109
admiration, 20, 31, 58, 59, 148
adoration, *see* worship
afraid, *see* fear
aggression, *see* hostility
Akkadian, 19n11, 28n39, 35n52, 38, 42n64, 73, 83, 88n57, 106, 120, 127, 129n1, 131, 136n16
alliance, 39, 70, 103, 105, 111, 123–25, *see also* covenant
amazement, 8, 9, 45, 46, 53, 63, 64, 127, 134, 152,
anger, 9, 10, 14, 32, 34, 35, 37, 38, 38n55, 40, 63, 142, 149, 152
anoint, 16, 25–27, 37, 48, 91, 125, 126, 133, 135
Apocrypha, 2
appease, 34, 93
apprehension, *see* fear
Arabic, 13n37, 18n10, 106, 129
arbitration, 126
arm, 14, 24, 25, 78, 86, 95–98, 100–105, 107, 109, 111–18, 113n41, 118n61, 122, 149
arrogance, *see* pride
ashes, *see* dust
Assyria, 91, 92, 103, 111, 116, 122, 124, 126, 131, *see also* Mesopotamia
astonishment, *see* amazement
awe, 34, 48, 79, 80

Babylon, 6, 15, 20, 45, 61, 63, 70, 76, 86, 88, 93, 100n6, 106, 118, 120, 123, 136, 137, 140, *see also* Mesopotamia
back, 50, 67, 68, 72–74
baldness, 16–18, 93
banquet, *see* feasting
beard, 18–19, 18n10, 51, 88
beat, *see* strike
bend, 19, 36, 77, 82, 86, 102, 103, 117, 138
bless, 16, 32, 47, 77, 86, 87, 112, 115, 116, 118, 119
blind, 25, 51, 53–56, 111, 134
blink, 55, 56
blink, *see* wink
body language, *see* nonverbal communication
bow, 3, 7, 21, 32, 48, 77, 86, 125, 130, 130n2, 135, 138, 150
breast, 14, 21, 61, 71, 72, 130, 149
breath, 36–38, 68, 145, 149
brow, *see* forehead

call, 43, 55, 143, 145
Canaan, 10, 26, 69, 78, 80
carry, 70, 82, 90, 111–13, 133
characterization, 11, 151, 151n6
cheek, 35, 36, 51, 149
chest, 71–72, 117
chin, 117
clap, xi, 3, 14, 42, 123, 126, 127, 127n92, 142
classical, 2, 11, 12, 80, 96, 101, 125, *see also* Greece, Rome

SUBJECT INDEX

clench, 4, 103, 104
cloak, *see* dress
clothing, *see* dress
clutch, *see* hold
co-verbal communication, 1
coals, 7, 8, 27
comfort, 22, 66, 105, 111, 115
compassion, *see* pity
confidence, 20, 28, 30–32, 60, 96, 135, 142
consecration, 16, 26, 119, 120
contempt, 10, 37, 45, 56, 62, 63, 67, 132, 144
control, 6, 36, 37, 44, 66, 107, 108, 113, 131, 139
conversation, 3, 46, 57, 148
cosmetics, 26, 28, 53, 93
covenant, 13, 39, 73, 121–23, 125, 141, *see also* alliance
cover, xi, 1, 5, 7, 19, 22–24, 33–35, 92, 102, 118, 149
crown, 17, 22, 22n23, 23, 83, 126
cry, 35, 43, 44, 66, 100, 127, *see also* weep
culture, xi, 5–7, 10–13, 12n35, 13n38, 17, 22, 53, 64, 77, 89, 90, 103, 106, 129, 140, 149, 150

dancing, 86, 126, 151
deictic, 57, 100, 100n8, 120
dejection, *see* sorrow
depression, 38, 77, 138, 139
derision, *see* mockery
determination, 30, 36, 58, 139
dirt, *see* dust
disfigurement, 32, 88
disguise, *see* dissimulate
dishonor, *see* shame
disinterest, *see* indifference
dissimulate, 16, 66n24, 89, 148
distress, 14, 16, 18, 20, 21, 23, 30, 33, 40, 43, 53, 64, 67, 71, 73, 80, 84, 92, 93, 142, 150
double entendre, 94, 122, 123, 144, 149
dress, 2, 14, 18, 24, 46, 65, 73, 76, 88–95, 90n64, 91n66, 94n74, 96, 102, 112, 122, 127, 134, 147, 149, 150

drink, 38, 39, 41
dust, 21, 23, 24, 41, 50, 63, 76, 88, 93, 97, 132, 147, 150

ear, 3, 8, 19, 55, 56, 68, 114
eat, *see* meals
Egypt, xi, 10, 12, 13, 17, 18, 24–27, 32n42, 33, 34, 39n60, 43, 45, 47n71, 48, 53, 58, 59n12, 66n24, 68n4, 69, 69n6, 72, 73, 77–80, 82, 83, 91, 98, 102–4, 108, 111, 113, 115, 116, 122, 123, 125, 127, 130n2, 131, 135, 136, 140, 142
elbow, 76, 117
embarrassment, *see* shame
embrace, 47, 67, 71, 112, 142
emotion, 1, 2, 4, 6–10, 14, 20, 27, 35, 36, 38, 40, 43–45, 47, 52, 56, 57, 61–64, 67, 72, 77, 79, 80, 85, 87, 149, 151
encouragement, 20, 86, 98, 103, 109, 111, 130
endurance, 7, 38, 70, 141
entreat, *see* plea, plead
envy, 53, 62
eye, 3, 7, 14, 14n41, 15, 21, 24, 25, 33, 34, 49, 52–66, 52n1, 52n2, 53n3, 63n15, 70n7, 75, 77, 102, 113, 114, 116, 118, 138, 143
eye contact, 57–61
eyebrow, 54
eyelid, 53–55

face, 1, 2–4, 5, 8, 9, 14–18, 21, 24, 27–38, 50, 51, 53, 56–58, 60, 66, 67, 72, 77–80, 84–86, 93, 94, 117, 129, 132, 146, 147–49, 152
fall, xi, 3, 4, 7, 9, 14, 32, 35, 61, 67, 74, 77–80, 83–85, 101, 135, 146, 147, 151
farewell, 5, 47, 65, 67, 78, 80, 112, 125
fast, 21, 32, 40, 76, 93, 134, 138
favor, 3, 28, 28n39, 29, 31, 32, 40, 44, 54, 60, 61, 81, 82, 87, 89, 90, 148

SUBJECT INDEX

fear, 8, 9, 15, 21, 33, 34, 43, 45, 47, 53, 57, 60, 61, 74, 77, 80, 84, 86, 87, 105, 130, 139, 143, 148, 149, 152
feasting, 39, 44, 48, 75n26, 76, 93, 133, 150
finger, 19, 56, 96, 102, 106, 107, 129n1, 143
fist, 5, 42, 103, 104, 113, 127
follow, 140, 141, 143, 145
foot, 14, 18, 28, 47, 48, 50, 56, 62, 69, 69n6, 75, 76, 78, 80, 81, 83–85, 91, 93, 106, 126, 131–33, 132n10, 138, 140, 142, 143, 145, 149
footstool, 23, 132, 149
footwear, xi, 2, 121, 131–33, 147, 149
forehead, 36, 78, 97, 118
friendship, 4, 5, 29, 39, 47, 49, 76, 109, 123, 125, 133, 144
fringe, *see* hem

gape, *see* scrutiny
garment, *see* dress
gaze, 30, 52, 56–61, 63, 148, 149
gender, 20, 73, 89, 110, 150
generosity, 3, 8, 34, 39, 62, 107, 108
gesture, xi, 1–8, 10–14, 16, 19–21, 23n27, 24, 32, 34, 35, 37–39, 41, 42, 45, 47, 49, 50, 56, 57, 60, 65–68, 71, 76, 77, 82, 84, 85, 88, 93, 94, 96–98, 100, 100n8, 101–3, 103n14, 105–7, 108n30, 110–27, 113n41, 118n58, 118n61, 121n74, 122n76, 123n80, 129, 132, 133, 135, 142, 146, 147n3, 148–51
glance, 53, 56, 57, 138, 148
glare, *see* scrutiny
gloat, 63, 142
gnash, 42, 50, 63, 149
grasp, *see* hold
gratitude, 18, 48, 72, 75, 80, 82, 84, 133
Greece, 2, 11, 12, 13, 18, 24, 76, 84, 109, 115, 125, 138n21
greeting, 44, 47–49, 67, 78, 79, 82, 109, 112, 118, 125, 135, 136, 150
grief, 9, 18–21, 23, 24, 35, 40, 43, 46n70, 64–66, 68, 71, 72, 76, 80, 87, 88, 92, 126, 129, 134, 142, 147, 149, 150
grind, 50
groan, 43
guide, *see* lead
guilt, 28, 31, 46, 107, 110, 114

hair, 13, 16–19, 23, 32n42, 149, 150
hand, 1, 2, 3n7, 4–9, 11, 14, 16, 19, 20, 24, 29, 33, 34, 39, 42, 45, 46, 46n69, 48, 55, 57, 58, 60, 62, 63, 69, 73, 74, 75, 77, 78, 80, 84, 94, 98–127, 118n64, 121n74, 122n75, 130, 137, 142, 146–49
handclasp, 121, 123–25, 123n82, 148
handshake, *see* handclasp
happiness, *see* joy
head, 1, 7, 8, 13, 14, 15–51, 65, 93, 99, 101, 110, 112, 118, 119, 121, 138, 147–49, 152
head covering, 7, 17, 17n4, 18, 22–25, 33, 33n45, 38, 89, 92
heal, 16, 26, 43, 51, 63, 64, 72, 83, 89, 94, 101, 110, 113–15, 119, 127, 130, 140, 142
heart, 1, 7, 8, 16, 31, 39, 42, 52, 52n1, 53, 55, 58, 59n12, 62, 63, 65, 68, 72, 87, 93, 99, 106, 148, 149
Hellenistic, 12, 18, 22, 76, 92, 141
hem, 90, 90n64, 91n66, 93, 94, 147
hiss, 2, 42, 43, 126, 127
Hittite, 26, 81, 83, 131
hold, 38, 73, 77, 81–84, 94, 98, 104, 105, 107–9, 111–13, 125, 127, 133, 149
homage, *see* obeisance
honor, 3, 17, 22, 31, 39, 42, 45, 49, 62, 77, 79, 80, 84–87, 93, 98, 105, 118n64, 131, 133, 135, 144, 148, 150
horror, 63, 68
hostility, 4, 27, 28, 30, 41, 49, 51, 57, 62, 63, 101, 113, 123n80, 134, 135
hubris, *see* pride
hug, 67, 112
humiliation, 17, 23, 35, 35n52, 40, 41, 50, 61, 69, 71, 86, 92, 117

SUBJECT INDEX

humility, 18, 29, 48, 61, 76, 87, 95, 138, 144, 147
hunger, 41

idiom, xi, 7, 7n21, 8, 10–15, 10n26, 19, 28, 28n39, 29–31, 34, 35n52, 37, 38, 40–42, 54, 55, 58, 61, 62, 65, 68, 70, 72, 73, 78, 96–98, 104, 105, 112, 116, 118, 122, 123, 129, 133, 140, 141, 148, 149
idolatry, 16, 30, 41, 46, 48, 60, 72, 92, 101, 129
impudence, 30
indifference, 27, 30, 35, 67, 132
indignation, *see* anger
insult, *see* mockery

joy, 9, 10, 20, 26–28, 32n42, 35, 39, 41, 43, 44, 54, 59, 64–66, 126, 136, 141, 142, 149, 152
judge, 31, 48, 55, 73, 75, 112, 137
jump, *see* leap

kick, 133
kiss, 3, 35, 38, 47–49, 47n71, 59n12, 67, 80, 82, 84, 105, 117, 125, 133, 150
knee, 20, 77, 78, 78n30, 80, 81, 83–85, 87, 88, 106, 129, 130, 130n2, 134, 149
kneel, 3, 77, 77n28, 80, 84, 85, 116, 118, 130, 130n2, 137

lament, *see* mourn
laughter, 2, 6, 41, 44, 74, 147, 149
lead, 16, 111, 119, 125, 140, 145
leap, 86, 142–43
leg, 14, 27, 83, 84, 129, 130
lick, 50
lie, 2, 59, 74–77, 94, 134, 145
lift, *see* raise
liminal, 150
limp, 141–43
lip, 3, 4, 31, 35, 42, 44, 47–49, 47n71, 56, 87
loins, 33, 73, 74, 87, 93
look, 1, 4, 14, 20, 28–30, 32–34, 43, 46, 52, 53, 57–63, 106, 108, 108n30, 112, 116, 134, 136, 146–48, 152

look, 1, 4, 14, 20, 28–30, 32–34, 43, 46, 52, 53, 57, 62, 108, 108n30, 112, 116, 134, 146–48, 152
lower, 20, 21, 31, 32, 76, 77, 117

meals, 38–41, 38n55, 54, 75n26, 131, 150, *see also* feasting
mediation, 42, 126
Mesopotamia, 10, 13, 18, 33, 35, 38, 73, 75, 77, 91n66, 102n13, 118n64, 140, *see also* Assyria, Babylon
metaphor, xi, 7, 8, 14, 17, 22, 26, 28, 36, 37, 40, 45, 52, 55, 67–69, 71, 95, 98, 106, 107, 111, 116, 128, 132, 135, 138–41, 143, 149
Middle East, *see* Western Asia
miracle, 113, 114
moan, 21, 43, 60, 65
mockery, 22, 24, 34, 35, 37, 38, 44, 47, 50, 51, 55, 57, 63, 68, 72, 74, 75, 80, 88, 90, 122, 124, 126, 127, 129, 142, 147, 148, 152
mood, 15, 147
mourning, 10, 17, 18, 23, 24, 35, 46, 65, 66, 71, 74, 74n21, 76, 86, 88, 91–93, 111, 131, 138, 148, 150
mouth, 5, 35, 38–50, 61, 101, 111, 117, 129, 140

nakedness, 3, 55, 91, 92, 95, 131
neck, 8, 14, 20, 36, 42, 67–71, 69n6, 76, 96, 108, 121, 131, 151
necklace, 67, 67n2, 96
nod, 20, 21, 77
nonverbal communication, 1–14, 9n23, 37, 44, 49, 53, 55, 96, 129, 146, 148–52
nose, 36–38

oath, *see* swear
obeisance, 10n26, 47, 77, 78, 80–85, 133
obstinate, *see* stubborn
open, 3, 19, 34, 42, 43, 47, 49, 50, 53–56, 62, 108, 118, 140

palm, 4, 48, 97, 107, 115–18, 118n58, 121, 121n74

SUBJECT INDEX

partiality, 3
patience, 36, 37, 70, 95, 109
performance, 151, 151n7
performative, 10, 121, 147, 148
perfume, *see* cosmetics
perplexity, 8, 45, 93
petition, *see* supplication
physiognomy, 2, 14, 41, 53
pity, 21, 22, 56, 57, 61, 64, 66, 95
plea, plead, 8, 19, 28, 30, 34, 55, 62, 63, 77, 81, 84, 85, 94, 105, 109, 115, 118, 130, 137, 141, 146, 149
pledge, *see* swear
point, 4, 48, 56, 100, 106, 117, 143
politeness, 78, 82, 82n39
possession, 103, 107, 108, 131
posture, 1–3, 3n7, 4, 5, 6n13, 13, 21, 69, 75, 76, 78, 80, 83–86, 83n45, 118n61, 130, 133, 135–37, 146
prayer, 3, 8, 9, 13, 17, 19–21, 26, 28–32, 42, 43, 54, 55, 60, 61, 65, 66, 71, 77, 80, 84, 93, 98, 113n41, 115–19, 118n58, 118n61, 121, 122, 134, 136, 137, 144, 145
pretence, *see* dissimulate
pride, 20, 27, 33, 49, 53, 61, 63, 67, 68, 72, 117, 132, 138
priest, 18, 22, 26, 35, 36, 46, 92, 110, 111, 119, 120, 124, 131, 136, 144
prophet, 3, 9, 16, 18, 26, 30, 35, 42, 45, 50, 55, 68, 84, 87–89, 88n57, 91–94, 102, 106, 111, 113, 127, 131, 136, 138, 140, 143, 146–48
prostration, 35, 41, 77–85, 101, 120n69, 148
proxemics, 1, 4, 6n13, 143–45
public speaking, 2, 57, 101, 135
pupil, *see* eye

raise, xi, 3, 4, 7–9, 14, 20, 21, 23, 24, 31, 34, 36, 39, 43, 60, 60n13, 61, 63, 70n7, 78, 97, 98, 100, 103, 104, 106, 109, 111, 113, 115–23, 118n64, 130, 131, 133, 146–49, 152
rank (social), *see* status
reach, 3, 103, 108–13, 115, 122

rebuke, 32, 37, 56
regard, *see* look, respect
rejoicing, *see* joy
remorse, *see* sorrow
resentment, 27, 30, 53
resist, 36, 135
respect, *see* honor
reverence, 47, 72, 77, 82, 86, 87, 116
right hand, 5, 20, 74, 75, 96–101, 100n6, 105, 112, 119, 122–25, 127
ring, 36, 37, 96
rise, 70, 72, 76, 134–36, 146, *see also* stand
Rome, 2, 11, 13, 18, 20, 24, 28, 34, 48, 77, 77n28, 84, 101, 101n9, 103, 116, 123, 141
royalty, 22, 29, 39, 67n2, 74, 78–82, 89–91, 127, 136
run, 3, 129, 130, 137–42, 144

sackcloth, 18, 21, 65, 92, 93, 138
sadness, *see* sorrow
sandal, *see* footwear
scepter, 127, 127n94, 147
scoff, *see* mockery
scorn, 22, 37, 44, 50, 63, 127
scorn, *see* mockery
scowl, 32
scrape, 88, 106, 120, 142–43
scrutiny, 9, 30, 35, 47, 58, 63, 64, 118, 148
see, 16, 28, 29, 32–34, 53, 55–57, 59, 61–63, 65, 89, 112, 136
Septuagint, 56, 63, 71, 82, 85, 122
shake, xi, 5, 20–22, 26, 42, 83, 86, 87, 93, 103, 104, 107, 123, 125, 127, 132, 148, 152
shame, 5, 9, 10, 17, 20, 24, 27, 30, 31, 33–35, 44, 45, 58, 68, 88, 91, 92, 95, 97, 127, 129, 144, 149, 151
shine, 28, 31, 32, 148
shock, 9, 46n70, 130
shoe, *see* footwear
shoulder, 67, 70, 71, 97, 100, 112
shuffle, 56, 138, 143
sigh, 42, 43
sight, 24, 54, 56, 57, 63, 81

167

SUBJECT INDEX

signal, 1, 6, 21, 37, 43, 74, 100, 100n7, 101, 147
silence, xi, 4, 5, 9, 16, 21, 45, 46, 46n70, 49, 50, 101, 117, 149
sit, 3, 23, 45, 57–60, 74–76, 75n26, 87, 88, 98, 136, 137, 145, 149
slap, 35, 36, 127, 129
smile, 1, 5–7, 31, 32, 41, 44, 148, 149
smite, *see* strike
sorrow, 8, 21, 24, 29, 32, 43, 65, 71, 91, 92, 127, 134, 138, 149
speechless, *see* silence
spit, 50, 51, 132, 144
staff, 2, 82, 127, 128
stagger, 142–43
stamp, 142–43
stance, *see* posture, stand
stand, 7, 14, 20, 38, 50, 70, 74–76, 78, 85, 92, 98, 116, 129, 130, 134–37, 136n16, 139, 142–45, 149
stare, *see* scrutiny
status, 1, 2, 11, 16–18, 22, 36, 39, 45, 47, 74, 76, 77, 80–82, 89, 90, 92, 93, 116, 133, 135–37, 150
stiffnecked, *see* stubborn
stretch, 4, 8, 14, 68, 78, 84, 87, 97, 98, 101–5, 113–17, 118n61, 119, 122, 124, 128, 138
stride, 138, 139
strike, 5, 14, 31, 35, 36, 50, 51, 71, 72, 103, 104n18, 123, 126, 129, 149
stubborn, 8, 30, 36, 68, 71
stumble, 106, 140, 143
subjection, 45, 69, 80, 81, 108, 131, 132
subjugation, *see* subjection,
submission, 19, 25, 41, 45, 46, 50, 70, 84, 122, 123n80, 131
subservience, *see* submission
supplication, 10n26, 74, 77, 81, 83, 84, 93, 94, 118, 137, 149
surrender, 14, 98, 118, 122, 123
swear, 7, 10, 68, 73, 74, 82, 97, 109, 120–26, 120n69, 120n70, 121n74, 122n75, 144, 147
sword, 40, 42, 65, 88, 93, 127, 128
sympathy, 21, 23, 42, 47, 71, 78, 148

tears, *see* weep
teeth, 42, 50, 63, 149
tenderness, 27, 35–37, 61, 66, 105, 111, 130
terror, *see* fear
thanks, *see* gratitude
thanksgiving, *see* gratitude
thigh, 6, 73, 74, 127, 129, 147
thirst, 41, 55, 68
threaten, 5, 50, 90, 92, 102–5, 120, 122, 128, 149
throat, xi, 20, 41, 68, 68n3, 68n4, 120n69
throne, 23, 34, 45n68, 58, 60, 74, 74n21, 75, 77n28, 78, 82, 83, 98, 104, 104n21, 121, 127, 127n94, 132, 136, 141, 150
tongue, 32, 42, 47, 49, 50, 114
tonsure, *see* baldness
torso, 14, 67–95
touch, xi, 3–5, 42, 47, 77, 78, 93, 94, 109–114, 118–20, 120n69, 124
treaty, *see* alliance
tremble, 9, 47, 61, 63, 86, 87, 130, 148
tribute, 2, 82, 83, 83n45, 123
turn, 3, 5, 14, 21, 28–31, 36, 58, 60, 67, 68, 70–72, 77, 93, 94, 97, 107, 116, 140
twinkle, 56

Ugarit, 10, 20, 21n17, 23, 50, 60n13, 65, 74n21, 78, 78n30, 84, 88, 94, 98, 107n28, 116

veil, *see* head covering

wag, *see* shake
wail, 24, 43, 65, *see also* weep
waist, 73
walk, 7, 9, 75, 111, 129–31, 134, 137–44, 138n21, 149
wander, 138, 142
wash, 32, 62, 66, 66n24, 106, 107, 132, 132n10, 133
wave, 100, 107, 113
weapon, 15n2, 103, 104, 116, 127, *see also* sword
wedding, 22, 39, 46, 90, 150

weep, 6, 14, 21, 23, 24, 27, 35, 43, 47, 54, 58, 61, 64–66, 64n19, 80, 147, 149, 151
welcome, *see* acceptance, greeting
Western Asia, xi, 10, 12, 13, 47, 50, 53, 56, 65, 67, 71, 77, 88, 94, 104, 116, 121, 122, 138
whistle, 2, 42, 43, 149
widow, 90, 132, 143

wink, 3, 49, 55, 56, 106, 143
withdraw, 66, 101, 105
worship, 3, 7, 8, 10n26, 17, 23, 29, 38, 39, 48, 59, 62, 72, 75, 78–80, 83–86, 97, 109–11, 115, 116, 130, 136, 144–46, 149
wrath, *see* anger

yoke, 3, 68, 70, 70n7, 108

Scripture Index

Genesis

2:7	23, 37	15:5	46	23:11	54
2:25	91	16:4	62	24:2	6, 73
3:6	59	16:5	62, 71, 112	24:14	41
3:7	55, 91	16:6	141	24:15	70
3:8	139	17:1	140	24:22	36
3:10	91	17:3	78, 79	24:26	84
3:11	91	17:11–14	73	24:29	141
3:14	41, 50	17:14	67	24:30	36
3:19	23	17:17	44, 80	24:32	132
4:4–5	62	18:2	141	24:47	36
4:5–6	32	18:4	132	24:63	139
4:5	9, 38	18:7	141	24:65	33
4:8	134	18:12–15	6, 44	25:26	133
4:11	106	18:23	143, 144	26:28–31	39
5:29	101	18:27	23	27:17	107
6:5	72	18:30	38	27:21	144
6:6	72	18:32	38	27:26	47
6:8	97	19:2	70, 132	27:27	47
7:15	37	19:17	58	27:33	86, 152
7:22	37	19:21	31	27:36	133
8:21	72	19:26	58	27:38	64, 65
9:2	108	19:35	134	27:40	70
9:20–27	95	21:6	44	27:45	37
11:1	47	21:8	39	28:12	5
11:4	20	21:14	70	29:11	47
11:5	58	21:16	65	29:13	47, 112, 141
12:17	5	21:19	55	29:17	53
13:9	99	22:3	70, 137	29:22	39
13:17	139	22:6	9	30:3	130
14:18–19	39	22:16	121	30:20	152
14:22–23	121	23:2	64, 65	30:35	107
14:22	7	23:6	81	31:5	4, 28
		23:7	81	31:13	26

SCRIPTURE INDEX

Genesis
(continued)

31:21	30	40:19–20	20	2:24	43
31:28	40	40:20	39	3:1	82
31:36	38	41:14	18	3:5	131, 144
31:40	40	41:42	67, 96	3:6	34
31:42	74	41:43	130	3:19–20	104
31:48–54	39	42:1	58	4:3	127
31:53	74	42:21	2	4:4	127
32:16	107	42:24	6, 151	4:17	127
32:20	31, 34	42:28	87	4:20	127
32:30	29	43:3	29	4:27	47
33:1–7	143	43:5	29	4:31	62, 84, 86
33:3–8	82	43:28	81	5:9	62
33:3–6	81	43:29	57	5:21	58
33:3	78	43:30	6, 64, 151	6:5	43
33:4	47, 65, 67, 112, 141	43:31	66	6:6	104
		44:14	78	6:8	121
		44:18	143	6:12	47
33:5	57	45:1	6	7:4–5	103
33:10	31	45:2	6	7:5	104
34:7	38	45:4	4, 144	7:9	127
34:13	72	45:14	65, 67, 151	7:10	127
35:18	68	45:15	47	7:17	127
36:6	67	46:4	55	7:19	103, 127
37:3	89, 90	46:26	73	7:20	127
37:6–11	81	46:29	65, 67, 151	8:5	127
37:29	14, 92	46:30	28	8:6	127
37:34	64, 65, 92, 93	47:29	73	8:16	127
38:14	90	47:31	82	8:17	127
38:15	33, 34	48:5–12	130	8:20	70
38:18	127	48:10	47, 112	9:3	102
38:19	90	48:11	29	9:8–11	24
38:20	105	48:13–20	99	9:11	135
38:21–22	32	48:14	119	9:13	70
38:23	44	49:6	37	9:22–23	127
38:25	127	49:7	37	9:22	113
38:28	122	49:8	69, 70, 108	9:29	117, 118
39:2	108	49:10	127	9:33	8, 117, 118
39:3	101	49:15	70	9:35	105
39:7	59, 94	49:26	16	10:12–13	127
39:8	107, 108	49:27	40	10:12	113
39:10	94	50:1	35, 47	10:21	113
39:12	94	50:23	130	10:22	113
39:23	62			12:11	73, 131
40:7	27, 32	**Exodus**		12:27	86
40:13	8, 20	1:5	73	12:29	74
		2:6	64	12:34	70
		2:23	43	13:9	36

13:11	125	29:6	22	8:11	26
13:21	129, 140	29:7	25, 26	8:12	25
14:6	102	29:9	120	8:30	26
14:8	103	29:10	110	8:36	105
14:13	7	29:15	110	9:5	136
14:16	113, 127	29:21	26	9:7	145
14:26	113	29:29	120	9:22	97, 118
14:27	113	29:33	120	9:24	40, 80
15:6	98	29:35	120	10:3	46
15:7	40	29:36	26	10:6	17
15:9	128	29:37	110	10:11	105
15:14	87	30:19	106	13	110
15:16	102	30:25	25	13:1–17	114
15:20	86	30:26	26	13:33	18
15:25	43	30:30	26	13:45	17, 92
17:9	127	31:18	96	14:8	18
17:11–12	113	32	32	14:9	18
17:12	74	32:9	68	14:15–29	119
17:16	104	32:12	38	14:18	26
18:7	47, 82	32:13	121	15:19–33	114
18:12	39	32:15–16	96	16:21	110
18:13	75, 136	32:20	41	16:29	40
18:22	112	33:11	29	16:31	40
19	145	33:20	29	16:32	120
19:6	22, 27	34	145	17:10	30
19:16	87	34:6	37	17:11	41
19:17	136	34:8	86	18:8	95
19:18	87	34:20	29	19:15	31
20:5	86	34:29–30	32	19:19	90
20:18	87	40:10	26	19:27	16
20:26	91	47:3	91	19:28	88
21:2–6	19			19:32	136
22:6	40	**Leviticus**		20:3	30
23:1	123	1:4	110	20:4	55, 60
23:8	55	3	39	20:5	30
23:15	29	3:2	110	20:6	30
23:27	72	3:8	110	20:11	95
23:31	108	3:13	110	21:1–4	110
24	145	4:4	110	21:5	17, 18, 88
24:1	85	4:15	110	21:10	17, 18, 26
24:7	151	4:24	110	22:4–6	114
24:11	39, 40, 59	4:29	110	24:14	110
24:17	40	4:33	110	26:13	70
25:6	25	5:2–3	110	26:16	65, 68
28:31–42	90	7:11–35	39	26:17	30
28:36–38	36	8:10	26	27:32	127
28:41	26, 120				

Numbers

4:37	105
5:2	110
6:1–21	18
6:25	32
9:23	105
10:35	134
11:1	40
11:4	65
11:8	139
11:12	71
11:17	112
11:27	141
12:14	51
14:1	65
14:5	80
14:6	92
14:14	29
14:18	37
14:30	121
14:43	141
15:30	103
15:38–39	90
15:39	59
16:4	80
16:15	28, 38
16:22	85
16:47	141
19:11	110
19:13–16	114
20:8	127
20:11	103, 127
20:17	140
21:2	108
21:4	37
22:22	135
22:27	127
22:31	55
23:25	40
24:1	30
24:3	58
24:10	127
24:15	58
24:17	127
24:20	57
24:21	57
25:2	85
25:3	70
25:4	38
26:10	40
27:2	137
27:18–23	119
30:1	16
32:6	75
32:11	141
32:12	141
32:13	138
32:15	141
33:3	103
35:12	137
36:1	16

Deuteronomy

1:12	112
1:17	31
1:27	108
1:36	131
2:25	87
2:27	140
3:8	107
4:3	141
4:10	136
4:11	136
4:19	59
4:24	40
4:28	102
4:34	97, 104
5:4	29
5:9	85
5:15	97, 104
5:32	140
6:5	68
6:8	36
6:14	141
7:4	141
7:8	125
7:16	40
7:19	97, 104
7:24	108, 135
8:19	141
9:2	135
9:3	40
9:27	28
9:29	97, 104
10:16	68
10:17	31
10:18	136
11:2	97, 104
11:12	62
11:18	36
11:24	131
11:25	131
11:28	141
12:40	121, 135
13:2	141
13:4	141
13:5	140
13:6	71, 112
13:17	38
14:1	17, 88
14:28–29	101
15:7	108
15:8	108
15:9	62
15:11	108
15:12–18	19
16:19	31, 55
17:11	140
17:20	140
18:5	136
18:7	136
19:17	137
20:9	16
21:6–9	107
22:5	89
22:10	70
22:12	90
23:14	30
24:1	107
24:3	107
25:9	50, 132
26:4	107
26:8	97, 104
26:15	61
27:20	95
28:7	134
28:14	140, 141
28:32	65
28:48	70
28:50	31
28:56	71

28:65	52, 54, 65, 68, 87, 131	8:34-35	151	9:48	70
29:4	52, 56	9:14	39	9:49	140
29:10	136	10:6	106	10:16	37
30:14	42	10:24	131	11:11	16
31:11	151	11:10	16	11:34	86
31:17	35	14:2	105	11:35	42, 92, 147
31:18	35	14:8	141	11:36	42
32:10	52	18:4	139	11:37	139
32:11	94	18:8	139	13:5	18
32:15	133	20:2	105	13:9	74
32:20	35	20:4	137	13:20	80
32:22	38	21:1	144	14:10-12	39
32:24	40	22:5	140	14:16	66
32:27	103	22:18	30	14:17	66
32:35	143	22:23	30	15:14	43
32:39-40	122	22:31	102	16:3	70, 134
32:40	121, 122			16:16	37
32:42	40	**Judges**		16:26	111
33:27	111	1:2	107	16:27	63
33:29	131	2:1	125	17:5	120
34:9	119	2:4	65	17:12	120
34:10	29	2:12	141	18:19	46
		2:14	135	20:5	134
Joshua		2:15	102	20:16	100
1:3	131	2:19	141	20:26	76
1:5	135	2:22	140	20:38	1
1:7	140	3:15	100	21:2	65, 76
2:18	1	3:20	134, 136		
2:24	107	4:5	75	**Ruth**	
3:3	141	4:7	108	1:9	47, 65
4:5	70	5:10	74	1:13	102
5:11	81	5:27	80	1:14	47, 105, 112
5:15	131	5:30	15	1:16-17	145
6:5	43	6:13	108	1:17	120
6:10	43	6:22	29	2:3	145
6:15	139	7:3	87	2:8	145
6:16	43	7:11	106	2:9	5
6:20	43	7:15	84	2:10	80
7:6	23, 80	7:21	141	2:14	145
7:10	135	8:3	37	2:20	145
7:12	72, 92, 135	8:6	108	3:3	26
7:13	135	8:26	89	3:8	145
7:26	38	8:28	20	3:9	94
8:1	108	9:4	140	4:1-2	75
8:18	113, 128	9:8	26	4:4	19
8:26	128	9:15	26	4:7	132
		9:24	106	4:13	145

Ruth
(continued)

4:16	71, 130
4:17	130

1 Samuel

1:3	84
1:7	40, 65
1:8	40, 64, 72
1:15	68
1:18	8, 27, 28
1:26	137
2:1	42
2:8	74
2:32	53
2:33	65, 68
2:36	85
3:5	141
3:17	120
4:4	74
4:5	44
4:12	23, 141
4:13	87
5:4	15, 101
5:6	102
5:11	102
8:11	141
9:8	107
9:15	19
9:16	26
10:1	25, 26, 48
10:4	107
10:9	71
10:10	26
11:4	65
11:7	105, 120
12:3–4	107
12:3	55, 60
12:15	102
12:20	141
13:7	140
13:15	140
14:15	87
14:19	101
14:27	54
14:29	54
14:38	144
14:44	120
15:11	38
15:24–31	94
15:25	84, 85
15:27	94, 147
15:28	91
16:4	87
16:11	75
16:12	53
16:13	26
16:20	105
17:15	135
17:51–54	15
18:2	68
18:4	91
18:6	86
18:8	38
18:9	53
20:2	19
20:7	38
20:12	19
20:13	19, 120
20:36	141
20:41	47, 64, 78, 80, 151
21:1	87
21:3	107
21:4	107
21:11	86
21:13	148
22:6	136
22:8	19
22:17	19
24:3–5	91
23:4	108
23:16	106
24:6	26
24:8	81
24:10	26
24:16	65
24:20	91, 137
25:22	88, 120
25:23	81
25:24	81
25:27	140
25:34	88
25:35	107
25:36	39
25:41	81, 132, 134
26:9	26
26:11	26
26:16	26
26:18	106
26:23	26
28:2	15
28:5	87
28:14	81, 90
28:18	38
28:20	40, 78
28:21	108
29:5	86
29:10	70
30:4	65

2 Samuel

1:2	23, 71
1:10	22
1:11	92
1:12	65
1:14	26
1:16	26
2:7	106
2:19	140
2:22	31
2:23	135
2:26	40
3:8	38
3:9	120
3:20	39
3:31	65
3:32	64, 65
3:35	40, 120
4:1	106
4:7–12	16
4:11	106
6:2	74
6:5	86
6:8	38
6:12	9
6:14–21	86
6:14	126
6:15	44
6:16	142, 151

6:20	147	19:13	120	3:20	71
7:6	139	19:24	18	5:3	131
7:27	19	19:39	47	6:12	140
8:1	107	19:42	38	8:14	136
9:6	81	20:8	90	8:15	42
9:8	28	20:9–10	18	8:22	85, 117, 118, 137
10:2	105	20:9	47		
10:4	18	20:21	103	8:24	42
11:2	134	20:22	16	8:29	62
11:4	105	21:1	30	8:32	15
12	150	22:8	38	8:38	117
12:3	71	22:9	37	8:41–42	97
12:8	71	22:16	37	8:52	55
12:16–17	40	22:25	54	8:53	105
12:16	76	22:28	58	8:54	84, 117
12:21	65	22:30	142	8:61	140
12:30	22	22:37	143	9:3	52
13:6	148	22:39	131	9:8	42
13:18–19	89, 90	22:41	72	10:8	136
13:19	23, 24, 92	22:42	60	10:15	123
13:21	38	22:44	16	10:24	29
13:27	39	23:12	135	11:5	141
13:29	137	24:8	139	11:10	141
13:31	76, 92	24:20	81	11:26–27	103
13:36	65			11:29–32	92
14:2–4	148	**1 Kings**		11:31	107
14:4	81, 86	1:2	71	11:34–35	107
14:16	108	1:5	141	11:37	68
14:19	140	1:16	82	11:38	91
14:22	81, 86	1:20	60	12:4–14	70
14:33	47, 81, 82	1:23	81	13:1	137
15:1	141	1:31	81, 82	13:13	137
15:2	70	1:35	140	13:33	120
15:5	47, 109	1:38	137	14:8	11
15:30	24, 131	1:39	26	14:9	72
15:32	23	1:40	140	14:10	88
16:12	58	1:41	39	14:11	40
16:21	106	1:49	87	15:18	107
17:2	87, 106	2:4	140	16:11	88
18:3	144	2:19	74, 82, 98	16:31	85
18:12	103	2:23	120	17:1	136
18:19–27	141	2:25	105	17:10	41, 143
18:28	81, 98, 103	2:32	15	17:19	71
18:33	64, 65, 87	2:37	15	18:7	81, 147
19:4	35, 43	2:44	15	18:21	46, 141, 143, 144
19:5	34	3:15	39, 137		
19:8	74	3:16	137	18:26	143

1 Kings
(continued)

18:27	88, 147
18:28	88
18:30	144
18:42	77
18:46	73, 102, 141
19:2	120
19:11	137
19:13	34
19:15	26
19:16	26, 91
19:18	48, 84
19:19	91
19:20	47, 140, 141
20:8	108
20:10	120
20:19	140
20:22	144
20:28	144
20:31	93
20:41	16
20:43	53
21:4	30, 40, 53, 76
21:21	88
21:27	92, 93, 138
22:3	107
22:10	89
22:15–16	147
22:21	136
22:24	35
22:30	89

2 Kings

1:8	89
1:13	81
1:14	40
2:5	144
2:23	16
3:14	31, 62
3:21	73
4:16	112
4:26	141
4:27	84
4:29	73, 128
4:34	113
4:35	55
4:37	86
4:38	75
5:1	31
5:7	92
5:9	137
5:11	113
5:13	143, 144
5:18	78, 85, 105
5:20	107
6:17	55
6:30	92, 93
6:31	120
7:2	78, 105
7:3–4	75
7:17	78, 105
8:10	58
8:11	9, 30, 58, 64
9:1	73
9:3	25, 26
9:6	26
9:8	88
9:13	93
9:17	137
9:30	54
10:4	135
11:12	22, 26, 125
11:14	92
12:17	30
12:20	134
13:14	64
13:23	28
13:25	107
14:8	30
14:11	30
15:19	106
17:36	85, 97
19:1	92
19:8	74
19:15	74
19:16	19, 55
19:21	22
19:22	63
19:26	105
19:28	45
20:5	64
20:11	43
21:8	138
22:2	140
22:8–10	151
22:11	92
22:19	65
23:2	151
23:26	38
24:20	37
25:27	20

1 Chronicles

5:20	43
6:39	98
12:2	99, 100
12:17	106
12:19	120
13:6	74
13:8	86
13:11	38
15:15	70
15:28	44
15:29	86, 142
16:22	26
17:16	75
17:25	19
19:4	18
20:2	22
21:16	80, 93, 128
21:21	81
23:30	137
28:2	132
29:5	120
29:20	85
29:22	39
29:24	122

2 Chronicles

5:14	137
6:4	42
6:12–13	117
6:12	137
6:13	84
6:15	42
6:19	28
6:29	117
6:32	97

SCRIPTURE INDEX

6:40	55	36:13	68	8:8	151
6:42	26	36:21	42	8:18	151
7:6	136, 137	36:22	42	9:1	23, 93
7:14	29			9:2	137
7:15	55	**Ezra**		9:3	136, 151
7:16	52			9:5	136
9:18	132	1:1	42	9:15	121
10:8	136	3:11–13	44	9:16	68
13:15	43	3:11	43	9:17	37, 68
13:9	120	3:12	65	9:26	72
15:7	106	4:4	106	9:29	68, 71
15:14	43	4:18	151	12:46	16
18:9	74, 89	4:23	151	13:1	151
18:18	136	5:5	62	13:25	17
18:29	89	5:8	101		
19:7	31	6:22	106	**Esther**	
20:3	30	7:6	102		
20:13	137	7:9	111	1:3–9	39
20:17	135	8:18	111	1:11	22
20:18	84	9:3	17, 18, 92	1:12	40
20:19	136, 137	9:4	87	1:14	29
22:27	84	9:5	84, 117, 118, 134	1:17	63
23:11	22			2:3–12	26
23:13	92	9:6	31	2:11	139
23:18	105	9:8	54	2:17	22
25:14	85	10:1	66	3:2	86
25:17	30	10:3	87, 123	3:6	63
26:20	5	10:6	64, 66	3:10	96
28:11	38	10:9	87	4:1–4	93
29:2	84	10:14	38	4:1	92
29:6	30, 67	10:19	122, 123	4:3	71, 76
29:8	43			4:11	127
29:11	136	**Nehemiah**		4:16	40
29:23	110			5:1	89
29:26	136	1:4	64, 65, 76	5:2	127
30:6	108	1:6	3, 55	5:9	87, 136
30:8	68, 121	2:2	32, 72	6:8	22, 89
30:10	44	2:3	32	6:9	137
30:12	102	2:8	111	6:12	24
30:27	136	2:19	44	7:7–8	149
34:2	140	3:5	70	7:8	34
34:18	151	4:1	38	8:2	96
34:19	91	4:7	38	8:3	81
34:30	151	5:6	38	8:4	127
34:33	30	5:13	93	8:15	22, 89
35:10	136	6:9	106	9:17–19	39
35:25	65	8:3	151	9:25	15
36:12	42	8:5	137		
		8:6	116		

SCRIPTURE INDEX

Job

1:4	39
1:6	136
1:7	139
1:10	101
1:20	14, 17, 80, 92
2:1	136
2:8	76, 88
2:10	102
2:11	21, 22
2:12	23, 65, 92
2:13	76
3:1	42
3:12	130
3:24	43
4:3	106
4:4	85, 130
4:9	37
4:14	87
5:15	42
5:16	44, 45
5:22	44
6:28	28
7:4	77
7:16	37
7:19	60
8:20	125
8:21	44
9:20	41
9:23	44
9:27	28
9:30	107
9:33	126
10:3	101
10:9	23
10:15	21
11:13–15	118
11:13	118
11:15	31
11:20	54, 65
12:4	44
12:24	139
12:25	143
13:8	31
13:10	31
13:21	105
13:24	35
14:3	58
14:6	60
14:20	28, 33
15:6	41
15:12	52, 63
15:25	103
16:4	22, 149
16:5	47
16:9	50, 63
16:10	35, 47
16:15	93
16:16	23, 27
16:17	106
17:2	57
17:3	123
17:5	54, 64, 65
17:6	51
17:7	54
17:9	106
17:16	23
19:9	23
19:18	72
19:21	102
20:11	23
20:23	38
21:5	28, 45
21:6	87
22:8	31
22:19	44
22:29	61
23:4	41
27:4	47
27:11	102
27:23	43, 126
29:3	139
29:8	136
29:9	45
29:14	95
29:24	27, 32, 44
29:25	16
30:10	51, 144
30:28	139
31:7	52
31:12	104
31:16	54, 65
31:26–28	48
31:27	48
32:21	31
33:2	42, 49
33:4	37
33:16	19
34:15	23
34:19	31, 101
34:29	35
34:37	126
35:7	107
36:10	19
36:15	19
37:1	87
38:3	73
38:15	105
40:4–5	45
40:7	73
40:9	102
41–42	45
41:20	38
41:26	58
41:29	44
42:2	46
42:8–10	31
42:11	22
44:14	22

Psalms

1:1	7, 75
2:2	135
2:4	44, 74
2:5	38
2:11	87
2:12	48
3:3	20
3:7	35
4:6	32
5:2	43
5:9	49
6:3	64
6:6	65
7:3	106
7:16	15
8:3	102
8:6	69, 102, 131
9:7	74
9:16	106
10:1	145

SCRIPTURE INDEX

10:2	98	22:17	63	35:14	86, 138		
10:4	27, 33	22:18	90	35:16	50		
10:6	16	22:19	145	35:19	55		
10:7	49	22:24	35	35:22	145		
10:11	16, 35, 60	22:27	85	35:27	43		
10:12	104	23:4	127	35:28	49		
10:15	105	23:5	25, 26, 39, 41	36:1	52		
10:17	19	23:6	76	36:11	69, 131		
11:4	58	24:3–4	118	37:12	50		
11:7	29	24:4	106, 139	37:13	44		
12:2	47, 72	24:6	30	37:14	128		
12:3	47	24:7	VI, 20	37:17	105		
12:4	49	25:15	58, 60	37:24	125		
12:5	43	25:16	28	37:30	49		
13:1	35	26:3	140	38:6	86, 139		
13:2	68	26:4–5	75	38:9	43		
13:3	54	26:6	107, 139	38:10	52, 54		
14:2	58	27:4	59	38:11	144		
15:3	49	27:6	20	38:21	145		
16:5	41	27:8	30	39:1	45		
16:8	98	27:9	35	39:5	37		
17:1	47	28:2	98, 116	39:11	37		
17:5	143	28:4	106	39:12	64		
17:6	19	28:5	102	39:13	32, 58, 60		
17:7	98	29:6	142	40:6	19		
17:8	52	29:10	74	40:9	47		
17:11	58	30:5	64	41:9	39, 133		
18:7	38	30:7	35	41:12	125		
18:8	37	30:11	86, 93	42:2	41, 59, 68		
18:15	37	31:2	19	42:9	139		
18:27	63	31:10	43	42:10	139		
18:29	142	31:16	32	43:2	139		
18:32–34	102	31:18	47	44:3	31, 32, 64, 102, 104		
18:35	98	31:22	145				
18:36	143	32:3	43	44:20	117		
18:38	69	32:8	62	44:24	35		
18:40	68, 72	32:11	44	45:6	127		
19:7	68	33:3	44	45:7	26		
19:8	52, 54, 56	33:13	58	45:9	98		
19:14	42	33:18	62	45:10	19		
20:5	44	34:1	41	45:13–14	89		
20:6	98	34:5	59	47:1	44, 126		
20:8	135	34:13	47	47:2	126		
21:3	23	34:14	139	47:3	69, 131		
22:1	145	34:15	62	47:5	44		
22:7	22, 44, 47	34:16	30	49:3	42		
22:11	145	35:13	21, 93	49:4	19		

SCRIPTURE INDEX

Psalms *(continued)*

Reference	Page(s)
50:19	41
50:20	72
51:14	49
51:15	47
52:2	49
52:6	44
54:7	63
54:9	63
55:2	139
55:5	87
56:8	64, 65
58:10	69
59:1	134
59:8	44
59:10	63
59:12	47
60:8	44, 132
62:9	37
63:1	41, 68
63:2	59
63:4	116
63:8	125
64:8	22
66:4	85
66:7	58
67:1	32
68:16	53
68:30	69
68:31	123
69:1–2	111
69:1	68
69:3	65
69:7	35
69:9	40
69:10	64
69:11	93
69:16	28
69:17	35
69:20	22
69:23	87
69:24	38
71:2	19
71:12	145
71:23	44
72:9	50
73:2	143
73:3	62
73:6	67
73:7	53
73:9	49
73:13	107
73:18	143
73:23–24	111
73:23	98, 125
74:11	103
75:5	68, 72
76:7	135
77:2	117
77:4	54
78:19	72
78:33	37
78:49	38
79:11	43
79:12	71
80:3	32
80:5	65
80:6	44
80:7	32
80:16	32
80:17	98
80:19	32
81:1	44
81:5	47
81:6	70
82:1	74
82:2	31
83:2	20
83:8	111
84:8	139
85:3	38
86:1	19
86:14	134
86:15	37
86:16	28
88:2	19
88:9	117
88:14	35
89:10	102
89:13	97, 102
89:15	32, 44
89:20	26
89:44	128
89:50	71
90:7	40
90:9	43
90:17	101
91:12	112
91:13	69, 131
92:4	102
94:11	37
95:1	44
95:6	84
96:9	87
98:1	104
98:4	44
98:8	44, 126
99:1	74, 87
99:5	84, 132
100:1	44
101:4	72
101:5	63
101:6	62
102:2	19, 35
102:4	40
102:5	43
102:7	77
102:9	65
102:17	28
102:19	61
102:20	43
102:25	102
103:8	37
103:14	23
104:14–15	39
104:15	26
104:27	60
104:28	108
104:29	23, 35, 37
105:15	26
106:23	70
106:26	121
106:30	137
107:5	68
107:7	140
107:40	139
107:42	45
108:9	44, 132
109:2	49

SCRIPTURE INDEX

109:24	130	140:3	47, 49	6:10	106
109:25	22	141:2	116	6:12–14	106
109:29	95	141:3	45	6:12	42, 143
109:31	98	141:5	26	6:13–14	143
110:1	74, 98, 132, 137	141:8	60	6:13	56
		141:12	9	6:14	72
110:2	127	143:6	41, 68, 117, 118	6:17	63
110:5	98			6:21	67
110:7	20	143:7	35	6:25	53, 55
112:8	63	144:1	124	6:33	5
112:10	50	144:4	37	6:35	31
115:4	102	145:8	37	7:2	52
115:7	101, 129	145:14	86	7:13	27, 30, 47
116:2	19	145:15	60	8:6	47
116:8	64	145:16	108	10:4	106
118:7	63	145:18	145	10:6	16
119:37	59	146:8	54, 86	10:10	56
119:48	116	147:17	135	10:13	47
119:82	54, 65	149:3	86	11:21	124
119:120	87	150:4	86	11:26	16
119:123	54, 65			12:4	22
119:132	28	**Proverbs**		12:14	101
119:135	32	1:9	67	13:3	45, 47
119:136	64	1:24	109, 121	13:19	30
121:5	98	1:26	44	14:2	140
123:1	60	3:3	67	14:13	44, 72
123:2	60, 108	3:7	30	14:16	30
124:2	134	3:16	99	14:24	23
124:4–5	68	3:22	67	14:29	37
126:2	42, 44	3:23	143	15:13	1
126:5	64	4:8	112	15:18	37
126:6	64	4:9	23	15:21	140
127:2	70	4:15	30	15:30	52
131:10	52	4:20	19	16:14	34
132:7	84, 132	4:21	62	16:15	32
132:9	44, 95	4:24	42	16:30	3, 49, 56
132:16	44	4:25	58	16:31	17
133:2	18, 26	4:27	140	16:32	37
134:1	136	5:1	19	16:33	71
134:2	116	5:3	47	17:6	23
135:15	102	5:11	43	17:18	123
136:10–12	97	5:13	19	17:24	30
136:12	104	5:20	112	18:5	31
137:1	65, 76	5:21	58	18:24	144
139:5	108	6:1	123	19:11	37
139:9	111	6:3	108	20:8	58
139:10	125	6:9–10	2	20:29	17

Proverbs
(continued)

21:4	52, 63
21:5	106
21:10	61
21:13	19
21:29	30
22:9	62
22:17	19
22:26	123
23:2	68
23:6	62
23:26	52
24:17	143
24:23	31
24:26	49
24:33	106
25:15	37
25:22	27
25:23	32
25:25	68
26:6	105
26:7	129
28:27	60
29:1	68
29:2	43
29:9	44
29:13	54
29:26	29
30:13	63
30:17	63
30:20	38
30:32	46
31:13	101
31:20	108
31:22	89

Ecclesiastes

2:2	44
2:10	52
2:12	28
2:24	102
3:4	86
3:20	23
4:5	106
4:12	135
5:2	42
5:6	101
6:7	41
7:3	32, 44
7:6	44
8:1	27, 31, 32
9:1	102
9:7	39
9:8	26
9:10	101
10:2	99
10:7	138
10:18	106
10:19	44
11:9	52, 58
11:10	58
12:5	65
12:7	23
19:16	39
19:17	39

Song of Solomon

1:2	47
1:6	63
1:10	36, 67
1:15	53
2:4	39
2:6	112
2:8	142
2:9	59
2:14	29
3:11	59
4:1	16, 53
4:3	36
4:9	53, 67
5:6	72
5:12	53
5:13	36
6:7	36
6:13	59
7:1	101
7:9	47
8:1	47

Isaiah

1:15	60, 116, 118
2:5	140
2:6	123
2:8	102
2:11	63
2:22	30, 37
3:3	31
3:8	54, 143
3:9	28
3:13	137
3:16	59, 68, 138
3:18–23	90
3:18	138
3:21	36
3:24	16, 17, 93
5:11	70
5:14	40
5:15	63, 86
5:25	104
5:26	43
6:2	34
6:5–7	47
6:10	19, 52, 55, 56
7:8–9	16
7:18	43
7:20	17
8:8	68
8:9	43
8:11	111
8:17	35
9:4	70
9:6	70
9:12	40, 104
9:15	16, 31
9:17	104
9:21	104
10:12	63
10:24	127
10:27	70
10:32	5, 103
11:4	37
11:15	37, 104
12:6	44
13:2	100, 121
13:7	106
13:8	33
13:9	38

SCRIPTURE INDEX

14:5	128	30:28	37, 68	44:5	97		
14:16	64	30:30	40, 102, 103	44:12	102		
14:25	70	30:32	103	44:18	52, 55, 56		
14:26–27	104	30:33	37	44:23	44		
15:2	18	31:1	60	45:1	26, 89, 98, 125		
15:3	65, 93, 139	31:3	104	45:12	102		
15:4	43	32:11	87, 93	45:22	30		
16:10	43	32:12	71	45:23	84, 85, 121		
17:7–8	60	33:2	104	46:2	86		
19:14	143	33:14	87	45:3–4	111		
19:16	87, 103, 104	33:15	19, 107, 140	47:1	74, 76		
19:25	101	33:19	47	48:4	36, 68		
20:1–6	3	35:3	106, 130	48:9	37		
20:2–4	91, 131	35:5	54	48:13	102		
21:3	86	35:6	142	48:20	44		
21:4	87	35:10	43	49:2	42, 105		
21:7	137	36:22—37:1	92	49:7	136		
22:4	60	37:2	93	49:15	71		
22:11	60	37:14	107	49:16	97		
22:12	65, 71, 93	37:16	74	49:18	90		
22:14	19	37:17	19	49:22	98, 100		
22:15–21	90	37:19	102	49:23	50		
22:21	119	37:22	22, 44	50:2	105		
22:22	70	37:23	63	50:6	51		
23:11	104	37:29	45	50:7	30		
24:14	44	38:2	30	50:8	144		
24:20	143	38:14	60	50:10	139		
25:6–8	39	38:17	72	51:5	104		
25:6	40	40:2	107	51:11	43		
25:8	66	40:7	37	51:16	105		
25:10–11	117	40:10	102	51:17–18	111		
25:10	107	40:11	111	51:17	41		
26:9	68	40:22	74	51:18	106, 125		
26:11	40, 148	40:26	57	51:19	22		
27:8	37	41:1	144	51:22	41		
27:13	85	41:2	131	51:23	85, 86, 131		
28:3	131	41:8–14	105	52:2	70, 76		
28:5	23	41:10	61, 125	52:10	103		
28:7	142, 143	41:13	98, 125	52:15	45		
29:6	40	41:23	61	53:1	103		
29:8	68	42:1	125	53:2	59		
29:9	143	42:5	37	53:7	46		
29:10	55	42:6	125	54:1	44		
29:13	42	42:7	54, 56	54:8	35		
29:22	33	42:11–13	44	55:1–5	39		
30:19	66	42:18–19	55	55:1–2	41		
30:27	38	43:8	55	55:3	19		

Isaiah
(continued)

55:12	126	2:25	68	16:6	17, 88
56:4	122	2:27	67	16:12	72
56:5	122	2:37	24	17:4	38
56:10	55	3:3	36	17:13	30, 97
57:4	50	3:10	148	17:23	68
57:16	37	3:12	32	18:15	143
57:17	35	3:19	141	18:16	21, 22, 43
58:5	21, 76, 86, 93	4:8	38, 71, 93	18:17	67
58:9	106	4:30	28, 54	18:18	49
58:10	68	4:31	118	18:20	136
59:1	19	5:1	139	18:23	143
59:2	35	5:3	30	19:14	136
59:3	47	5:21	52, 56	19:15	68
59:8	106	5:31	120	19:18	43
59:10	143	6:12	104	20:4	108
59:16	104	6:15	143	20:5–6	107
59:17	95	6:21	143	20:11	143
60:1	32	6:24	106	21:5	97, 104, 108
60:14	138	6:26	76, 93	21:10	30
60:16	71	7:2	135	22:5	121
61:1	26	7:19	35	22:10	22
61:3	26	7:23	140	22:17	52
61:10	22, 90, 95	7:26	68	22:24	96
62:3	23, 105	7:29	17	23:23	145
63:5	104	8:12	143	23:14	106
63:12	98	8:18	72	23:18	136
63:13	143	9:1	65	23:22	136
64:7	35	9:8	42	24:6	61
65:2	8, 109, 118	9:17–18	65	25:6–7	102
65:5	38	9:26	16	25:9	43
65:6–7	71	10:3	102	25:15	41
65:12	86	10:5	129	25:16	143
65:19	65	10:9	89, 102	25:18	43
65:25	41	12:5	141	25:23	16
66:1	132	13:11	73	25:28	107
66:2	61, 87	13:21	16	25:30	43
66:5	87	13:26	34, 91	25:34	76
66:12	130	14:4	23	26:2	135
		14:6	54, 65	27–28	3
		14:12	41	27:1–12	70
		15:1	136, 137	27:5	97
		15:3	40	28:5	137

Jeremiah

		15:5	22	29:18	43
1:9	42, 111	15:14	38	30:6	33, 73
1:16	102	15:15	37	30:10	87
1:17	73	15:16	41	31:4	86
2:16	17	16:5	22	31:7	16

SCRIPTURE INDEX

31:9	140, 143	51:51	35	2:1	136
31:13	86	51:61	151	3:1–3	40
31:15	65	51:63	151	3:5	47
31:18	22	52:31	20	3:6	47
31:19	127, 129			3:7–9	36
31:20	72	**Lamentations**		3:8	30
31:25	68	1:4	43	3:14	102
31:32	125	1:8	22	3:22–27	45
32:17	97, 104	1:17	115	3:22	102
32:18	71	2:10	21, 23, 74,	3:23	80
32:21	97, 104		76, 86, 93	4:3	30
32:33	67	2:1	132	4:7	30, 103
33:5	35	2:11	65	5:1–4	18
35:19	136	2:15–16	42	5:1	17
36:5–23	151	2:15	22, 126, 152	5:11	61
36:21	136	2:16	50	6:2	30
36:24	92	2:18	65	6:9	60
37:17	108	2:19	116, 118	6:11	127, 142
38:4	106	3:19	139	6:14	104
39:12	61	3:26–27	70	7:4	61
41:5	88	3:29–30	50	7:9	61
42:1	144	3:29	41	7:17	130
44:11	30	3:30	35	7:18	30, 93
44:25	42	3:34	131	8:1	102
46:27	87	3:41	116, 118	8:16	72
47:3	106	3:48	65	8:17	38
47:5	88	3:50	61	8:18	61
48:17	22, 128	3:54	68	9:4	36, 43
48:25	105	3:56	19	9:8	80
48:27	22	3:62	134	9:10	61
48:33	43	4:2	101	10:7	107
48:37	17, 18, 88, 93	4:7	16	11:13	80
48:39	68	4:5	89	11:21	15
49:3	88, 93, 139, 142	4:16	31	13:17	30
		4:17	54, 65	13:22	106
49:14	134	4:20	37	14:6	30
49:17	43	5:6	122, 123	14:8	30
49:32	16	5:13	142	14:9	104
50:4	66	5:15	86	14:13	104
50:13	43	5:16	23	15:7	30
50:15	43, 122	5:17	52, 54	16:2	2
50:43	106			16:8	91, 94
51:14	43	**Ezekiel**		16:9	26
51:25	104			16:10	90
51:31	141	1:3	102	16:11	67
51:37	43	1:28—2:1	135	16:12	23, 37
51:48	43	1:28	80	16:27	104

Ezekiel
(continued)

16:39	108
16:49	111
16:63	44, 45
17:18	122, 123
18:6	60
18:12	60
18:15	60
18:17	107
18:21	30
18:24	30
18:26	30
19:6	40
19:11	127
20:5–6	121
20:5	122
20:7	59, 60
20:8	59, 60
20:15	121
20:23	121
20:24	60
20:28	121
20:33–34	97, 108
20:35	29
20:42	121
20:46	30
21:2	30
21:3	128
21:7	106, 130
21:12	127, 129
21:14	127
21:17	127
21:19	100
21:26	22
22:13	127
22:14	106
22:25	40
22:26	60
23:32	44
23:33	41
23:34	41
23:40	28, 54
23:41	74
24:16	59, 66, 71
24:17	18, 35, 43, 131
24:25–27	45
25:2	30
25:6	126, 142
26:16	76, 87
27:30	23, 76
27:31	93
27:36	43
28:17	63
28:21	30
29:2	30
30:10	105
30:12	105
30:21–24	105
30:24	106
30:25	106, 128
32:10	87
33:12	143
33:21–22	45
33:22	102
33:31	42, 75
35:2	30
35:3	104
36:7	121, 122
36:9	28
37:1	102
37:5	37
38:2–3	16
38:2	30
39:23	35
39:24	35
39:29	35
40:1	102
43:3	80
43:8	40
43:19	145
43:26	120
44:4	80
44:12–13	122
44:12	121
44:20	17, 18
47:14	121

Daniel

1:5	136
1:10	15
2:28	16
2:46	81
3:19	32
4:33	17
4:34	60
5:1	39
5:6	33, 89, 130
5:7	67, 89
5:9	33
5:10	33
5:16	67
5:29	67
6:10	85
6:11	85
6:26	87
7:5	40
7:9	137
7:10	75, 136
7:13–14	137
7:26	75, 137
7:28	33
8:17	80
8:18	5, 80
8:23	30
9:3	30, 93
9:17	32
9:18	19
10:3	26
10:5	20
10:7	87
10:9–11	135
10:9	80
10:10	111
10:16	42, 47, 111
11:15	135
11:17	30
12:4	142
12:7	121, 122

Hosea

2:2	28
5:15	30
7:2	28
7:5	124
11:3–4	71
11:3	111
11:4	36
11:9	38
13:2	48

SCRIPTURE INDEX

14:3	102	1:11	91	2:15	43, 127
14:9	143	1:16	17	3:3	40
		2:3	70, 138	3:8	40
Joel		2:7	140	3:9	47, 70
1:8	93	3:4	35	3:14	44
1:13	93	4:4	87	3:16	106
2:12	71	4:9	43		
2:13	37	4:10	43	**Haggai**	
3:7	15	4:11	63	2:23	96
3:12	75	5:1	35	2:13	110
4:9	144	5:9	103, 104		
		5:13	102	**Zechariah**	
Amos		6:8	7, 138		
		6:15	26	1:10–11	139
1:5	127	6:16	43	1:21	20
3:3	144	7:5	45, 71	2:9	104
5:16	65	7:6	134	2:12	52
5:22	62	7:7	60	2:13	104
6:6	26	7:10	63	3:1	137
6:10	26	7:16	45	6:11	22
8:10	17, 93	7:17	50, 87	6:13	89
8:11	68			7:11	71
8:12	139, 142	**Nahum**		8:4	127
9:4	58			8:9	106
9:14	39	1:3	37	8:13	106
		1:6	38	8:17	72
Obadiah		1:13	70	8:19	40
		2:1	73	8:23	94
12	63	2:7	71	9:1	58
13	63	2:10	27, 87, 130	9:9	44
15	15	3:5	34, 91	10:11	128
		3:7	22	11:8	37
Jonah		3:19	126	12:4	58
2:5	68			13:4–6	88
3:5	93	**Habakkuk**		14:13	111
3:6	74, 76, 93	1:10	6, 44	14:17	84
3:8	93	2:16	143		
3:9	38	3:10	98, 123	**Malachi**	
4:1	38	3:13	27	2:6	41, 47
4:2	37	3:16	47, 87	2:7	47
4:4	38			2:9	31
4:9	38	**Zephaniah**		2:13	65, 107
4:11	100	1:4	104	3:2	135
		1:5	85	4:2	142
Micah		1:6	141	4:3	131
1:8	71, 91, 131	2:2	38		
1:10	76	2:13	104		

SCRIPTURE INDEX

Matthew

Reference	Page	Reference	Page	Reference	Page	Reference	Page
2:2	85	10:12	112	18:9	59		
2:10	9	10:13	21	19:13–15	119		
2:11	2, 83, 86	10:14	132	19:26	57		
2:18	65	10:21	134	19:28	74		
3:4	89	10:38	141	20:15	62		
3:11	133	10:42	41	20:32	134		
4:6	112	11:5	56, 134	20:34	114		
4:9	86	11:8	89	21:7	137		
4:10	85	11:17	65, 86	21:8	93		
4:19	141	11:19	40	21:42	16		
5:1	75	11:21	93	22:1–14	39		
5:2	42	11:29–30	70	22:2	40		
5:6	41, 68	12:10–13	101	22:4	39		
5:29	59	12:13	115	22:11–13	90		
5:30	106	12:15	141	22:12	46		
5:35	132	12:34	42	22:13	50		
5:36	120	12:41–42	134	22:34	46		
5:39	36	12:49	100	22:44	74, 98		
5:47	49	12:50	49	23:2	75		
6:3	99, 108	13:1–2	75	23:4	70		
6:16–18	40	13:15	19, 52, 55, 56	23:5	36, 90		
6:16	32	13:16	56	23:7	79		
6:17	26, 32	13:42	50	23:16–26	55		
6:22	7, 63	13:50	50	24:3	75		
6:28–29	89	13:54	152	24:4	140		
8:1	141	14:2	134	24:7	134		
8:2–3	114	14:8–12	16	24:51	50		
8:3	114	14:13	141	25:1–10	40		
8:12	50	14:19	60, 76	25:10	39		
8:15	114	14:31	111	25:30	50		
8:22	141	14:36	94, 114	25:33–34	100		
8:23	141	15:2	106, 107	26:7	26		
9:4	72	15:8	47	26:8	152		
9:9	141	15:11	41	26:23	39		
9:10–11	40	15:18	42	26:26–29	39		
9:14–15	40	15:19	72	26:36–46	145		
9:18	114	15:30	83	26:39	41, 80, 85		
9:20–22	114	15:31	56	26:42	41		
9:20–21	94	16:6	61	26:43	54		
9:23	65	16:16	26	26:45	108		
9:24	44	16:24	113	26:48	49		
9:25	114	17:6	84	26:50	108		
9:29	114	17:7	111	26:55	75		
9:30	54, 56	17:22	106	26:62	137		
9:33	152	18:8–9	143	26:63	26		
10:10	127	18:8	106	26:64	74, 98		
				26:65	92		

SCRIPTURE INDEX

26:67–68	35	6:13	26	13:3	75
26:67	51	6:17–29	16	13:5	140
26:75	64, 66	6:21	39	13:8	134
27:11	137	6:39	76	14:8	26
27:14	9	6:41	60	14:22–25	39
27:19	75	6:46	112	14:32–42	145
27:24–25	107	6:56	94, 114	14:35	85
27:24	62	7:2	107	14:36	41
27:29	23, 80	7:3	106	14:40	54
27:30	51	7:6	47	14:41	106, 108
27:32	113	7:9	147	14:44	49
27:39	22	7:21	72	14:46	108
27:50	44	7:22	62	14:52	91
27:54	152	7:32–33	114	14:58	102
27:55	145	7:34	43, 60, 152	14:60	137
27:63	134	8:12	43	14:61	46
28:2	74	8:15	61	14:62	74, 98
28:4	86	8:18	56	14:63	92
28:8	141	8:22–25	114	14:65	34, 51
28:9–10	9	8:23	51, 111	14:72	24, 64, 66
28:9	84, 86	8:24	152	15:5	46
		8:33	57	15:17	90
Mark		8:34	113	15:19	51, 80, 86
1:26	43	9:15	141	15:29	22
1:31	114	9:27	114	15:37	44
1:40–41	114	9:35	75	15:40	145
1:41	114	9:36	112	16:1	26
2:15–16	40	9:41	41	16:19	74, 98
3:1–5	63	9:43	106		
3:4	46	9:47	59	**Luke**	
3:5	115, 152	10:13	119	1:19	136
3:32–34	57	10:14	152	1:20–22	45
3:32	75	10:16	112, 119	1:22	100
5:22	81	10:17	80	1:51	102
5:23	114	10:21	57, 112	1:62–64	45
5:25–34	94, 114	10:22	9	1:62	101
5:25–29	89	10:26	152	1:63	101
5:30	94, 114	10:27	57	1:66	102, 111
5:31	94	10:32	140	1:70	42
5:33–34	114	10:34	51	1:71	108
5:33	9, 87	10:38	41	1:74	108
5:38–49	65	10:39	41	2:9	9, 28
5:40	44	10:49	134	2:28	112
5:41	114	10:52	56	2:37	40
6:2	114	11:25	137	2:46	75
6:5	114	12:36	74, 98, 131	4:8	84, 85
6:11	132	12:38	79	4:11	112

SCRIPTURE INDEX

Luke
(continued)

4:16	136, 151
4:18	26, 56
4:20	60, 75
4:40	114
4:41	26
5:3	75
5:7	100
5:8	77, 81
5:12	81
5:13	114
5:27–32	76
5:29	39
5:30	40
6:10	115
6:20	57
6:21	44
6:23	142
6:29	36
6:45	42
7:14	114
7:21–22	56
7:25	89
7:32	86
7:36–50	76
7:38	18, 26, 27, 49, 133
7:44	132
7:45	48, 49
8:25	152
8:41	81
8:43–44	88, 114
8:44–47	94
8:46	114
8:47	87
8:52	65
8:54	114
9:5	132
9:16	60
9:23	113
9:44	108
9:51	30
9:53	30
9:54	40
9:61	112
9:62	58
10:4	79, 131, 150
10:11	132
10:13	76, 93
10:23	56
10:25	135
10:31–33	144
10:34	26
10:39	75, 133
11:31–32	134
11:43	79
11:46	113
12:27	89
12:35	73
12:36	39
12:37	76
13:13	114
13:28	50
14:4	46, 113
14:7–11	76
14:15	40
14:21	152
14:27	113
14:31	75
15:5	70
15:20	47, 67, 112, 142, 144
15:22	90, 96
15:25	86
16:19	89
17:2	143
17:16	81
18:10–14	144
18:11–13	137
18:12	40
18:13	14, 61, 71
18:15	119
18:24	57
18:32	51
18:35–43	56
18:40	134, 144
19:5	152
19:41	64
19:42	56
20:17	57
20:19	108
20:21	31
20:26	46
20:43	132
20:46	90, 139
21:10	134
21:28	20
22:4	41
22:14–20	40
22:21	39, 106
22:30	74
22:35	131
22:40–46	145
22:41	85
22:47–48	49
22:47	48
22:51	114
22:53	108
22:55	75
22:61	58
22:62	66
22:64	34, 35
22:69	74, 98
23:26	113
23:27	71
23:35	37
23:46	44
23:48	71
23:49	145
24:5	21
24:7	106, 108
24:12	142
24:15	144
24:17	32, 134
24:31	55, 56
24:37	53
24:50	119

John

1:27	133
1:38	141
1:41	26
1:42	57
2:1–10	39
2:10	39
2:17	40
3:35	107, 108
4:6	74
4:13–14	68

SCRIPTURE INDEX

4:14	41	18:11	41	7:48	102
4:20–24	85	18:22	35	7:49	132
4:25	26	19:3	106	7:51	8, 19, 68
5:2	134	19:13	75	7:54	50
5:27	137	19:17	113	7:55	98
6:5	57	19:23	90	7:57	19, 43
6:10	76	19:30	21, 44	7:58	91
6:35	41	20:4	142	7:60	85
6:51–58	39	20:11	64	8:17	119
6:53–56	41	20:12	28, 74	8:18	119
7:30	108	20:13	64	8:27	85
7:37	68	20:15	64	8:28	138
7:44	108	20:22	37	8:35	42
8:1–11	96	20:31	26	9:7	45, 134
8:2	75	21:19	141	9:8	111
8:3	137			9:12	114
8:12	139, 140	**Acts**		9:17	114, 119
8:34	70	1:9	54	9:21	152
9:1–34	56	1:10	60	9:35	30
9:6	25, 51	1:16	42	9:40	55, 85
9:17	54	2:23	106	9:41	114
9:26	54	2:32	105	10:4	152
9:39–41	55	2:33–34	98, 108	10:25	86
10:12	141	2:34	74	10:34	31, 42
10:17	21	2:35	132	10:38	26
10:21	54	3:7	98	11:18	46
10:28	105	3:8	142	11:21	102, 111
10:39	108	3:12	64	11:28	135
11:2	18	3:18	42	11:30	105
11:9–10	143	3:19	30	12:1	106
11:27	26	3:21	42	12:14	53, 141
11:35	64	4:3	108	12:17	101
11:37	54	4:25	42	12:21	89
11:41	60, 152	4:26	135	13:2	40
12:3	18	4:30	104	13:3	40, 119
12:14	138	4:35	83	13:10	140
12:20	85	4:37	83	13:11	102, 111
12:35	7, 139, 140	5:12	114	13:15	151
12:38	103	5:18	108	13:16	101, 135
12:40	52, 56	5:31	98	13:17	104
13:3–14	132	5:36	140	13:46	29
13:3	107, 108	6:6	119	13:27	151
13:18	133	6:15	27, 28	13:51	132
13:24	21	7:10	136	14:3	114
14:9	59	7:25	60, 105	14:14	92
17:1	60, 152	7:33	131	14:15	30
18:6	80	7:41	106	14:19	104

Acts
(continued)

14:23	119
15:5	135
15:7	42, 135
15:10	70
15:19	30
15:21	151
17	86
17:22	135
17:25	37
17:30	60
18:6	15, 93, 132
18:8	18
18:14	42
18:15	62
18:20	21
19:6	119
19:11	114
19:12	94
19:22	110
19:26	102
19:33	101
20:1	112
20:29	40
20:31	64, 66
20:34	101
20:36	85
20:37	65, 67, 112
20:38	29
21:1	112
21:5	85
21:7	49
21:19	49
21:24	18
21:40	101, 135
22:3	133
22:7	84
22:11	111
22:23	93
22:30	137
23:1	58
23:2	35
23:3	75
23:9	135
23:23	138
24:10	21
24:25	152
25:10	137
26:1	101
26:6	137
26:14	84, 133
26:16	135
26:18	30, 56
26:20	30
27:9	40
27:21	135
28:8	114
28:27	19, 52, 55, 56

Romans

1:1	70
2:11	31
3:13	47, 49
3:18	54
5:2	135
6:4	140
6:16–20	70
7:1	49
7:14	70
7:25	70
8:4	140
8:26	43
8:34	98
9:32–33	143
10:8–10	42
10:9	49
10:21	109
11:4	84
11:8	52, 56
11:10	56
12:8	62
12:20	7, 8, 27
14:10	137
14:11	49, 84
14:4	135
16:3–16	112
16:3–15	49
16:4	68
16:16	49
16:20	131

1 Corinthians

2:1–5	3
2:3	86
2:9	52
4:6	72
4:12	101
4:18	72
4:19	72
5:2	72
8:1	72
9:24	141
9:26	141
10:12	61, 135
10:16–17	40
11:2–16	23
11:3	16
11:4–7	7
11:5	17
11:14–15	17
11:15	16
11:21	39
11:29	41
13:4	72
13:12	29
14:25	78, 84, 86
15:1	135
15:25–28	131
15:47–49	23
15:52	56
15:54	95
16:10	62
16:13	135
16:20	49

2 Corinthians

1:21–22	27
2:4	66
2:17	136
3:7–13	32
3:14	151
5:1	102
5:2	43, 95
5:4	43
5:7	140
5:11	86
5:12	148

SCRIPTURE INDEX

6:7	99
6:14	70
7:15	87
8:2	62
8:9	119
9:11	62
9:13	62
10:5	70
11:20	36
11:27	91
11:33	108
13:12	49

Galatians

1:10	70
2:2	141
2:9	5, 125
2:11–14	40
3:1	54
3:19	105
3:27	95
4:27	44
5:1	70, 135
5:7	141
5:15	40
6:2	113

Ephesians

1:18	52, 56
1:20	74
1:22	16, 131
2:13	145
3:14	85
4:15	16
4:24	95
4:28	101
5:14	134
5:23	16
6:5	87
6:6	70
6:9	31
6:11–14	135
6:13–17	91
6:13	7

Philippians

1:1	70
2:10	84
2:11	49
2:12	87
2:16	141
3:18	64, 66
4:1	7, 135
4:5	150
4:21	112

Colossians

1:18	16
2:10	16
2:18	72
3:1	98
3:12	95
3:25	31
4:12	70, 135
4:16	151

1 Thessalonians

1:9	30
2:17	29
3:8	135
3:10	29
4:11	101
5:26	49, 112
5:27	151

2 Thessalonians

2:8	37
2:15	135

1 Timothy

2:8	116
2:9	16, 90
4:13	151
4:14	119
5:15	141

2 Timothy

1:4	29
1:6	119
2:19	30
2:24	70
4:8	23
4:19	49, 112

Philemon

17	150

Hebrews

1:3	98
1:8	127
1:10	102
1:13	132
2:8	131
3:10	140
3:12	72
5:7	64
5:11	19
6:2	119
6:13	121
7:7	118
7:10	73
8:1	98
8:5	62
8:9	125
9:11	102
9:24	102
10:11	136
10:12	98
10:13	132
10:27	40
11:21	82
11:37	89
12:1	141
12:2	98
12:12	106, 130
12:13	140
12:21	87
13:17	43
13:24	112

James

1:1	70
1:5	61
1:12	23
2:1	31
2:3–4	76

James
(continued)

2:9	31
2:15	91
3:3	45
3:5–9	49
4:8	107, 145
4:9	44
5:1	65
5:14	26
5:17–18	77
5:19–20	140

1 Peter

1:13	73
2:8	143
2:16	70
2:17	49
2:21	141
2:25	140
3:3	16, 90
3:10	47
3:11	30
3:12	30, 55, 62
3:22	98
4:3	39
4:13	44
5:4	23
5:6	102
5:8	40, 49
5:12	135
5:14	49

2 Peter

1:9	55, 56
1:10	143
2:14	52, 59
2:15	140, 141

1 John

1:7	140
2:6	140
2:11	55, 56
2:16	59
2:20	27
2:27	27

2 John

4	140
6	140
12	29

3 John

13–14	29

Jude

16	31

Revelation

1:9	49
1:16	42
1:17	111
2:10	23
2:16	42
3:9	85
3:17	55, 56
3:18	56, 91
4:2	74
4:10	83, 86
5:4	65
5:6	52
5:14	86
6:17	135
7:3	36
7:9	136
7:11	84, 86
7:16	41
7:17	66
8:2	136
9:4	36
9:20	106
10:1	28, 129
10:3	43
10:5–6	121
10:8–10	40
11:3	93
11:5	40
11:11	37
11:16	84, 86
13:6	42
14:1	36
14:4	141
14:9	36
14:10	41
16:19	41
17:4	89
18:9	65
18:12	89
18:16	89
18:19	23, 65
19:9	39
19:10	62, 81, 84
19:15	42
19:17–18	39
19:21	42
20:1	108
20:4	36, 97
20:9	40
21:2	90
22:4	29, 36
22:17	68
22:8	81
22:18	151

www.ingramcontent.com/pod-product-compliance
Lightning Source LLC
Chambersburg PA
CBHW070326230426
43663CB00011B/2233